Tomás Gutiérrez Alea

Latin American Studies
David William Foster, *Series Editor*

Tomás Gutiérrez Alea

The Dialectics of a Filmmaker

Paul A. Schroeder

Routledge
New York and London

Published in 2002 by
Routledge
29 West 35th Street
New York, NY 10001

Published in Great Britain by
Routledge
11 New Fetter Lane
London EC4P 4EE

Routledge is an imprint of the Taylor & Francis Group.

Copyright © 2002 by Routledge

Printed in the United States of America on acid-free paper.

10   9   8   7   6   5   4   3   2   1

Library of Congress Cataloging-in-Publication Data

Schroeder, Paul A.
  Tomás Gutiérrez Alea : the dialectics of a filmmaker / Paul A. Schroeder.
      p. cm.—(Latin American studies)
    ISBN 0-415-93664-0
      1. Gutiérrez Alea, Tomás, 1928–Criticism and interpretation. I. Title.
  II. Latin American studies (Routledge (Firm))

PN1998.3.G874 S37 2002
791.43'0233'092—dc21   2001048688

For María, my love

Contents

Acknowledgments

This book owes much to the work of previous scholars who have written about Alea, especially to the writings of Michael Chanan, Julianne Burton, Paulo Antonio Paranaguá, Silvia Oroz, and José Antonio Evora. The most important source, however, has been Alea himself, through his numerous interviews and writings.

Like many books, this one began as a dissertation, and its completion would not have been possible without the constant support, encouragement, and feedback from my many friends at Stanford University: my professors Jorge Ruffinelli, Mary Louise Pratt, Claire Fox, and Michael Predmore, and my colleagues Consuelo Kenna, Jacqueline Lazú, Manel Camps, María Angélica Hernández, and the late Raquel Mendieta, among others.

I would also like to give special thanks to David William Foster for his enthusiasm toward this book and for his generosity of spirit.

Last but not least, my mother, Vidalina Rodríguez-Schroeder, and my sister, Ilse Schroeder-García, gave me the kind of moral support and unconditional faith that are needed to finish any project of this magnitude. With their help this book turned into something more than just an intellectual undertaking. It became a labor of love.

Preface

The first time I saw a Cuban film was at Spain's National Film Institute in the summer of 1994. Daniel Díaz Torres, the director of *Alice in Wondertown*, was in the theater to answer questions after the screening of his film, and that discussion opened my eyes to the fact that cinema plays a similar role to the novel in the nineteenth century, the role of modern foundational fictions. On my return to the United States from that summer in Spain, and with the support of David William Foster, I organized biweekly screenings of Latin American films at Arizona State University's Department of Spanish. The screenings were quite informal affairs on Friday afternoons, after which we'd walk across the street to a local pub and discuss the film and each other's lives. When I went to Stanford University to continue my studies, it was not with the idea that I'd study Latin American film, and yet as I look back, I see that my first contact with Cuban film in Spain, and the informal screenings at Arizona State University, were more than simple coincidences. I am even tempted to call them examples of "synchronicity," to coin Carl Jung's convenient term. That is to say, after all the "coincidences" that have led to this book, I can think of no better term than synchronicity to describe how this project came to fruition.

For example, one of the first courses I took at Stanford was Transnational Film Production, taught by Claire Fox. All the films we saw in that class, with one exception, were transnational in that they were produced by individuals or institutions of more than one nation, and that exception was none other than *Memories of Underdevelopment*, Alea's masterpiece and a classic of Latin American and world cinema. One year later, as I prepared for the qualifying exams, I was lucky enough to be able to include Latin American cinema as one of my three areas of concentration. This concentration had just been created a few months before, thanks mainly to Jorge Ruffinelli's interest in the field and his realization that in the current academic world of the United States, Spanish departments are better poised than film or communication departments to study Latin American film.

After the qualifying exams, and having secured a grant to travel to Cuba, I visited some of my relatives in San Juan, Puerto Rico, before moving on to Havana. In my grant proposal I had stated that my focus would be on how Cuban films of the 1960s had helped to redefine national, racial, and sexual identities in the island-nation and how they had in effect become the new foundational fictions of Cuba, taking on the role previously held by nineteenth century novels such as *Cecilia Valdés* and *Francisco*. That's what I was telling one of my cousins one morning in front of a bank, as we waited for my aunt to make a deposit. My cousin suggested that we go to the bookstore that was right next to the bank to look for books on film, and to my surprise, we found José Antonio Evora's book on Tomás Gutiérrez Alea, a collection of interviews with Alea that had just been published, which I had not seen before.

Once in Havana, the economic and moral crisis I encountered forced me to rethink my proposal. I now wanted to better understand how a revolution that had inspired so many people throughout the world (including myself) had come to the present crisis. The films of Tomás Gutiérrez Alea seemed a perfect way of approaching this question, and that's how my original project to study Cuban film in the 1960s turned into a study of Alea's oeuvre.

But the biggest coincidence of all was yet to come. After I finished the first draft of this study, I decided to reread Alea's theoretical treatise, *The Viewer's Dialectic*. When I went to the library to get it, the Spanish original was already checked out, so I picked the English translation instead. I distinctly remember I was standing when I opened the book because I had to sit down when I saw the dedication. Alea's handwriting was not very clear, and I had to read it several times before I could make out everything it said: "To Paul Schrader, with admiration and many wishes to meet you some day. TG Alea, January '89." After I got home, I realized that the dedication was not for me, but rather for Hollywood scriptwriter and director Paul Schrader. However, for a whole afternoon, and thinking (preposterously) that the book was indeed addressed to me, all sorts of questions raced through my mind, questions such as: Was I to look in *The Viewer's Dialectic* (as I eventually did) for the key to understand Alea's films? Or more to the point, how could Alea know I'd be writing a book about him, so many years before I even saw any of his films? Was Alea trying to tell me something from somewhere in the afterlife?

Today I acknowledge that finding that particular book in that particular library was a simple coincidence. But what a coincidence! Reading that dedication felt like a discovery, like stepping into an alternate, filmlike reality. Fortunately, the concept of synchronicity allows me to recover part of that feeling of discovery by giving a poetic meaning to an otherwise prosaic reality. Coincidentally (or not), this imbuing of life with poetic meaning is precisely what Alea's films do with the sometimes heroic, sometimes tragic, but always complex reality of revolutionary Cuba.

Introduction

The films of Tomás Gutiérrez Alea (1928–1996) have always defined the limits of expression in revolutionary Cuba. Many other filmmakers in Cuba have been either somewhat predictable in their treatment of revolutionary themes or else considered too hostile for their work to be shown without recrimination.[1] Alea always walked the middle path, supportive of the ideals of the Revolution but critical of the regime when it turned against those ideals. Alea, moreover, had a keen eye for identifying and then dramatizing the historical and cultural legacies that stand in the way of turning Cuba into a truly socialist society. For example, *Memories of Underdevelopment* explores the logical consequences of political apathy and cultural elitism, *The Last Supper* examines the dehumanizing effects of slavery on both masters and slaves, *Up to a Certain Point* gropes with the lingering machismo among Cuban men, and *Strawberry and Chocolate* offers friendship and love as the best antidotes to centuries of intolerance and homophobia. Just as important, the work of Alea is a window through which one can look into the cultural politics of revolutionary Cuba; it is a window that affords a panoramic view, since his career spans most of the Revolution, and also a very balanced view, as his films always steer clear of the double traps of revolutionary propaganda and reactionary vituperation.

Surprisingly, there are no other scholarly monographs on Alea, even though he is Cuba's most important film director and, along with Glauber Rocha, the most influential practitioner and theoretician of the New Latin American Cinema. There are, to be sure, four books dedicated to Alea,[2] but while all are valuable as primary sources of information, none offers an analysis of individual films within the context of Cuban cultural politics, much less a diachronic reading of his work. This book aims to fill these gaps in Cuban film scholarship and, in the process, provides me with a unique opportunity to engage in the broader study of the history of cultural politics in revolutionary Cuba. Finally, and unlike previous studies that tend to see Alea's work as limited to the confines of Cuba, this book places Alea's work within a global context that includes Italian neorealism, Soviet cinema, the French New Wave, Cinema Novo, and the theater of Bertolt Brecht.

Of the dozen feature films that Alea directed, I focus on three: *Memorias del subdesarrollo* (*Memories of Underdevelopment*, 1968), *La última cena* (*The Last Supper*, 1976), and *Fresa y chocolate* (*Strawberry and Chocolate*, 1993). Not only are these considered Alea's best films, but each is also symptomatic of an identifiable period in revolutionary Cuba. *Memories of Underdevelopment* corresponds to the period of triumph and affirmation of the Revolution in the 1960s, *The Last Supper* to the period of consolidation and institutionalization in the 1970s, and *Strawberry and Chocolate* to the period of crisis and radical questioning of the tenets of the Revolution since the fall of the Berlin Wall.

Notwithstanding the importance of a political and synchronic reading of Alea's three major films, such a reading would not do full justice to their complexity. For this one must also look diachronically at Alea's intellectual and artistic evolution within a specific context that includes politics, but is not reducible to it. With this in mind, I have identified five periods in Alea's intellectual and artistic evolution:

1. The Early Years: Idealism and Experimentation
   Historias de la Revolución (*Stories of the Revolution*, 1960)
   Las doce sillas (*The Twelve Chairs*, 1962)
   Cumbite (1964)
   La muerte de un burócrata (*Death of a Bureaucrat*, 1966)
2. *Memorias del subdesarrollo* (*Memories of Underdevelopment*, 1968)
3. The Search for Cuba's "Intra-Historia"
   Una pelea cubana contra los demonios (*A Cuban Fight against Demons*, 1971)
   La última cena (*The Last Supper*, 1976)
   Los sobrevivientes (*The Survivors*, 1978)
4. Turning the Lens on Himself: *Hasta cierto punto* (*Up to a Certain Point*, 1983)
5. Melodrama and the Crisis of the Revolution
   Cartas del parque (*Letters from the Park*, 1987)
   Fresa y chocolate (*Strawberry and Chocolate*, 1993)
   Guantanamera (1995)

By looking at Alea's total output, I was able to make connections and trace influences that would have remained clouded otherwise. For example, the first group of films is organic not only because of the films' common idealism, but also because of their debt to Italian neorealism. In *Memories of*

Underdevelopment, on the other hand, Alea successfully synthesized the comic with the tragic and incorporated the formal lessons of Godard, the narrative expressiveness of Eisenstein, the intellectualism of Brecht, and the political commitment of Cinema Novo to create a masterpiece that is not derivative, but highly original and contentious. In the third period, Alea's increased use of Brechtian theory and praxis responds to his desire to incite viewers to engage in a rational public debate about the material roots of contemporary Cuban reality. In *Up to a Point*, Alea turns the camera lens on himself by blurring the lines that separate the real-life director from the film's fictional scriptwriter, and documentary from fiction. Finally, and insofar as melodrama tends to flourish under conditions of crisis,[3] the use of this genre in the last period reflects the closing of the revolutionary cycle, even as the films open up and explore new forms of conceiving the Revolution. The book is organized around this periodization, with brief discussions of each, plus in-depth analyses of individual films. In addition, the book contextualizes Alea's work within the twin histories of Cuban and New Latin American Cinema, discusses his legacy in both, and concludes with a discussion of the three recurring themes in his oeuvre: the social role of the intellectual, religion, and the Cuban Revolution.

To view and study Alea's films is to see revolutionary Cuba through the eyes of the island-nation's most important and consistently critical filmmaker. On the whole, the picture that emerges is one of a complex reality that does not fit into the neat binarisms of the Cold War or the Manicheanism that has plagued discussions about the Revolution. Rather, all of his films give testimony to a collective project full of contradictions, a process that has been, successively, progressive and reactionary, machista and feminist, dogmatic and tolerant, heroic and tragic. To paraphrase Alea,[4] it is a project whose truth does not lie in any of these poles, but rather in their confrontation, and especially in what that confrontation suggests within a context that includes the Cold War, Latin America's revolutionary struggles for emancipation, and Cuba's own specific circumstances.

Where does this study fall within the debates taking place in U.S. academia and among Latin American intellectuals? Partly within the debates of cultural studies and partly within the older tradition of writing cultural histories. Of the two, the practice of writing cultural histories has a long tradition in Latin America, going back to the very first years of the Spanish Colonial Period. The practice of cultural studies in Latin America, on the other hand, is parallel but distinct from the cultural studies movement that began in 1964 at the Centre for Contemporary Cultural Studies at the University of Birmingham. The founders of the center—Richard Hoggart, Raymond Williams, E. P. Thompson, and Stuart Hall—all came from working-class backgrounds, and were all concerned with the question of culture in the class-based society of England. Over the years, their work expanded to include race, gender, and religion as well as class, partly in response to the demise of Marxism and partly in response to the real need to expand the horizon of explanations of cultural manifestations. In different parts of the world, cultural studies have taken on varying shades, depending on the context. In India, for example, there are three distinct schools of cultural studies, all based in Delhi and all interested, in varying degrees, with deconstructing the legacy of British colonialism: the Centre for the Study of Developing Societies (CSDC), the Centre of Contemporary Studies (CCS), and the Subaltern Studies Collective. Each of these centers is distinct in their approach to cultural phenomena, but all are Indocentric. The same may be said of cultural studies in different countries or regions. For example, Canadian cultural studies focus on what is broadly described as the "Canadian experience"; French cultural studies have focused on the hegemony of Paris over other parts of France and with the north-south divide within France; Australian cultural studies became concerned with identifying distinctive features of Australian life, especially as seen in Australian films; and in the United States, from where I'm presently writing, cultural studies have been preoccupied with the growing cultural diversity (or "multiculturalism") within U.S. borders.

What about Latin America? Can there be such a thing as Latin American cultural studies? Yes and no. Cultural studies in general are preoccupied with differences within a cultural space, but given the diversity of cultural, political, and economic histories in the vast territory called Latin America, such an approach runs the risk of oversimplifying a very complex reality. Another approach may be to identify regions or areas of study in Latin America that have enough in common to justify cultural studies. This has already happened, and today we hear of Mesoamerican studies, Caribbean studies, Southern Cone studies, and Andean studies, among others. Behind such fragmentation lies the acknowledgment that Latin America is in many ways an empty signifier, a signifier created by intellectuals in the metropolis to deal with a vast and heterogeneous region in terms that are favorable to that metropolis. From this perspective, many studies of Latin America fall into the trap of Orientalism, defined by Eduard Said as "the corporate institution for dealing with the Orient by making statements about it, authorizing views of it, describing it, teaching it, settling it and ruling over it: in short, Orientalism is a Western style for dominating, restructuring and having authority over the Orient."[5] Román de la Campa has picked up on this idea and applied it to Latin America in his recent book, *Latin Americanism*.[6] In it he argues, pace Said, that the Latin America that has been formulated and constructed in U.S. academic institutions does not correspond to the reality of Latin America. In place of a distorting and Anglocentric view of Latin America, de la Campa calls for a Latin America–centered cultural studies. For this he proposes a canon of several critics, foremost among them Fernando Ortiz, Angel Rama, Beatriz Sarlo, Antonio Benítez Rojo, Nelly Richard, and Edouard Glissant.

Yet not all interventions have to be made from Latin America, and de la Campa also cites metropolitan critics such as Jean Franco, Mary Louise Pratt, and Doris Sommer as examples of critics writing in the United States whose work attempts to theorize Latin America from within.

The problem with writing cultural studies about Latin America from a position of privilege in the U.S. academy is that one's interpretations will inevitably reflect the realities of the society within which one writes. In my own case, this reality includes liberal democracy as the preferred form of government (and civil society as its corollary), the intellectual as a marginalized figure, and in the cultural sphere, the ongoing battle between monoculturalism and multiculturalism. I have tried as much as possible not to impose my own personal and political concerns on the study of Alea's films. I know this is inevitable, so I should qualify the verb "tried" with the adverbs "somewhat successfully." That is to say, in this study I have somewhat successfully tried to look at Alea's films from within the context of Cuban cultural history and, just as importantly, from within a humanist tradition that is as distinctively Cuban as it is Western.

In this book I try to provide a just valorization of Alea's work using the tools of literary criticism and film studies, but also using the tools cultural studies and history. In doing so, I align myself with Latin America's own tradition of doing cultural studies, a tradition that emphasizes content and contextualization over form, but without doing away with the study of form, either. Aníbal González calls this approach "telluric" because it emphasizes the importance of place (or more generally, context) in deciphering texts.[7] A good example of this tradition is the work of Mexican critic Alfonso Reyes, who as early as 1952 had written that "So-called pure criticism—aesthetics and stylistics—only considers the specifically literary value of a work, in its form and its content. But this cannot lead to a complete evaluation and understanding of a work. If we do not take into account the social, historical, biographical, and psychological factors, we will never arrive at a just valorization."[8] Almost fifty years later, Reyes' observations still hold. Cultural studies have highlighted additional factors that may be taken into account in the process of evaluating and understanding a text, and I use them when appropriate. But more than an exercise in cultural studies, this book provides a cultural history of revolutionary Cuba as seen through the eyes of Tomás Gutiérrez Alea and his films. My aim has been to strike a balance between form, content, and context, a balance where each informs the others, but without pretending to exhaust all interpretative possibilities. That is, alas, a right that belongs to the reader and to future scholars of Tomás Gutiérrez Alea and Cuban film.

1
Context

Tomás Gutiérrez Alea: A Sketch

Tomás Gutiérrez Alea (a.k.a. Titón) was born on December 11, 1928, to a family of bourgeois tastes and progressive politics. For seven years he formally studied music, and he became good enough at the piano to entertain his university friends with interpretations of, among others, Debussy's "La plus que lente" and García Caturla's "Berceuse campesina".[1] An exemplary son, Alea agreed to his father's wishes that he study law. His interests during his studies (1948–1951), however, gravitated toward the political and the cultural. With another dozen students, among them Néstor Almendros and Guillermo Cabrera Infante, Alea founded Nuestro Tiempo, the legendary group that sought to link culture with progressive politics through manifestos, film screenings, and discussions. He also edited poetry and stories. Around 1950, for example, he published his own collection of poems, *Reflejos*, as well as Roberto Fernández Retamar's first publication, *Elegía como un himno*, using a printing press that his father kept in his house.[2] These were also the years of the university reform movement, which began in Argentina and spread throughout Latin America like wildfire. Alea was not immune to this influence, as may be evidenced by his signature on a manifesto of November 1950 that included a plan for the reform of the university and concluded with calls for anti-imperialism, national liberation, and agrarian reform. After receiving his law degree from the University of Havana in 1951 Alea went to study film at the Centro Sperimentale della Cinematografia in Rome, where he met Julio García Espinosa. Upon their return to Cuba they joined forces to direct Cuba's first neorealist film, *El Mégano* (*The Charcoal Worker*, 1954).

Alea's career as a filmmaker, however, did not really start until after the Revolution. Before 1959 there simply was no film industry in Cuba, and between 1954 and 1959 his directing was limited to newsreels and advertisements.[3] As soon as the Rebel Army took over Havana, it set up a Cultural

Department to promote literacy and culture. One of its divisions was called Cine Rebelde, and under the directorship of García Espinosa, it produced two documentaries. The first, *Esta tierra nuestra* (*This Is Our Land*, 1959), was directed by Alea, and the second, *La vivienda* (*Housing*, 1959), by García Espinosa. With this documentary Alea scored the first of many firsts in his career. Others include *Historias de la Revolución* (*Stories of the Revolution*, 1959), the first Cuban feature to be screened by the Cuban Film Institute (ICAIC); *Memories of Underdevelopment* (1968), the first Cuban feature to be banned by the U.S. government and, with Humberto Solás' *Lucia* (also of 1968), the first Cuban feature to receive international acclaim; *The Last Supper* (1976), the first Cuban film to be a commercial success, thanks mainly to its popularity in Brazil; and *Strawberry and Chocolate* (1993), the first Cuban feature to deal directly and sympathetically with homosexuality, as well as the first Cuban film to receive an Academy Award nomination. All these accomplishments are as much individual as collective, in the sense that without ICAIC Alea would not have been able to flourish as a director, and also in the sense that Alea's success is tied to the success of the New Latin American Cinema.

Alea may be studied as an auteur, and by choosing to organize this book around him I am contributing to this particular take on his work. However, Alea is not an auteur in the European sense of the word, with its emphasis on the search of an individual style while at the same time breaking free from Hollywood's commercialism. Rather, Alea and other Latin American auteurs emphasized their commitment to society. Indeed, the most important lessons that Latin American auteurs learned from the French New Wave (where the idea of a *cinema d'auteur* originated) had to do with how to produce a film with limited resources, not with how to edit, shoot, or tell a story. For Alea and other Latin American auteurs, being a director with a distinct voice was less important than the sense of belonging to a collective emancipatory project with national and continental dimensions. The history and philosophy behind ICAIC is a good example of this Latin American twist on the idea and practice of the *politique des auteurs*. Founded in 1959, ICAIC was entrusted with "the most direct and extensive vehicle for education and the popularization of ideas."[4] In terms of its potential to promote and cement a revolutionary consciousness, film was recognized as the most important of the arts. As such, ICAIC was showered with extensive financing and the appropriate facilities for the production, distribution, and exhibition of films.

The Immediate Context: ICAIC and the Cuban Revolution

ICAIC is for all practical purposes an independent organization whose independence can be attributed to Alfredo Guevara, its founder and subsequent director. At the same time, however, the films produced by ICAIC always responded to the priorities of the state. The most obvious example of this is the meteoric rise of the documentary, both in quantity and in quality. If one compares the number of documentaries against the number of fictional films produced by ICAIC, one gets the sense that ICAIC was mainly a company set up to make documentaries, and only incidentally a company to make fictional films. Compared with fictional films, documentaries have always received priority status at ICAIC. This is partly because documentaries are less expensive, but also, just as importantly, because of ICAIC's belief that documentaries deal with truth more directly than do fictional films, and are thus better suited to raising the revolutionary awareness of the masses. Julianne Burton explains this phenomenon in detail:

> [In the first 24 years after the Revolution] ICAIC produced 112 full-length films (feature and documentary), some 900 documentary shorts—educational, scientific, and technical as well as animated and fictional films—and more than 1,300 weekly newsreels.
>
> As these production statistics demonstrate, ICAIC has given priority to documentary over fictional subjects. Both economic and ideological factors motivate the preference. The economic motivations are obvious: when funds and equipment are limited, professional actors, elaborate scripts, costuming, as studio sets can be regarded as nonessentials. [Moreover], in a society which subscribes to the principles of Marxism-Leninism, it is believed fitting that creative activity be based on the confrontation with material reality.[5]

What this means for a director of feature films such as Alea is that his output would be limited, as indeed it was. In a period of over thirty years, he directed only twelve feature films. It also means that the aesthetics, theory, and practice of documentary filmmaking would influence (and be influenced by) Alea. Indeed, Alea directed at least one short documentary before the Revolution (on the 1762 British occupation of Havana), and after the Revolution he directed four more: *Esta tierra nuestra* (1959), a before-and-after docudrama of the agrarian reforms of that year; *Asamblea general* (1960), a news report without narration of a speech by Fidel Castro at the Plaza de la Revolución; *Muerte al invasor* (1961), on the Bay of Pigs fiasco (parts of which he would incorporate into *Memories of Underdevelopment*); and *El Arte del Tabaco* (1974), a visual collage of cigar boxes and fine tobaccos. This last documentary apart, Alea's documentaries after the Revolution responded to the desire to capture the incredible reality of these first years. Again, Julianne Burton:

> This attempt to record the first convulsive moments of revolutionary victory had a profound effect on artists who had previously conceived of filmmaking as above all a vehicle for personal expression. In their documentary

apprenticeship, Cuban filmmakers came face to face with unimagined aspects of national life. Their newly found growth in awareness and social sensitivity is largely responsible for the intense dialectic between historical circumstance and individual response which informs fictional as well as documentary production in post-revolutionary Cuban cinema.[6]

This "intense dialectic between historical circumstance and individual response" carried over from Alea's documentary practice and into his features. In *Memories of Underdevelopment*, for example, Alea incorporates documentary footage as an important and even organic element of the film. Further experimentation with the style and technique of documentary filmmaking—handheld cameras, outdoor shooting, and direct sound, for example—reached a climax in *Una pelea cubana contra los demonios* (*A Cuban Fight against Demons*, 1973), in which concern with plot seems to have given way to a barrage of images, as if truth were in the "documented" imagery rather than the "fabricated" narration. But perhaps the most obvious example of the influence of documentary practices on the work of Alea is *Hasta cierto punto* (*Up to a Certain Point*, 1983), a film that explores the very process of documentary filmmaking.

The production of a large number of good documentaries undoubtedly served to cement ICAIC's reputation in the eyes of the central government. A similar phenomenon occurred at Casa de las Américas with the incorporation in 1970 of the testimonial genre as a category in its annual competition. In both institutions, the promotion of genres with popular values—documentary in film and testimony in literature—responded to a concern at the highest echelons of the government to develop what Tzvi Medin calls a "monolithic democracy" whose aim is "to emphasize the importance of the involvement of the masses—but masses who are uniform in their revolutionary outlook."[7] Under these circumstances, the production of feature films takes on secondary importance, and then is only permitted to the extent that these films promote the creation of a monolithic democracy.

Alea's films, however, do not promote uniformity or any kind of monolithic worldview. What *is* uniform throughout his filmography is the *desirability* of an idealized revolutionary process. Only his last two films, *Strawberry and Chocolate* and *Guantanamera*, openly question the *feasibility* of that process, and only because by then, the central government had become an impediment rather than a facilitator of that process.

Alea's privileged position as an intellectual of the Revolution made him doubly *comprometido*. The two possible translations of this word into English—committed and compromised—give a hint of the complexity of the problem. On the one hand, to be committed or, as the French would say, *engagé*, entails the moral choice to align oneself with the more progressive forces in society. This Alea always did. On the other hand, *compromiso* suggests being compromised, or at least implicitly involved, with those forces. The problem arises: What if the progressive forces to which one is committed become reactive, entrenched, and authoritarian? As this became more and more the case in Cuba, especially after 1970, Alea became more compromised with the very authoritarianism that his films decried. Like many other Cuban intellectuals, Alea was torn between the defense of the Revolution as a utopian project and the condemnation of its bureaucratization. In fact, Alea became one of many contentious intellectuals in Cuba, simultaneously defending the Revolution abroad while criticizing it from within.

Having said that, I would caution the reader that, while a reading of Alea's films according to their political stance vis-à-vis the Cuban Revolution helps to explain their political meaning, such a reading would not do full justice to the complexity of the films. For this, one must look beyond politics to the intellectual and artistic evolution of Alea within a specific context that includes politics, but is not reducible to it. Therefore, in this study I also aim to present Alea's films as the symbolic expression of an incessant intellectual activity[8], an activity that calls for additional parameters of interpretation. To this end, I identified in the Introduction five periods in Alea's intellectual and artistic evolution, always keeping in mind that periodizations are tools, not ends in themselves. The purpose of this periodization is to help organize what would otherwise remain unintelligible. It is not intended as the final word on Alea's development, but as a point of departure for future studies. More specifically, this periodization will help to conceive Alea's work as evolutionary, keeping in mind that evolution is not positivism and that it can include ups as well as downs.

The Broad Context: New Latin American Cinema

Cuba has always been an avid consumer of Western art, a fact explained by Havana's strategic location as entry port to the Americas. Yet apart from popular music, Cuban art before the Revolution was little known and hardly influential beyond its shores. Only occasionally did nonmusicians—Wifredo Lam, Alejo Carpentier—leave their mark on the Western artistic tradition, and then always mediated by France or Spain. The Revolution permanently changed this sorry state of affairs. After 1959, Havana briefly joined Buenos Aires, Mexico City, and Barcelona as a major publishing center for Spanish-language books and periodicals, while artists from all over Latin America, Europe, and North America converged on the island for congresses, exhibits, and intellectual debates of all kinds. In film, Cuba's coming of age occurred in 1968, with the releases of *Memories of Underdevelopment* and *Lucia*. Only a year before, the first Festival of Latin American Cinema had taken place at Viña del Mar in Chile, with the participation of a Cuban delegation headed by Alfredo Guevara. And since 1979, Havana has been the permanent home of the festival, a sponsorship that reflects the central role Cuba has played in the development of a pan-American film community. The effects of these changes on Cuban film have been remarkable. Instead of always looking to Europe and North America for models and inspiration, Cubans can now seek inspiration in a Latin American film tradition that they themselves helped create and shape: the New Latin American Cinema.

The New Latin American Cinema began as an unconnected web of politically engaged filmmakers and cooperatives working within the boundaries of their respective nations. Some of the most important of these groups were the Documentary Film School in Santa Fe, Argentina; the Ukamau Group in Bolivia; Cinema Novo in Brazil; and ICAIC in Cuba. Despite the independence of each of these groups from each other and of the very different circumstances in which they developed, all of them shared the common belief that cinema was an effective weapon in combating the grave injustices that plagued their respective societies. Before the first Festival of Latin American Cinema in 1967, there were already a number of films that were made with this belief in mind—for example, Julio García Espinosa's *El Mégano* (1955), Nelson Pereira dos Santos' *Rio Zona Norte* (*Rio, North Zone*, 1957) Fernando Birri's *Tire dié* (*Throw a Dime*, 1958), and Glauber Rocha's *Deus e diabo na terra do sol* (*Black God, White Devil*, 1964). But it was not until after the Viña del Mar festival that extensive networking between filmmakers from throughout Latin America began in earnest. The following year, participants at the First Encounter of Latin American Documentary Film at the University of Mérida in Venezuela ratified the movement's ideological commitment to three basic principles:

> (1) To contribute to the development and reinforcement of national culture and, at the same time, challenge the penetration of imperialist ideology and any other manifestation of cultural colonialism; (2) to assume a continental perspective towards common problems and objectives, struggling for the future generation of a Great Latin American Nation; and (3) to deal critically with the individual and social conflicts of our peoples as a means of raising the consciousness of the popular masses.[9]

These three principles define the project of the New Latin American Cinema (building a Latin American cultural consciousness with national cultures as the building blocks), its intended audience (the popular masses), and the common enemy (imperialism and colonialism) during the euphoric sixties and early seventies.

Symptomatic of these years was *La hora de los hornos* (*Hour of the Furnaces*, 1965–1968), an agitational documentary by Argentinean filmmakers Fernando Solanas and Octavio Getino, which had its Latin American premier at the 1968 festival in Mérida. The documentary explores the antagonisms between nationalist populism and bourgeois liberalism in Argentina since the military coup that toppled Juan Perón in 1956. Many other films of the time explore this same antagonism, most notably Glauber Rocha's *Land in Anguish* (1967) and Alea's *Memories of Underdevelopment* (1968).[10]

These three films were all filmed and screened at a time when it seemed as if most of Latin America was on the verge of adopting socialism. Cuba had set an early example of how to go about it, but other countries experimented with their own paths to socialism. In the Dominican Republic, the election of Juan Bosch in 1962 was followed by a series of agrarian reforms and social programs designed to undo the legacy of Rafael Trujillo. In Brazil, João Goulart's use of radical rhetoric, plus his mobilization of peasants and workers, seemed to promote the creation of conditions for a worker-peasant alliance against the socioeconomic establishment[11]—again, nationalist populism versus bourgeois liberalism. In Peru, a military coup led by General Juan Velasco ushered a series of progressive measures to end the "unjust social and economic order which places the usufruct of the national wealth solely within the reach of the privileged, while the majority suffer the consequences of a marginalization injurious to human dignity."[12] The most important of these measures were an ambitious land reform program and the organization and mobilization of workers and peasants under a cleverly named umbrella organization, the National System for Support of Social Mobilization, whose acronym in Spanish spells SINAMOS, sometimes written as two words—*sin amos*, "without masters."[13] In Argentina, nationalist populism was held back through a series of legal maneuverings, but Peronism refused to die. Chile, of course, was the first Latin American country to have a socialist government democratically installed, in 1970. And in Panama, General Omar Torrijos began a similar set of reforms as those in Peru after his coup in 1968 against an unpopular president who had been in office for only eleven days.

In many of these shifts to the left, intellectuals played a key role, sometimes even a decisive one. Their impact was strongest at the rhetorical level, with concepts such as anti-imperialism, dependence, and underdevelopment crossing over from academic discourse to political and even popular discussions. Part of being a Latin American intellectual now included an awareness of these concepts and the forces behind them, plus a commitment to combat them in whatever capacity the intellectual could, within his or her circumstances. In *Hour of the Furnaces* this meant taking to the streets to protest right-wing governments; in the first half of *Land in Anguish*, the commitment meant giving advice to a populist politician; and in *Memories of Underdevelopment*, commitment meant making the transition between passive awareness to active participation, a transition the film's protagonist never completes. In fact, much of the success of *Memories of Underdevelopment* among Latin American intellectuals may be due to the expectation that they too would soon find themselves in the protagonist's position—that is, a bourgeois intellectual in a socialist country—and that they too would have to make the transition from passive awareness to active participation, if they had not already done so.

In a few years, however, all the hopes of the sixties turned to dashed dreams, as a backlash to the events described here turned Latin America into a checkerboard of repressive military dictatorships. In the Dominican Republic, a military coup against Bosch in 1963 eventually led to U.S. occupation in 1965. In Brazil, a military coup deposed Goulart in 1964. In 1975, Peru's revolutionary junta replaced General Velasco with General Francisco Morales Bermúdez, who then presided over the dismantling of the 1968–1975 experiment. A U.S.-backed coup deposed Salvador Allende's government in 1973; Panama's Torrijos was followed by General Manuel Noriega; and in 1976, Argentina's generals took over the country and began their infamous Dirty War. In this new context, it is understandable that Latin American filmmakers would want to make sense of it all. In fact, many of the films made during this backlash explore the ways in which a small conservative elite achieves and maintains power through force—for example, Leon Hirszman's *Eles nao usam black tie* (*They Don't Wear Black Tie*, 1980), Nelson Pereira dos Santos' *Memorias do carcere* (*Memories of Prison*, 1984), Hector Olivera's *La Patagonia rebelde* (*Rebellion in Patagonia*, 1974), and Alea's *The Last Supper* (1976). All of these films address the ways in which intimidation and brute physical force are used to serve the interests of a few well-placed individuals at the expense of the masses, be these slaves, wage laborers, political dissidents, or farmhands.

The Last Supper should also be seen as part of a hemispheric debate on the origins, forms, and consequences of African slavery in the Americas. In Brazil these debates centered on the repudiation of Gilberto Freyre's domestication of slavery in *Casa-grande e senzala* (*The Masters and the Slaves*, 1933). *The Last Supper*'s box office success in that country—the first commercial success for ICAIC outside of Cuba—is perhaps explained by the film's candid portrayal of everyday brutality in a slave plantation, a portrayal that goes against the grain of Freyre's book. In film, Carlos Diegue's beautiful and poignant *Xica da Silva*, also of 1976, mythologizes the real-life story of a slave woman in the middle of the eighteenth century who attained freedom, wealth, and power by becoming the lover of Brazil's richest diamond contractor. (Also of 1976, but in the United States, is Alex Haley's epic *Roots: The Saga of an American Family*, a runaway bestseller that was successfully adapted for television in 1977.) These films mark a shift in the New Latin American Cinema away from a prevalent concern with politics as conventionally defined (a concern evident in films such as *Hour of the Furnaces*, *Land in Anguish*, and *Memories of Underdevelopment*) to the exploration of other politics, such as the politics of race, gender, and ethnicity.

The expansion of subject matter deemed worthy of being filmed continued throughout the 1980s and into the 1990s. Thirty years after its inception, the New Latin American Cinema "no longer yields to an appraisal based exclusively on the filmmaker's political responses to social and political changes."[14] Such is the case with films as varied as *Mujer transparente* (*Transparent Woman*, 1990), a Cuban composite film made up of five dramatic shorts, each exploring a different aspect of female subjectivity; Federico García Hurtado's *La lengua de los zorros* (*The Language of Foxes*, 1992), a Peruvian film that aims to explain the guerilla war within the context of Andean mythology; and Alea's own *Strawberry and Chocolate* (1993), a melodrama that explores the intersections between sexuality, nationalism, and exile. What stands out in these and other recent films from Latin America is their emphasis on subjectivity, a far cry from the early attempts in the New Latin American Cinema to create an awareness based on the objective conditions in the region. At the same time, the change in focus proves the movement's capacity to adapt and incorporate new forms of expression and points of view without abandoning its initial resolve to use film as a tool for social change and assert cultural autonomy.[15]

This introduction makes clear that Alea was both the most distinguished director of revolutionary Cuban cinema and a founding figure of the New Latin American Cinema. Argentine filmmaker Fernando Birri has stated that the New Latin American Cinema was born in Cuba with *El Mégano* (1955), a neorealist film by Julio García Espinosa that Alea helped to direct.[16] Yet Alea's legacy goes beyond that of a founding figure, either of ICAIC or of the New Latin American Cinema. His writings and pronouncements on the dangers of bureaucratizing art by imposing socialist realism had cemented his reputation within ICAIC several years before *Death of a Bureaucrat* made him the most renowned director inside Cuba, and well before *Memories of Underdevelopment* became a model in terms of its approach to a complex social reality through the construction of an intimate narrative. This could perhaps be Alea's most important contribution to Latin American film in terms of narrative strategy, for even twenty or thirty years after the screening of *Memories of Underdevelopment*, one can see this approach used to great effect in such films as Nelson Pereira dos Santos' *Memorias do carcere* (*Memories of Prison*, 1984), Luis Puenzo's *La historia oficial* (*The Official Story*, 1985), and Walter Salles' *Central do Brasil* (*Central Station*, 1998).

Like Alfredo Guevara, ICAIC's longtime director and personal friend of Fidel Castro, Alea fought bureaucracy, socialist realism, "machismoleninismo," and other deformations of the revolutionary process. All of these themes would be taken up again and again by other filmmakers such as Juan Carlos Tabío, Manuel Octavio Gómez, Sergio Giral, Daniel Díaz Torres, Gerardo Chijona, and others. Some of the specific films that stand out as direct responses to Alea's films and ideas are Humberto Solás' *Un día de noviembre*

(*A Day in November*, 1972), which takes up the theme of *Memories of Underdevelopment*; Juan Carlos Tabío's *Plaff!*, based on an idea by Alea; and Sara Gómez's *De cierta manera* (*One Way or Another*, 1974), finished by Alea after Gómez died during the final stages of filming. But besides helping Tabío and Gómez as a mentor and a friend, Alea also contributed to the development of many other young directors at ICAIC through working groups designed specifically for that purpose. In effect, Alea saw his roles as filmmaker and teacher as inseparable and his own legacy as collective rather than individual.

I have subtitled the book "The Dialectics of a Filmmaker" for three reasons. First, Alea never settled for a final synthesis in theme or in style. Instead, he always searched for new ways of understanding and expressing the social, political, and historical dimensions of the revolutionary process. And whether it was through comedy or drama, historical fiction or documentary footage, Alea always sought to expand the mind of the viewer by calling into question stale categories from Cuba's colonial and neocolonial past and rethinking more recent concepts from the revolutionary present. Second, his films reflect an intense dialectic between historical circumstance and individual response. These two poles—individual and society—are always fluid and inseparable, but in Alea's case we have a man whose films are living testimony of the intensity with which he lived that dialectic. Finally, the subtitle of this book is a tribute to Alea's theoretical study, *The Viewer's Dialectic*, which summarizes not only the theory behind many of Alea's films but also much of New Latin American Cinema.

2
The Early Years:
Idealism and Experimentation

Before the Revolution, Alea had worked for three years (1956–1959) at Cine-Revista, a Mexican-owned production company, directing shorts that were shown before regular screenings. He had also worked on a total of seven film projects, three with photography by Néstor Almendros, one in collaboration with Julio García Espinosa, and one as assistant director for a student project at the Centro Sperimentale in Rome. None of these experiences, he explains, prepared him for the kind of films he would direct after the Revolution:

> Camilo Cienfuegos, who at the time [early 1959] headed the Rebel Army, had the idea of creating within the Rebel Army, a Cultural Section with a department of film. He called on Julio [García Espinosa] and me [Alea] to make documentaries with *urgent* themes. We were happy to comply. The project satisfied our yearning to make a *useful* cinema, and so we organized the department enveloped by great *fervor* and *effervescence*. That was in the first months after the Revolution, and we slept an average of three or four hours a day: we did not want to miss a thing of what was going on.[1] [emphasis mine]

Urgency, usefulness, fervor, and effervescence: These four words describe Alea's state of mind while working on the documentary *Esta tierra nuestra* for the Rebel Army, and also during the filming of his first feature, *Stories of the Revolution*. Alea, then thirty-one years old and already slim, seems to have literally fed off his work, for he lost twenty pounds during the process. Exhausted both physically and mentally, he decided to make his next film a comedy. It would be a *divertimento*, a chance to please himself, but also a chance to experiment more freely with narration techniques and style:

One may say that making *Stories of the Revolution* was traumatizing. That film was . . . more achievement of the Revolution, and therefore had to reach an acceptable level, especially if one keeps in mind that the subject matter is directly related to the Revolution. And the situation only got worse because it was also my first film and I had absolutely no experience in this kind of production. Today I can reveal, for example, that I had never been present at the filming of a feature film, even though I had studied at a film school. We found ourselves, all of the sudden, in that delicate situation and did not want to be accused of wasting film stock. . . . It was, in the end, a solution built on compromises, and the results in such cases can never be extraordinary. That is why I felt the need to make a film that would not entail such a high degree of responsibility; that is to say, a sort of "divertimento." This would permit a greater degree of freedom, a greater audacity, and of course, a greater sense of pleasure from our work.[2]

The Twelve Chairs was screened in December 1962, a few months after the Bay of Pigs fiasco. Yet unlike *Stories of the Revolution, The Twelve Chairs* does not reflect the solemnity or militarism of these early years. Rather, Alea takes for granted that the Revolution is secure and focuses instead on the new social dynamics, as exemplified by the relationship between the two main characters: a *pícaro* (Oscar) and his ex-boss (Hipólito). They use each other to find a hidden treasure, but in the end the treasure is found by a group of workers who use it to finance a community center. In the final sequence, Oscar joins a game of baseball at the community center, while Hipólito runs away and out of the frame. The message is clear: Those who stay in Cuba must join the game of the Revolution, or else leave the island.

After finishing *The Twelve Chairs* Alea felt he had finally reached the sought-after status of film director. Ironically, this left him with a feeling of emptiness that he tackled by assuming greater administrative responsibilities at ICAIC and by accepting, more than deciding, to film *Cumbite*.[3] Following that film, Alea began work on adapting Fernando Ortiz' *A Cuban Fight against Demons*. Two things stood in the way of that project: one, he felt "it was a difficult task for which we still lack[ed] the maturity necessary to confront it,"[4] and two, he was too frustrated from having to deal with ineffective bureaucrats as he tried to finalize a divorce while at the same time solving the myriad of small crises that inevitably came up because of the shortages caused by the blockade.[5]

Alea solved the first problem by putting aside the project of filming *A Cuban Fight* until after *Memories of Underdevelopment*, by which time ICAIC and Alea had acquired the necessary experience to tackle such a project. For the second problem, on the other hand, he decided to channel his anger into making *Death of a Bureaucrat:*

The decision to make that film was an incredible form of psychotherapy: it allowed me to channel the violence that I had been accumulating into a film. I continued running errands, visited the necessary offices, met with many bureaucrats, and wasted much time. But now it was different. I always carried with me a small notebook where I would write down different situations, behaviors, facts, and my errands turned into a most interesting research project, and I began to confront the situation with a great sense of humor.[6]

With this film, Alea's years of idealism and apprenticeship ended. From *Memories of Underdevelopment* onward, his attitude toward life and art matured into a healthy skepticism, and he developed his own dramatic style of filmmaking, a style that used narration to explore internal conflicts.

Stories of the Revolution

In the early meetings to discuss what to do for Alea's first feature, the working group arrived at the following consensus:

Taking into account our inexperience and also the fact that we did not have adequate technical resources, we could not promise to make "the great film" of the Revolution, nor anything close to it. We remembered *Paisà* and thus the key to the film, the model with which to work, with our feet firmly planted on the ground.

Rosellini's film had five different episodes about the Second World War in Italy, and we saw that such a structure reduced the risks of our project. . . . This structure also allowed us to approach different aspects of the revolutionary struggle: the clandestine struggle in the city, in the Sierra Maestra, and the final triumph.[7]

Implicit in this structure is the official historiography of the Revolution as a struggle on two fronts (city and country), which bore fruit when the two successfully came together in the Battle of Santa Clara. In the film these three aspects of the struggle—city, country, and their coming together—are not tied together in a single narrative, so the force of the argument is somewhat diluted. (It would be up to Humberto Solás to successfully incorporate this idea into a workable narrative in *Manuela*, 1966). Another major weakness of the film is that its first two episodes waver between the epic and the dramatic, without succeeding in either mode. Only the last episode overcomes this problem, but at the expense of doing away with the dramatic element that is Alea's forte.

Seen today, *Stories of the Revolution* is a dated film that assumes the viewer's familiarity with the specifics of the revolutionary struggle. The three episodes—"El herido" ("The Wounded Man"), "Rebeldes" ("The Rebels"), and "La batalla de Santa Clara" ("The Battle of Santa Clara")—each deal with a precise moment in history. In "The Wounded Man" that moment is the assault on the Presidential Palace mounted by the urban revolutionary group

Directorio Revolucionario on March 13, 1957, in "The Rebels" it is the struggle of the guerrillas in the Sierra Maestra, and in "The Battle of Santa Clara" it is the battle that convinced Fulgencio Batista to flee Cuba, lest the same thing happen in Havana.

Stylistically and ideologically, *Stories of the Revolution* is heir to Italian neorealism. The direct model was Rosellini's *Paisà* (1946), and the elements in common with that film are the use of nonactors (along with professionals, in Alea's case), shots on location (for "The Rebels" Alea used a site in the Sierra Maestra where Che Guevara had conducted an ambush), the episodic form, and the dignity and sacredness of everyday life. This last point brings us to the ideological coincidences between Italian neorealism and Alea's art, coincidences that will be of even greater importance for Alea's future development than the stylistic ones. Like Umberto Barbaro (1902–1959), the film critic and lecturer at the Centro Sperimentale in Rome where Alea had studied, Alea believed in art's potential to serve and improve the human condition. His use of neorealist techniques therefore responds to his faith in the humanistic project underpinning neorealism as much as to the need to make a film with few resources. Specifically, the realism that Barbaro and others like him advocated was the Soviet expressive realism of Eisenstein, Pudovkin, and Dovzhenko. This influence was less technical than ideological, however, and the stylistic resemblances between Italian neorealism, Soviet expressive realism, and Cuban cinema in the 1960s, although they do exist, are slight.[8]

The Twelve Chairs

The Twelve Chairs is based on a novel of the same title by two Soviet writers, Ilya Ilf and Eugene Petrov. The novel, set in 1927 in the Soviet Union, tells the story of the search for a chair filled with jewels. A wealthy woman, fearing expropriation, had hid the treasure in one of the twelve chairs of her dining set. Gassat Vorobianinof, her nephew and heir to the family fortune, finds out about it after her death, when the dining room has already been nationalized and its twelve chairs dispersed throughout the land. Therein begins a frantic search for each and every one of the chairs. Vorobianinof enlists the help of an adventurer (Ostap) to help him get the coveted chair, but in the end Ostap dies and Vorobianinof is left penniless, the chair having ended up in the headquarters of a workers' union and the jewels used for the common good. In Alea's adaptation of the novel, the basic outline of the original narrative remains, except that Alea combines the roles of Ostap and Vorobianinof's servant into one (Oscar), and more importantly, Oscar does not die but rather ends up poised to constructively join the new, socialist reality.

The Twelve Chairs is the first attempt to film a comedy after the Revolution, and it is a very conscious exercise to explore and expand the arsenal of narrative and technical tools available to Alea and others at ICAIC:

> The principal collaborators during the filming were young men and women without much previous experience. The director of photography [Ramón F. Suárez], the camera operator, the person in charge of lighting, and the assistants were all working on their first feature. Also new to this kind of project were the assistant director and the notetaker. Even the film stock that we used (Agfa NP20 and Ultrafast) presented problems which had not yet been solved by our cameramen.[9]

This lack of experience, coupled with Alea's desire to experiment with form, led to some achievements and many imperfections. Sometimes these would coexist in a single space, as when, during the third sequence, an ICAIC newsreel on hidden treasures gives Oscar the idea to go back to his ex-boss' mansion to try his luck at finding one such treasure. This clever use of preexisting material, however, loses much of its cleverness because of the off-voice comments explaining what Oscar is thinking and why. Such didacticism borders on pamphletism when one considers the characterization of the two protagonists, Oscar and his ex-master, Hipólito. At best, the film is an attempt to demystify the bourgeoisie (through Hipólito) and at the same time criticize the remains of bourgeois thought in Cuba (through Oscar).

In any event, the film is set right after the Cuban Revolution, and the only people who know about the jewels are a petty priest who got the information while administering the woman's last rites of confession, her nephew Hipólito, and Oscar, the faithful ex-servant whom Hipólito recruits because he is not street-smart enough to track the chairs down by himself. The people who actually find the jewels—a group of workers who in turn donate them to their Railway Workers' Social Institute—constitute a fourth, collective character: the new society that is now history's agent, which Oscar joins at the end of the film.

These four characters—Hipólito, Oscar, the priest, and the workers—suffer a rather schematic treatment. Oscar is the sympathetic ex-servant who in the end joins the workers, Hipólito is the aristocratic bourgeois who cannot or will not work, the priest is a simple puppet controlled from afar, and the workers are an idealized mass who charm us with their good will and common sense, as in the scene when they conclude that the artist commissioned to paint a mural in their new compound is a bit crazy because of the way he describes how he will depict the forces of the Revolution against the forces of imperialism, all in the style of socialist realism.

In 1961, during a cultural debate that culminated in Fidel Castro's "Words to the Intellectuals," Alea had criticized those who advocate state control over art's form and content, especially if the prescription was to be socialist realism. This bit about the muralist is a continuation of that argument. The scene, in fact, seems to have caused a bit of a controversy. In an interview published a month after the film's release, Edmundo Desnoes asked Alea why he had called *The Twelve Chairs* a socialist realist film. Alea responded as follows:

Let me clarify: I was not referring to *The Twelve Chairs*, but rather to the majority of works—in film, in painting, and in literature—that are presented to us as examples of socialist realism, but which have little in the way of realism. Is it necessary to give examples? I think they are too obvious. One need only remember all those works where the bourgeois character embodies all that is evil, all the corruption, all the possible rottenness; and the working class character is on the other hand an immaculate being, exceptionally talented and pasteurized, and then when there appears a political commissary, he reminds us too much of Superman, the one from the American comic strips. This, you will agree, has nothing at all to do with realism. I would say it's the worst kind of idealism. And that's why I referred to these sort of works as representative of socialist idealism.

Now I'm ready to answer your question: *The Twelve Chairs* is an example of socialist realism because it presents in a very direct way a critical moment for our society, a moment of transition when one can observe very clearly the fight between the old and the new. And in that fight the film reflects a tendency in favor of the new, in favor of the disappearance of the last interests of the bourgeoisie and in favor of the integration into society of healthy and productive elements.[10]

In other words, the characters in *The Twelve Chairs* are schematized, but not to the extent of becoming caricatures. Indeed, Oscar is not a pasteurized figure but a *pícaro* who would survive and thrive regardless of the circumstances. Hipólito, on the other hand, is far from evil and is really nothing but a poor devil whom we wish would join the baseball game at the end of the film. One possible solution to the debate over the film's use of socialist realism may be to see *The Twelve Chairs* as a parody of socialist realism, an inside joke for those who had been following the debates on this issue.

The importance of the film, however, lies outside this debate. As Ugo Ulive, the film's codirector, wrote, "*The Twelve Chairs* is important because it goes beyond the theme of resistance, of clandestine struggle, of the difficult past, and shows, from a humorous perspective, the problem of adaptation that a new reality creates, in people of very different origins."[11] Important? Yes. Humorous? Well . . . The film, according to its publicists, is about "three characters in search of a chair." The nod to Pirandello is, however astute it may sound, misleading. After all, the humor in *The Twelve Chairs* is not caustic or penetrating, but rather shallow and ineffective, a light version of *choteo*, Cuba's national brand of corrosive humor. This may sound harsh, considering that critics agree that the film is humorous. And yet, Alea tells the story that "when we were finishing with the shooting of the film, one of the technicians who was working with us asked me if I was going to make a funny movie after finishing this one."[12]

Cumbite

Cumbite is an adaptation of a Haitian novel, Jacques Romain's *Les Gov-erneurs de la Rosée* (literally, *The Governors of the Dew*). It is ICAIC's last neorealist film and Alea's own farewell to the style that taught him so much. It's a simple story, a *Romeo and Juliet* set in Haiti in 1942, with the differ-ence that when Manuel (Romeo) dies, Anaisa (Juliet) decides to honor his memory by convincing the townsfolk to leave family feuds behind and work together in order to build the water canal that her beloved had envisioned.

Cumbite was Alea's least favorite film:

> I did not succeed in achieving the authenticity of speech of the Haitians, simply because it is not my culture. I saw things as one who observes from outside. That is the main flaw of the film. . . .
>
> I think that the film has some beautiful scenes: Manuel's funeral with the Haitian prayer for the dead, and the Voudou dances, for example. But these are things that one finds in folklore, and what I want is to make films with core human values, not folk.[13]

Notwithstanding the harsh self-criticism, *Cumbite* was Alea's best film to date, with its beautifully stark black-and-white photography, a uniform rhythm that contrasts sharply with the erratic tempo of *Stories of the Revolu-tion* and *The Twelve Chairs*, and a narrative that is compact and clear, not dif-fuse and episodic as in *Stories of the Revolution*, nor drawn-out as in *The Twelve Chairs*. It is, contradictory as it may sound, a neorealist film that feels like a dream . . . and a farewell.

Death of a Bureaucrat

Had Kafka been a Cuban, instead of being a writer of the absurd, he would have been a writer of customs and manners.

—VIRGILIO PIÑERA[14]

In *Death of a Bureaucrat*, Alea continues the deliberate experimentation with narrative techniques and style that began in *The Twelve Chairs*, and while the results are considerably better, the film still suffers from a narrative that moves in fits and starts and from drawn-out sequences that could have been solved with more daring editing.

The film is a satiric comedy about one man's efforts to secure his aunt's widow's pension. The day after his uncle dies, he goes with his aunt to a government office in order to apply for her pension. The office worker asks for her dead husband's work ID, but she can't give it to him because the uncle had asked to be buried with it. So begins a series of bureaucratic and illegal adventures to get that ID, culminating in a final sequence of mayhem in which the nephew goes crazy and strangles the head bureaucrat at the cemetery.

In between these two deaths—that of the uncle and that of the bureaucrat—Alea pokes fun at the bureaucrats who had made his own life miserable over the past couple of years. He also continues the polemic over official art (or, more specifically, the influence of bureaucrats in art), which he had touched on in *The Twelve Chairs*. This time, however, the target is not only socialist realism, as in the scene where an artist describes his idea for a mural depicting an imperialist octopus, but also the mechanical reproduction of art, as in the opening sequence, which shows a Rube Goldberg–type of machine that the uncle had invented in order to mass-produce plaster busts of José Martí. Bernardo Callejas, a Cuban film critic, has called this sequence "a satire on those who by dint of mechanistic thinking cut themselves off from the thought of great men, turning them into hollow symbols."[15] I agree, and the observation makes me ask if this sort of mechanical reproduction is not what Alea came close to doing in *Death of a Bureaucrat*, with all the explicit references to past movie greats. In the film there are direct visual quotes of Harold Lloyd's *Safety Last* in the clock sequence, of Laurel and Hardy's *Two Tars* in the final sequence, of Buñuel's *Un chien andalou* and Bergman's *Wild Strawberries* in two different flashdreams, and of Chaplin's *Modern Times* in the opening sequence. Alea explained that these homages "emerged spontaneously while we worked on the script. During our discussions we used references to known films in order to understand each other better. For instance, we might say something like 'This scene is solved in a Laurel and Hardy approach.' This would give us a model which made the work easier."[16] This sentence sounds like a description of the machine in the film, and its mechanistic reproduction of art, and yet to call the film's references to movie classics "mechanical reproductions" would be unfair. I rather see these tributes as a good examples (at the formal level) of Alea's double-voicing: the references are both creative homages and a playfully mechanical approach to staging narrative situations. Moreover, the film's stylistic eclecticism may be seen as Alea's way of claiming the body of world film production as his heritage (and the heritage of Cuba),[17] while simultaneously bidding farewell to the cinematic forms of the past. This last point is of particular importance when considering Alea's development because it functions as a necessary exhumation[18] of these influences before he could tackle the more complex proposals of the French New Wave, Brecht, Eisenstein, and the New Latin American Cinema. All of these, as we'll see, were skillfully assimilated and put to use in *Memories of Underdevelopment*, Alea's next film and itself a classic of world cinema.

3
Memories of Underdevelopment:
The Dialectics of Identification and Alienation

Genesis and Reception

Alea continued his research for *A Cuban Fight against Demons* after the completion of *Death of a Bureaucrat*. One day, however, he read Edmundo Desnoes' *Inconsolable Memories* and immediately called the author to tell him he wanted to make a film based on it. The action in both the novel and the film takes place in Havana, between two defining moments in postrevolutionary Cuban history: the Bay of Pigs invasion in 1961 and the Cuban Missile Crisis in 1962. Sergio, the protagonist, is an aspiring intellectual from the merchant middle class. When his wife and parents leave for the United States, he sees their departure as an opportunity to try his luck in writing. Instead, he spends his days reflecting upon his past life and looking for love. In the end, Sergio's failure to fall in love with the women he courts parallels his failure to join in the larger social transformations unfolding all around him.

Desnoes did not think his novel, a highly subjective diary with hardly any action, could lend itself to film. But Alea liked what he read (he felt that "something interesting could come out of it")[1], and decided that what the novel lacked the film could provide:

> What the film process could contribute to the novel was the "objective" vision of reality in order to make it clash with the subjective vision of the protagonist. Photography, direct documentation, fragments of newsreels, recorded speeches, filming on the street with a hidden camera on some occasions were resources which we could count on and needed to develop to the fullest . . . . In this way, we were able to develop to a greater degree than in the novel that thread which reveals the "objective" reality surrounding the character and which little by little tightens its grip until it suffocates him at the end.[2]

Alea and Desnoes worked closely on the script, and Desnoes would eventually add some chapters to his novel based on his experiences with the film. Alea also had the good fortune of working with Leo Brouwer (music) and Ramón Suárez (cinematography). Both had already worked with Alea in previous films, but in *Memories* they took their respective arts to a higher qualitative level. Suárez, for example, "discovered" the handheld camera, and Brouwer created a soundtrack that enriched—instead of simply embellishing—the film. Finally, Alea recruited Nelson Rodríguez for the editing. This was a crucial decision, since the success of the film depended on the degree to which it could create (mostly through editing) a dialectic between the protagonist's individual subjectivity and the collective subjectivity of a society in the throes of radical change. As Rodríguez recounted it:

> Titón had always worked with Mario [González]; that is, Mario had edited *The Twelve Chairs*, *Stories of the Revolution*, *Cumbite* and *Death of a Bureaucrat*. But when he came up against *Memories*, something happened and that something is that Mario was an editor, let us say, totally academic, an older person, who had stayed a little bit with the idea that editing was the academic form, he did not . . . . For example, we had been discussing by that time, I'm talking about the year . . . end of 66, beginning of 67, about Godard and all that Godard had contributed to cinematographic montage, all that about liberating all the academic stuff of the years before the 1950s. All that liberty in the cutting, in the montage, in the way of telling a story without transitions, et cetera. So there was that problem with Mario, and then Titón comes up to me and says: "Look, Nelson, I want to edit this film with you because this film has a lot of different forms in the mise-en-scene that need a fresh vision, a vision of a young person who's up to date with this stuff, and Mario is going to put up a fight because he's always going to want to have everything in a very formal way, a very . . ." That was the problem. That's how my relationship with Titón began. And in fact, the film did have a bit of everything, it had fiction, pure fiction, it had free-cinema, that is, hidden camera, a lot of material filmed that way, it had archive material, and it had reconstruction. And then all of that had to be mixed, and it had to be solid, unified.[3]

The narration's unity, so easily achieved in the novel because of its monologism, becomes in the film a problem that, thanks to the mastery of Rodríguez and Alea, is no longer a problem of the film, but of the spectator. For what Alea and his team have done is transform a monologistic novel into a dialogistic film, therefore forcing the spectator to actively participate in the film's cognitive reconstruction. Julianne Burton has pointed out the difficulty of this task, noting, "The resonance between the documentary and fictional segments, their complex and multifaceted interaction, are what make this such a thought-provoking and fertile film. Through this interaction, and often as a function of dramatic irony, the vision of the film not only exceeds that of its protagonist but often undermines and contradicts it."[4] These contradictions, so disturbing to some and so laudable to others, is why there are so many conflicting readings of the film. When it first came out in 1968, audiences in Cuba were mostly disturbed, thinking that the portrayal of a decaying and uncommitted petit-bourgeois was not a fitting subject for revolutionary Cuban cinema. Twenty years later, however, audiences were not only accepting but proud of the film. Alea recounts one such transformation:

> Two or three years ago, I talked to a high government official who in 1968 had considered it inadmissible (he did not question the artistic quality of the film, but rather its provocative nature) and to my delight he told me that now he is happy that *Memories* is a film of the Revolution. In light of what happened after the film's release he came to see it not simply as a good Cuban film, but as a film of the Revolution, and even recognized its militant character.[5]

What happened after the film's release is that perceptive critics in Cuba and abroad praised the film's subtle demystification of bourgeois individualism, particularly effective in the film because of the dramatic social cataclysms that frame the narrative and ultimately render Sergio's individualism obsolete: the Bay of Pigs invasion and the Cuban Missile Crisis. Consider the following reviews:[6]

> *Memories* offers a solid structure in which two realities are interwoven and played off against each other: the reality as seen through the subjective prism of an individual, and reality as it is [*sic*]. . . . The point of departure of the film is the presentation of a problematic from the first of these points of view. . . . The justification for this inversion can be found in the film's double objective: to present clearly a focus that responds to the ideological limitations of a determined individual and, at the same time, to offer the tools for its negation. The result is a dynamic relationship in which the film's argument is enriched, and which permits a profound analysis of the protagonist's most subtle contradictions. (Fernando Pérez *Pensamiento Crítico*, Havana, 1970)

> While the protagonist of *Memories of Underdevelopment* slowly becomes an endangered species in Cuba, with each passing day the film has taken on greater importance in Chile. So much so, that for us, Alea's film is now much more valid than when it was first screened in 1968. A product of a Europeanized culture, frustrated writer, given to vague philosophical ramblings, [Sergio] never comes into real contact with the new conditions in his country. This film . . . combines what happens to the protagonist with images that show precisely that external world which he does not capture: history in the making, the people in the streets. (Hans Ehrmann, *Última Hora*, Santiago de Chile, February 1973)

Throughout the film Sergio confronts the new reality, a reality that includes remains of the past, and everything we see is his boredom, his being washed away by the enthusiasm of the others, the vital angst that springs from the lack of certitude about his present and future, the ineffectiveness of his efforts to integrate into the new society, using the old methods that used to work but no longer do; we see how the old society molded his way of being, a way of being that has been adultered by century upon century of classist conformity and which he, because he finds them normal and valid, does not see it as the element that makes him "different" in that Cuba of '61, barely changed, but already different. (Armando Almánzar, *¡Ahora!*, Santo Domingo, 1978)

The critics I cite here emphasized Sergio's contradictions and his inability to integrate into the new order. Other critics tended to go in the opposite direction, emphasizing Sergio's lucidity and how it enables him to criticize some aspects of the new reality:

All the chaos of revolutionary Cuba is seen reflected by an uncomprehending yet "open" mind. And what better way to present the Cuban revolution to the bourgeois world than through the eyes of a man who might be any well-meaning liberal (like you or me) when faced with a totally new society? It seemed at the time very courageous of the Cubans to produce and export a film so eminently *fair*. (Richard Roud, *New York Times*, 1978)

I would submit that *Memories of Underdevelopment* has no more been honored by us [the National Society of Film Critics in New York] as a product of socialist Cuba than *Day for Night* has been honored as a product of capitalist France . . . . We vote the works of individuals, not of systems. Indeed, what struck most of us favorably about *Memories of Underdevelopment* is its very personal and very courageous confrontation of the artist's doubts and ambivalence regarding the Cuban Revolution. (Andrew Sarris, *The Village Voice*, New York, 1974)[7]

This kind of praise of Sergio's capacity for critical thought even led some critics to conclude that the film was a scathing critique of the Revolution,[8] since many of his criticisms were aimed at the inconsistencies of that historical process. Yet this is only partly true, as Alea himself has indicated:

There is a special group of people with whom we have to live, who we have to count on, to our daily disgust, in this project of building a new society. They are those who believe themselves to be the sole depository of the revolutionary legacy; those who know what is the socialist morality and who have institutionalized mediocrity and provincialism; the bureaucrats (with or without bureau); those who know the people's soul and speak of it as if it were a very promising child, but a child that must be well understood, et cetera, et cetera. . . . They are the same ones who tell us how we have to speak to the people, how we have to dress ourselves and under what terms we must struggle; they know what can and cannot be shown, because the people are not mature enough yet to know the truth. . . . This film is also directed to them, and is also intended, among other things, to annoy them, to provoke them, to irritate them.[9]

The key to this quote is the word "also" in the last sentence. Many of Sergio's criticisms against certain aspects of the new reality (those "directed to them") often apply to the old order and to Sergio's own inconsistencies. The problem in interpretation begins when critics—on both sides of the debate—point out one target of Sergio's criticisms while failing to acknowledge the other. In reality, both of these interpretations of the film (as criticism of some aspects of bourgeois individuality and as criticism of some aspects of the Revolution) may be sustained with examples from the film. That is, the film is a demystification of bourgeois individualism made through a lucid character who embodies much of what can be positive about bourgeois life (a high level of education, cosmopolitanism, lots of free time, disposable income, and a capacity for critical thought) but also much of what can be negative about it (the objectification of women, compulsory heterosexuality, the twin brothers of racism and classism, and the reification of individualism at the expense of solidarity with one's fellow humans). Because the demystification of bourgeois individualism is not categorical, the film lends itself to various and varying ideological interpretations, many of which fall short because they are partial. Julianne Burton has so far come up with the best explanation for this phenomenon:

In a film of such structural intricacy and thematic complexity, the viewer is compelled to exercise certain perceptual priorities. These are culturally conditioned and reinforced, and tend, I believe, to generate a selective and fragmented view of the film among American audiences when the film's most outstanding achievement is its synthesis—the integration of diverse components into a unified whole.[10]

I agree with the first half of this argument. From the example of the high government official cited by Alea, however, we know that Cuban audiences (and any audience, for that matter) are also capable of generating a selective and fragmented view of the film. The interesting question is not so much whether audiences exercise certain perceptual priorities. Clearly, all of us do. A more interesting approach to a film like *Memories* (which because of its dialogism *requires* that the viewer exercise certain perceptual priorities) is to ask where these priorities come from and what they entail. In the worst of cases, these priorities are dictated by a Cold War Manichaeism (cf. Andrew Sarris and the Cuban high government official who considered *Memories* "inadmissible", while in the best of cases, they are nurtured by an understanding of the context in which the film is situated and filmed (cf. Hans Ehrmann and Armando Almánzar). In the following pages I first describe and comment on the film sequence-by-sequence in an attempt to avoid the pitfall of selective reading that Burton so perceptively pointed out. This description is followed by a consideration of Alea's own explanations of the film as a dialectical play between identification and alienation, spectacle and analysis. The reason for privileging Alea's reading is that his are the most coherent and developed published explanations so far, and also because his role as director and coscriptwriter of the film gives him an insight into the film that critics can only hope to approximate. Finally, this study of *Memories* concludes with my own contribution to the film's criticism: a reading of the film as a tragedy, with special consideration given to the allegorical significance of the women in the film.

Description of the Film

Formally the film is a collage of film material broadly divided into the categories of fiction and narrative. Each category is in turn a mixture of modes. In the fiction segments, the film draws from several currents, although the more obvious ones are from Second Cinema, specifically Italian neorealism and French New Wave. Alea's knowledge of post–World War II Italian cinema was intimate and already fully assimilated before filming *Memories*. In *Memories*, the use of black-and-white film stock, of hidden cameras to record street scenes, and of real audio all remit us to films such as *La strada*. More contemporary Italian cinema also comes to mind, especially Antonioni and Fellini—Antonioni because of his popularizing the theme of the brooding intellectual and Fellini for his sympathetic portrayals of middle-age men looking for love in all the wrong places. Indeed, Sergio bears a striking resemblance in terms of taste, outlook, luck, and even looks to Marcello Mastroiani in *La dolce vita* and *8 1/2*: a good-looking, intelligent, and cultivated man with money, time, and wit to spare. From the French New Wave, *Memories* seems closest to the films of Godard (at least in terms of formal experimentation with montage and handheld camera) and Resnais, whose *Hiroshima, mon amour* (1959) continuously shifted between objective and subjective modes of narration. William Alexander explains the effect of using these cinematic styles:

> Gutiérrez Alea has chosen to work within his own language structure—that
> of the middle-class intellectual—for he seeks an audience of such intellec-
> tuals, especially those who remain dangerous spectators of the Cuban Rev-
> olution. He hooks them with Second Cinema, a subtle film language that
> appeals to their sophistication, and through it enables them to see them-

selves for what they are. Here then is one use of film language for empow-
erment, for changing some spectators into actors in the revolution, and for
further isolating those who will not change.[11]

This masterful use of Second Cinema styles does not imply that Alea was
interested in the same issues as Second Cinema auteurs. As I pointed out in
the Introduction, Alea was politically closer to New Latin American Cinema
than Second Cinema, and his use of Second Cinema techniques was as
means to "hook" people, not an end in itself or as a means of showing off his
versatility.

The documentary portions of the film are also diverse in origin and style.
Here the more important antecedents are not so much European as Cuban,
specifically, the documentaries of Santiago Alvarez. Virtually all kinds of
"documents" are used in the film: hidden camera footage, photo-essays,
newsreels, TV reports, radio broadcasts, newspaper clippings, and even a
sociological treatise. All of this material is interwoven with Sergio's fiction
so that the result is, as Eisenstein put it, a montage of ideas, an intellectual
montage whereby "an idea results from the collision of independent takes—
takes which may in fact be opposed to each other."[12] The accumulation of
many such collisions throughout the film is what gives it the feeling of a collage, which is how Alea described it during his cameo appearance in the film
itself (talk about self-reflexivity!). Two years before the film, however, Alea
had already articulated how he wanted to make this film:

> Not only in cinema, but also in literature, in painting, in music, language is
> developing towards ever greater atomization, . . . a fragmentation that
> makes it the most appropriate vehicle of expression for the new rhythm in
> life. . . . Today, Eisenstein's "intellectual montage" is being developed
> starting from Resnais. That offers new resources to capture a reality that is
> elusive, complex, ever-changing, and to establish new relations . . .
> between the different aspects of that reality that is recorded directly by the
> camera.[13]

In an article published in *Film Quarterly* in 1970 (two years after the film
and four years after Alea's remarks), Brian Henderson defined collage using
strikingly similar language. In traditional montage, he notes, fragments of
reality are reconstituted in a "highly organized, synthetic emotional and intellectual patterns. Collage, [on the other hand], collects or sticks its fragments
together in a way that does not entirely overcome their fragmentation."[14] The
best example of how *Memories* is more of a collage than a montage in this
sense is the way in which the story of Noemi is incorporated into the narrative.
Like Elena, she gets her own intertitle, but unlike Elena, Noemi's narrative is
dispersed throughout the film. Moreover, the relationship between the takes
where she appears is not causal (as with Elena, where one thing leads to

another), but instead is determined by Sergio's own fragmented imagination. The main drawback of this conceptualization of the film as a collage is the fact that collages are taken in all at once, whereas film must be seen in time. In other words, it is impossible to step back from the film as one would step back from a two-dimensional collage. The ability to associate the fragments into a coherent whole will, in the case of film, depend on the viewer's ability to remember many details, make the necessary connections between fragments that are close in time (easily done as the film is projected on the screen), and make the necessary connections between fragments that are not close in time (not so easily done). In the next few pages I will describe the film sequence-by-sequence to point out details that may escape the viewer, thus hampering his or her ability to construct a coherent whole out of the fragments.

Memories has a total of thirty-one sequences:

1.   Opening sequence: popular dance and credits
2.   At the airport (intertitle: HAVANA 1961. MANY PEOPLE ARE LEAVING)
3.   At the apartment with Laura's belongings
4.   First foray into the city (of markets): "I'm not like them"
5.   With Pablo in town (intertitle: PABLO; "The truth of the group is in the murderer")
6.   First meeting with Noemi (intertitle: NOEMI); erotic fantasies
7.   Second foray into the city (of tourists): "There is an exquisite moment bet. 30 and 35"
8.   Back in the apartment (TV: Marilyn Monroe and Guantánamo)
9.   Third foray into the city (of pleasure): Pick-up scene at La Rampa (intertitle: ELENA)
10. With Elena at ICAIC
11. Making out with Elena in the apartment, Elena leaves, flashback to Laura
12. Elena returns the next day
13. Farewell to Pablo
14. Fourth foray into the city (of memories): Flashbacks to childhood, school, and brothel
15. Last time with Elena (visits to library, art museum, and Hemingway's house)
16. At Hemingway's house (intertitle: A TROPICAL ADVENTURE)
17. Round table: Literature and underdevelopment
18. Letter from mom
19. Fifth foray into the city (of lost love): Flashbacks to Hanna
20. Elena comes back; Sergio does not let her in
21. Urban Reform surveyors
22. Sixth foray into the city (of workers): May Day demonstration, flashback to the opening sequence, and photo-essay of Sergio's family life

23. Seventh foray into the city (of nostalgia): Photo-essay of Sergio's family life
24. Elena's brother pays a visit
25. Arguing with Elena's family in front of the mannequin display
26. At the police station
27. The trial
28. At the apartment with newspaper and Noemi's photos; erotic fantasies interrupted
29. Reality encroaches I (intertitle: OCTOBER 22, 1962/KENNEDY SPEAKS)
30. Reality encroaches II: Castro answers; Sergio increasingly tense
31. Eighth (and final) foray into the city (of war): Malecón scene, pacing in the apartment, views of Havana

A survey of these sequences reveals that the main characters in the fictional side of the narrative are Sergio, Elena, Noemi, Hanna, Laura, Pablo, the judges, the surveyors, and the city of Havana. On the documentary side of the narrative, the main characters are Fidel Castro, John F. Kennedy, the captured invaders of the Bay of Pigs, common people in the streets, and (once again) the city of Havana, a city whose transformation—from city of markets, to city of tourists, of pleasure, of memories, of lost love, of workers, of nostalgia, and finally, of war—reflects not only an economic and political reality, but also Sergio's subjective transformation. Let's see how they interact.[15]

1. Opening Sequence: Popular Dance and Credits[16]

The film opens with people dancing outside at night. The scene is shot with a handheld camera moving and jostling through the crowd of dancing, sweating bodies. The camera loses focus at times and its view is obstructed by the dancers, seemingly unaware of its presence. In the midst of this cinema verité shooting, one of the dancers, an Afro-Cuban woman, looks directly into the camera. The camera moves on. Several gunshots sound above the rhythmic music (an Afro-Cuban *mozambique* by Pello "el Afrokán"); confusion follows as people gather around the victim on the ground; the camera moves rapidly through the crowd, calling more attention to its subjective use and reminding the viewer of its operator (or is it Sergio, the protagonist, whom we haven't seen yet?). The camera then comes to rest on the face of the same Afro-Cuban woman, who addresses the camera (Sergio?) with her bold gaze. The frame freezes on the woman; music fades out, then the image cuts to the next sequence.

This first sequence has the effect of jolting the viewer out of complacency. The setting used here was virtually de rigueur in films made before the Revolution: exotic, sexually charged dance scenes where violence is quickly absorbed and the party goes on.[17] Yet what may have been exotic and seducing (for the typical viewer of such films) is now pedestrian and unsettling. The closing shot shows a woman who may have been, in prerevolutionary films, a line dancer at the Tropicana. Here, however, she is no longer an object on stage, but a subject among us. Her intense gaze, made insistent by the freeze of the shot, shifts the viewer from the safe position of an unacknowledged voyeur to the responsible position of a conscious observer, perhaps even participant, in the process of the film about to unfold.

2. At the Airport (Intertitle: HAVANA 1961: MANY PEOPLE ARE LEAVING)

The camera work is still cinema verité style. There is no focused sound; rather, a direct track of ambient noise in the airport runs synchronously with the images. The roving, handheld camera randomly follows various people who will board planes to the United States. Some of them are clearly suffering, some of them look stoic, and some children play, unaware of what's going on. All of them are white and middle class, with the exception of some (white) nuns. An immigration official stamps "SALIDA" on a passport. The film could be a documentary up to this point. Then Sergio is finally revealed hugging his parents goodbye. Next, he approaches Laura, mouths what looks like "Well, bye, bye" (in English), and they hug each other. Sergio, clearly unmoved, proceeds to wipe off his mouth, as if Laura's goodbye kiss were an unwelcome gesture. Laura walks toward the runway, hesitates for a second, looks back at Sergio, then keeps walking. The plane rolls down the runway in long shot, with the camera set up behind the many people waving to the plane. In the foreground—set apart from the others—is Sergio, the camera looking over his shoulder. In this critical shot Sergio is established as the locus of subjectivity and (simultaneously) the object of the viewer's attention. The camera begins with an almost subjective, over-the-shoulder shot behind Sergio (as described above), then it tracks around him (remaining in close-up), and ends in front (a 180-degree track). The shot is held—a close-up of him looking straight on— as he whistles and watches the plane take off, so that the viewer ends up looking *at* him as well as *with* him. This crucial shot begins a pattern of identification/distantiation that becomes a model for perception throughout the film, which will be discussed in more detail in the next section.

Sergio then takes a bus home. Flashbacks to the airport, only this time we see the farewells from another point of view, with the camera over Sergio's shoulder. Unlike Sergio, his relatives are not detached or unmoved. As Sergio remembers Laura walking toward the airplane (a sign next to the steps announces that it's bound to Miami), he says to himself in voice-over, "She'll really have to work there . . . well, that is, until she finds some dumb guy who'll marry her. To tell the truth, she's still something to look at. She'll remember me when things get bad. After that . . . I'm the one who's really been stupid. Working so that she could live like someone who had been born in New York or Paris, and not on this underdeveloped island . . ." Back in the bus, we see (from Sergio's point of view) a billboard celebrating the victory at Playa Girón (Bay of Pigs).

3. At the Apartment with Laura's Belongings

The camera continues the lateral movement of the last shot; that is, it continues Sergio's point of view as he steps into his apartment. It's a modern apartment, with Cuban paintings and framed family pictures on the walls and solid, American-style furniture. Sergio's side of the apartment is filled with books, objects d'art, and his typewriter, while Laura's side of the apartment is filled with cosmetics, perfumes, and other beauty enhancers—two incompatible people occupying the same space, a story that will be partly repeated with Elena. Scattered around are copies of American magazines (*Vogue, Life, Harper's Bazaar*). Offscreen, Sergio whistles "Adelita," a song from the Mexican Revolution (does he think this revolution will be like the Mexican one, where bourgeois values and privileges survived under different guise?).

Sergio goes to the bedroom, then to his typewriter, where he types the first words of Desnoes' novel: "All those who loved me and kept bothering me right up to the last minute have left now." Camera tracking shows more objects in his side of the apartment, one of which is a collage showing Pope John Paul framed by a toilet seat. The next morning Sergio is having breakfast: toasted bread, café au lait and a cigarette. He's wearing his undershirt, his hair is undone, and he burps. He is clearly alone. On the balcony, Sergio observes the city through a telescope, a symbol of his detachment. He sees a couple kissing as they sit by the rooftop pool at the Hotel Capri and ships entering the harbor. "Everything remains the same," he says. "Here everything remains the same. All of a sudden it looks like a set, a city made of cardboard." More shots of Havana through the telescope: children playing in school; a statue of General Antonio Maceo, a Dominican black leader and martyr of the Wars of Independence against Spain (1868–1878); and the foundation of the monument to the U.S. Battleship Maine, from which the imperial eagle has been torn down. "The Bronze Titan . . ." Sergio says ironically. "Cuba free and independent . . . who would have thought that this could happen? Without the imperial eagle. And what about the dove Picasso was going to send? It's very comfortable being a communist millionaire in Paris." The telescope keeps panning: left to focus on a freighter in the harbor, right to focus on a small torpedo boat. Things are, after all, not the same. The next telescopic shot is of a billboard that reads "ESTA HUMANIDAD HA DICHO BASTA Y HA ECHADO A ANDAR," a phrase that comes from the last paragraph of the Second Declaration of Havana, proclaimed by Castro on February 4, 1962. Sergio reads the sign with an ironic intonation and adds: "Like my parents, like Laura, and they won't stop until they get to Miami. Yet today everything looks so different. Have I changed, or has this city changed?" Both, in fact, have changed, although in the last sequence we will see that the city has changed much more than Sergio ever will.

Sergio's voyeurism is interrupted by the chirping of his birds. He goes to feed them, but one of them, symbolizing Laura, is dead. He lifts it out by its feet and lets it fall from the balcony to the street. Ever-ironic, he recites the following verses from one of the poems in Pablo Neruda's *20 poemas de amor y una canción desesperada* (*Twenty Love Poems and a Desperate Song*, 1924): "It's the time of departure. Oh! abandoned like the wharves at dawn. Everything in you was shipwrecked." Here is a good example of Sergio's unintended irony, for whose shipwreck is he referring to, Laura's or his own? The next shot shows Sergio pressing the PLAY button on a reel-to-reel tape recorder, and as he rummages through Laura's belongings, we hear a heated tape-recorded argument between them. Sergio's irony is unbearable, as he points out Laura's artificiality while hinting at his own shallowness in choosing women based solely on external attributes. The shot of him playing with a lipstick underscores his phallocentrism, and as he looks at himself in the mirror, his face disfigured by a stocking, Laura's tape-recorded voice says: "You're a monster! You're sick!" The stocking that previously enhanced Laura's beauty now enhances Sergio's monstrosity.

4. First Foray into the City (of Markets): "I'm Not Like Them"

The camera's eye corresponds to Sergio's point of view as he walks alone in the streets of Havana: people getting off a bus, people crossing the street in opposite direction, a woman wearing metal rollers in her hair, a young woman licking an ice cream cone, an *iyabó* (someone who is being initiated into Santería and who, as part of that process, wears white for at least a year) whose beautiful legs catch the camera's attention, more people, shop windows, and a bookstore display rack, where he stops and walks in. It is as if Sergio was shopping around for a woman, but since he does not like anything he sees, he walks into a bookstore. The camera follows him. Again, the camera allows us to look with Sergio and then at Sergio.

In the bookstore we see a novel by Mikhail Sholokhov, a book on Soviet cosmonaut Yuri Gagarin, the works of José Martí, and Argentinean Leon Rozitchner's book *Moral burguesa y revolución* (*Bourgeois Morality and Revolution*, 1963). Sergio picks up a copy of this last book, all the while claiming to have a clear conscience. As he leafs thorough the book, he observes a beautiful young woman who in turn looks suggestively at him. This makes him a bit uncomfortable, as he likes to gaze, but not to be gazed upon. "Here," he says, "women look straight into your eyes as if they want to be touched by your look. That doesn't happen anywhere else in the world. Maybe Italian women stare a little more, but no, it's never like here."

Back in the streets, he walks by a relatively empty park where there used to be a department store called "El Encanto." Flashback to the night the building burned down, commenting on how Havana has changed from being the "Paris of the Caribbean" (i.e., with luxury stores) to a "Tegucigalpa of the

Caribbean," with almost empty shop windows. Empty, that is, except for a few knick-knacks. In one window, for example, there is a poster of Fidel Castro, a bust of José Martí, and a piece of cardboard with Martí's line, "Our wine is bitter, but it is our wine"; in another window, a large photograph of Fidel in battle dress; in another, an empty window with a sign advertising Kodak film; in another, a window displaying a photograph of Fidel against a cloth backdrop, and next to it a crudely lettered sign that reads: "Aquilimbo. This concern is united in fulfilling the golden rule"; in another, an empty store window with strips of tape forming an "X" across the window and a picture of José Martí in the background; and finally, in the last window shown, we see a naked Santa Barbara, a bust of a suffering Christ, figurines of Mary and Christ, and a portrait of Fidel Castro. The suggestiveness of this last shot is all the more striking because the portrait of Fidel is directly below that of the naked figurine of Santa Barbara, Cuba's patron saint.

The sequence ends as it began, with shots of common people. Only this time Sergio is beginning to doubt his own superiority. "What meaning does life have for them?" he asks. "What meaning does it have for me? . . . But I'm not like them!" Sergio's face looks contorted, somewhat wasted, grave, and sad, as the ones just seen. When the camera closes in on him, the frame freezes, thus forcing the viewer to ask himself or herself: "Am I (the viewer) also like Sergio?" A "yes" would be flattering for the viewer if he or she was thinking about Sergio's intelligence and good taste, but it would not be so flattering if that same viewer were to consider that he or she may be, like Sergio, hopelessly detached, unproductively ironic, utterly egocentric, disgustingly snobbish. For every penny's worth of redeeming qualities, it seems, Sergio has a whole bank account of condemnatory defects.

5. With Pablo in Town (Intertitle: PABLO: "The Truth of the Group Is in the Murderer")

In this sequence we learn that Sergio is not a caricature of the bourgeoisie. That honor belongs to Pablo: opportunistic, materialistic, and highly critical of the Revolution. First we see them driving down the Malecón in Pablo's convertible. Sergio is accompanying Pablo to fix a few dents in the car because the government won't allow him to emigrate unless the things he leaves behind (in this case, the car) are in top shape. Pablo discusses politics, and how Cuba is just a pawn in the international game called the Cold War. That is, Pablo fails to recognize the national roots of the Revolution. When they stop at a gas station, Pablo complains that without the American "know-how" the country won't develop economically. He fails to recognize the reason why the economy was underdeveloped in the first place. And finally, when they return to Pablo's apartment building, Pablo implies that the solution to all the shortages is to imitate the Americans: "Listen, they say the latest American cars are incredible. I was reading a magazine Julio Gómez lent me. Sealed motors with two spark plugs and a two-year guarantee. If it breaks down, they give you another one. You don't have to fix it. . . . Imagine, with the kind of mechanics we have here, that's the solution." In other words, Pablo fails to recognize that Cuba's specific problems cannot be solved by indiscriminately applying solutions that were tailored for the specific circumstances of another, totally different system. To me, Pablo seems to embody the collective character in Rubén Blades' song about materialistic men and women: the *chicos plásticos que van por ahí*. Even Sergio grows sick of him. "To think," Sergio muses in one of the flashbacks to his buddy days with Pablo, "[to think] that we've been running around together all the time for more than five years."

In the next shot Sergio and Pablo are in Sergio's apartment. Pablo is in the bathroom washing his hands and talking nonsense, while Sergio reads from *Moral burguesa y revolución*, the book he had purchased earlier at the bookstore. "That's what they said," adds Sergio, referring to Pablo's nonsense. "Who?" asks Pablo. "The Bay of Pigs prisoners. Listen." And so Sergio (of all people!) begins to narrate, in reporter style, the longest and most thorough documentary piece in the film, with segments taken from Alea's own documentary, *Muerte al invasor* (1961); TV footage of the four-day public trial that followed their capture; and footage of Batista's death squads and high-society events during his dictatorship. Sergio narrates, and the visual images support, how the invading brigades had "a hierarchy of social functions which epitomizes the division in the moral and social work of the bourgeoisie: the priest, the businessman, dilettante official, the torturer, the philosopher, the politician, and the innumerable sons of good families. Each one of them carried out specific duties, and yet, it was the whole, the group, which gave meaning to each individual activity."

Next are scenes of a woman explaining (during a public trial) how one of the invaders tortured her and killed a man in front of her. These are perhaps the film's most powerful documentary images. The sequence continues, but words and images, instead of reinforcing each other, now increasingly contradict each other. Thus, for example, a priest is shown offering communion on a ship, while Father Lugo, one of the captured invaders, says in voice-over: "It seems as though you want to accuse me of being the originator of the invasion and all those things. I want to insist that my mission was purely spiritual. I have never handled a weapon, before or after. The fact that one is mixed up in a conspiracy doesn't make one a conspirator." The hypocrisy and brutality of the invaders is demonstrated clearly here. What becomes problematized, however, is Sergio's position vis-a-vis the Revolution. What is Sergio's relation to the events that he narrates? At best, Sergio represents the lag between consciousness and action. At worst, he is just like Father Lugo, a man who cannot or will not see (in the documentary's own words) "the true dialectical relationship between individuals and the group."

6. First Meeting with Noemi (Intertitle: NOEMI); Erotic Fantasies

The sequence introduces us to Noemi, Sergio's cleaning lady for over a year. He's never noticed her before, he says, but thinks that "if she would fix herself up and dress better, she would be very attractive." They have breakfast together, and she tells him about the time she was baptized in a river. Sergio's imagination runs wild, and in a "flashdream" he imagines the two of them alone in the river. He holds her in his arms, and her nipples show through her wet white shirt.

The movement is extremely slow, unreal, and is accompanied by the "Spring" movement from Vivaldi's *The Four Seasons*. The rest of the sequence is an intercalation of Sergio in the apartment pretending to be busy as Noemi cleans, when in fact he's having erotic fantasies about her.

7. Second Foray into the City (of Tourists): "There Is an Exquisite Moment bet. 30 and 35"

This is a very short sequence, not very important. In it Sergio visits the Riviera Hotel and wistfully comments on other people's exhibitionism, even as he wears a bikini and a pullover with the logo of Kent State University. We also learn more about his view of women: "There is an exquisite moment between thirty and thirty five when Cuban women suddenly go from maturity to decay. They are fruits that rot at an amazing speed." Later in the film, Sergio would say of himself: "I'm thirty-eight years old and I'm already an old man. I don't feel wiser or more mature. More stupid. More rotten than mature, like a piece of rotten fruit."

8. Back in the Apartment (TV: Marilyn Monroe and Guantánamo)

A TV screen with a succession of images. The first is Marilyn Monroe singing the closing bars of the song "Baby, I'm Through with Love." This foreshadows the next sequence, in which Sergio picks up Elena for purely sexual reasons. The rest of the images have to do with Guantánamo Bay and the increase in tensions between the United States and Cuba because of the American base there. Sergio turns the TV off. The world outside is in crisis, but he believes that by turning off the TV these problems will go away, or at least not affect him.

9. Third Foray into the City (of Pleasure): Pick-Up Scene at La Rampa (Intertitle: ELENA)

Walking along La Rampa, Havana's glitzy red-light district before the Revolution (and again for the past few years), Sergio picks up Elena. First, Sergio removes his glasses, stares at Elena, and as he walks by, tells her, "You have beautiful knees." Elena responds by scoping Sergio as he climbs the stairs. Sergio looks down and sees Elena inspecting her knees. She took the bait!

Next thing we know, Elena is upstairs flirting with Sergio and saying "Are you crazy?" to every one of Sergio's advances. Finally, Elena agrees to have dinner with Sergio, partly out of self-interest (he tells her he can take her to meet some of his friends at ICAIC) and partly out of pleasure. After the waiter finishes taking their order, Sergio orders a martini, and Elena declines his offer of a drink because "they're giving me shots for my nerves." The cut to the next sequence is a stroke of genius.

SERGIO: Why do you want to be in films?
ELENA: Because I'm tired of always being the same. That way I can be
          someone else without people thinking I'm crazy. I want to be able
          to unfold my personality.
SERGIO: But all those characters in theater and film are like broken records.
          The only thing an actress does is to repeat the same gestures and
          the same words thousands of times. The same gestures and the
          same words . . . the same gestures and the same words . . ."

As Sergio finishes these words, we begin to see repetitions of clips from Hollywood movies where women submit to men or strip for them. In the context of the relationship that will develop between Sergio and Elena, these clips underscore how Sergio's sexist attitudes are reinforced by capitalist media, and they also foreshadow the kind of hypocritical sexual elusiveness and game-playing that Elena herself is about to engage in with Sergio.[18] This is Alea at his best: First he rids the film clips of their original erotic charge by decontextualizing and repeating them. Next he uses them to illuminate the subjectivities of the new lovebirds Sergio and Elena. Then he uses them as documents of the hypocrisy of Batista's censors. And finally, Alea drives the point home that such hypocrisy is no longer part of the new society.

10. With Elena at ICAIC

When these repetitions are over we are no longer in the Chinese restaurant but at ICAIC, watching Sergio, Elena, Alea, and Ramón Suárez (the film's director of photography) as they watch the very clips we have just seen. We are no longer spectators but part of the film's narrative! As fellow spectators of those clips, we situate ourselves in the same company as Sergio and Alea, and the question comes up: Which model do I choose for myself, Sergio's unproductive detachment or Alea's creative engagement with society? Here for the first time in the film, the double position of observer and observed—a position that so far only applied only to Sergio—applies also to the viewer.

As we consider this question, Alea spoofs censors and proceeds to inject a level of self-reflexivity and self-referentiality that is both smooth and astute:

SERGIO: What are you going to do with them [the clips]?
ALEA: I'm thinking of using them.
SERGIO: In a film?
ALEA: Yes. It'll be a collage that'll have a bit of everything.
SERGIO: It will have to have some meaning.
ALEA: It's coming along. You'll see.
SERGIO: Will they approve it?
ALEA: [Nonchalant] Yes.

The film that will "have a bit of everything" is of course *Memories of Underdevelopment*, and thus Sergio's doubts about the new government's openness are shown to be unfounded. The sequence ends with a light touch, as Elena gives a dismal performance of a romantic ballad to her puzzled "suitors."

11. Making Out with Elena in the Apartment, Elena Leaves, Flashback to Laura

Sergio keeps his eyes on the prize, and as soon as they exit ICAIC, he begins flirting with Elena, but she keeps her distance because of her doubts about his marital status. Sergio tells her that he's divorced, that his wife left him, and eventually gets her to agree to come up to his apartment. He'll go in first, and she'll follow a few minutes later, in order to keep appearances. In the apartment by himself, Sergio is all excited as he carries a bottle of brandy and a glass to the kitchen, while the radio begins to play Renaissance music for lute. When Elena comes in, she's visibly frightened. He asks her to get comfortable while he prepares some coffee, whereupon she goes to the living room, changes the radio station to one playing a popular song by Elena Burke (one of the most popular of Cuban singers of ballads), and begins to study the photographs on top of the console.

SERGIO: They're my parents, and that's Laura. They left the same day.
ELENA: And you?
SERGIO: What about me?
ELENA: Aren't you going to leave?
SERGIO: No, I'm fine right here.
ELENA: Are you a revolutionary?
SERGIO: [Laughing] What do you think?
ELENA: That you're neither a revolutionary nor a counterrevolutionary.
SERGIO: Then, what am I?
ELENA: Nothing. You're nothing.

Elena stands up while Sergio remains on the couch looking thoughtful. Sergio's question—"What do you think?"—was apparently directed at himself as much as to Elena, and one would think that it was also addressed to us, the viewers who have by now seen enough of Sergio to venture a judgment. In the end, it is this being "nothing" that condemns Sergio. Fidel Castro's words to the intellectuals (although given in a different context) come to mind: "Within the Revolution, everything, outside of the Revolution, *nothing*" (my emphasis). By being "nothing," Sergio is, in effect, outside the Revolution. And as long as he remains outside the Revolution, detached and cynical, he will be "nothing."

The heaviness of Elena's verdict does not last for long. She begins to leaf through some fashion magazines, which gives Sergio the terrible idea of offering her some of Laura's fashionable dresses. Elena accepts, and so begins the "game" of love, only in this game the players are not themselves, but surrogates of others: Elena plays Laura and Sergio plays Prince Charming. Each one gets something they want, but also something they don't. Sergio gets some sex (which he clearly wants), but he also gets a puerile companion who (to his chagrin) listens to popular ballads instead of classical music. Elena, on the other hand, gets some material rewards, but also a self-centered man who will not commit to anything. When they finish making love, she pretends to be ashamed of it, and Sergio sends her off with a bag of dresses as payment for services rendered. Alone in his apartment, Sergio lights a cigarette, and the radio, still on, carries news of subversive activities in Venezuela. He shuts off the radio (cf. sequence 8) and moves toward the balcony. Elena, it seems, has brought back memories of Laura, and so begins a flashback to the same fight we heard in sequence 2. This time, however, we also get a visual of the fight (from Sergio's point of view), and we learn that the reason why she left him was because she couldn't stand his distasteful gimmicks and his corrosive sarcasm.

12. Elena Returns the Next Day

The next day Elena comes back to the apartment, wearing one of Laura's dresses and cheerfully singing a love ballad: "Before your lips confirmed / That you loved me / I already knew it / I already knew it." Sergio looks surprised, perhaps because he thought Elena would do as Laura did and leave him. His surprise turns to coldness when Elena moves closer to caress him, whereupon she begins to express her feelings with another ballad: "Go on and say it / It couldn't last / It's all finished / It couldn't be / You don't love me anymore." Sergio finds her theatricality amusing, and he bursts into laughter. They end up kissing again, and the frame freezes.

The next few shots show still photographs of Elena at different moments in the previous scenes, followed by shots of people in the streets. Sergio narrates thoughtfully:

> One of the things that really gets me about people is their inability to sustain a feeling, an idea, without falling apart. Elena turned out to be totally

inconsistent. It's pure deterioration, as Ortega [y Gasset] would say. She doesn't connect one thing with another. That's one of the signs of underdevelopment: the inability to connect things . . . to accumulate experience and to develop . . . . It is difficult here to produce a woman shaped by sentiments and culture. It's a bland environment. Cubans waste their talents adapting themselves to every moment. People aren't consistent. And they always need somebody to do their thinking for them.

Here is another key to the film's understanding. On the one hand, the term "underdevelopment" is transformed from an economic descriptor to a description of one's ability to connect things. This means that the title of the film is not about Sergio's memories of an underdeveloped economy (as the term is usually applied), but about the underdevelopment of people's cultural and social awareness, of their ability to accumulate experience and be consistent. Second, this underdevelopment applies not only to people like Elena (which is obvious), but also to people like Sergio himself, people who fail to make the connection between individual and society. Sergio, in other words, cannot grasp "the true dialectical relationship between individuals and the group" (cf. sequence 5), and this makes him as underdeveloped as Elena and Pablo, precisely the two people he loathes most.

13. Farewell to Pablo

As if to drive the previous point home, this sequence begins with a long shot of a billboard displaying Fidel's face and the words "PLAYA GIRÓN." The image comes as the last words of Sergio's voice-over are still fresh in our minds: "Cubans waste their talents adapting themselves to every moment. People aren't consistent. And they always need somebody to do their thinking for them." This shot alerts the viewers (Cuban or otherwise) that they are as prone as Sergio and Elena to suffer from mental underdevelopment, especially if they let others do the thinking that they themselves must do in order to be fully developed. Asked if this was a warning to Cubans, Alea responded:

> It's an alert: people should be able to think for themselves, independently from the orientations that come "from above." The tendentious interpretation that the film generated in certain sectors of the West became a boomerang, because in the end we have come to convince ourselves that if the film reveals contradictions, these are no more and no less than the latent expression of a vital culture that is nurtured, and not destroyed or impoverished, by the Revolution.[19]

This is quite a generous reading, but one that merits as much consideration as the more literal one, for two reasons. First, it was part of an interview that appeared in *Juventud Rebelde* (an independent-minded periodical in Cuba), and second, the interview was conducted in 1988, at a time when the film was already a consecrated classic and its discussion no longer generated the partisanship evident in earlier critiques of the film.

After this polemical intellectual montage, the narrative continues as Sergio accompanies Pablo to the airport. On the way there, the conversation shows how distant the two old friends have become. Pablo complains, as usual, and Sergio defends those who stay behind by using a term they can both understand even though it has become anachronistic. "There are also *decent* people among them," says Sergio. "Did you hear me? Really *decent* people" (my emphasis). At the airport, Pablo is visibly crippled, like the villain of countless stories. When the two are finally separated by a glass partition, Pablo gesticulates something, but neither Sergio nor the viewer can make out what Pablo is saying. The line has been drawn: Communication between exiled Cubans and those who stay is no longer possible. Sergio's interior monologue reveals the worst sentiments on either side of the Florida Straits: "Was I like him, before? It's possible. Although it may destroy me, this revolution is my *revenge* against the stupid Cuban bourgeoisie. Against idiots like Pablo" (my emphasis).

14. Fourth Foray into the City (of Memories): Flashbacks to Childhood, School, and Brothel

With Pablo gone and with no woman to take Laura's place, Sergio ventures into the city by himself. As he walks, he has three flashbacks: one to his privileged childhood, another to school as a twelve-year-old boy (where he learned "for the first time, the relationship between Justice and Power"), and a last to his first visit to a brothel as a fifteen-year-old adolescent.

15. Last Time with Elena (Visits to Library, Art Museum, and Hemingway's House)

Sergio's estimation of Elena was not so low after all. He thinks he can Euro-Americanize her interior just as he Euro-Americanized her exterior by giving her some of Laura's dresses. First they visit a library, where he picks up a copy of Vladimir Nabokov's *Lolita*. This apparently innocent gesture has two functions. First, it contrasts Cuba's openness with that of other countries where *Lolita* had been banned, and second, it calls attention to the differences in age between Sergio (thirty-eight years old) and Elena (sixteen years old). After the bookstore they attend an exhibition of paintings by Cuban artist Acosta León at Havana's Museo de Bellas Artes. Sergio tries to explain one of the paintings to Elena, but all she does is straighten his tie. Now he is convinced that he cannot change her: "I also tried to change Elena, just like I tried with Laura . . . but she doesn't understand anything. She has another world in her head, very different from mine." Were it not for the context, this might have been a failed love story between a man and a woman of different worldviews. But the next sequence proves this hypothesis wrong.

16. At Hemingway's House (Intertitle: A TROPICAL ADVENTURE)

Sergio continues his attempts to educate Elena at Hemingway's villa in San Francisco de Paula, some nine miles south of Havana. The main function of the sequence is to comment further on Sergio's mental world. Almost everything he says about Hemingway applies to himself. The viewer only has to change from the third person to the first in order to understand Sergio's analysis of himself:

What Sergio says of Hemingway:	*As it applies to himself:*
"This was his refuge, his tower, his island in the tropics."	"My apartment is my refuge, my tower, my island in the tropics."
"He modeled [René Villareal] to his needs. The faithful servant and the great lord. The colonialist and Gunga Din."	"I modeled Elena and Laura to my needs. The faithful servant and the great lord. The colonialist and Gunga Din."
"Hemingway must have been unbearable."	"I must be unbearable."

The most revealing of these parallelisms comes when Sergio reads from Hemingway's story "The Short Happy Life of Francis Macomber": " 'You know I don't think I'd ever be afraid of anything again,' Macomber said to Wilson. 'Something happened in me after we first saw the buff and started after him. Like a dam bursting. It was pure excitement.' " Sergio raises his head and looks at the head of the buffalo hanging on the wall behind him. He puts down the book, walks toward the gun, and, in a very suggestive gesture, touches it, adding: "As if running after a buffalo was enough to conquer fear. Anyway, there are no buffaloes in Cuba. I'm an idiot. He conquered the fear of death but he couldn't stand the fear of life, of time, of a world that was beginning to get too large for him." Sergio could have been speaking of himself, thus: "As if running after a girl was enough to conquer my isolation. I'm an idiot. I may have taken my revenge on the stupid Cuban bourgeoisie, but I can't stand my fear of commitment to a new reality that is beginning to get too large for me." Sergio's slip of the tongue—"I'm an idiot" instead of "He's an idiot"—followed by references to Hemingway's suicide is the first of many foreshadows of death in the film.

The secondary function of the "Hemingway sequence" is to draw a parallelism between the United States and Russia and to the possibility that Cuba may be substituting one master for another:

ELENA: Is this where Mr. Way used to live? I don't see anything so special. Books and dead animals. Just like the American house in Preston [a sugar mill town in eastern Cuba]. The same furniture and the same American smell.

SERGIO: What is an American smell?
ELENA: I don't know. You feel it.
SERGIO: Which do you like best, the smell of the Russians or the smell of
           the Americans?

As if to underscore the point, the next scene shows a group of Russians asking Elena to pose for them. "There you have her," Sergio says to himself, "the
[in English] beautiful Cuban señorita." The sequence ends with Sergio hiding
from Elena and Elena hitching a ride back with the group of Russian tourists.

17. Round Table: Literature and Underdevelopment

Sergio has given up on Elena, but not on Cuban culture. The sequence opens
with a screen title that reads:

ROUND TABLE: LITERATURE AND UNDERDEVELOPMENT

René Depestre [Haitian poet]	Gianni Toti [Italian writer]
Edmundo Desnoes [Cuban writer]	David Viñas [Argentinean writer]

Moderator: Salvador Bueno [Cuban critic]

Tuesday at 7	Salón de Actos [at the Casa de las Américas]

ENTRANCE FREE

Sergio sits among the public. Desnoes talks about discrimination against
Latin Americans in the United States: "Now I know that, although I look
white, Anglo-Saxon, and Protestant, I am really a Southern Negro." As he
says this, a black man brings water to the panelists. Toti and Viñas begin to
argue in circles. Sergio observes Desnoes: "What are you doing up there with
a cigar?" he says in voice-over. "You must feel pretty important because
there's not much competition here. Outside Cuba, you'd be a nobody . . . .
But here, you're well placed." Like his comments about Hemingway, Sergio's comments here are really directed at himself and at others like him who
use the Revolution for personal goals—in Sergio's case, to escape his family,
and in other cases, well, for a myriad of reasons. Jack Gelber, an American
playwright sitting close to Sergio, asks for permission to speak:

> Could I ask a question in English? It's all right? Ah . . . ah . . . [He stands
> up.] Why is it that if the Cuban Revolution is a total revolution, they have to
> resort to an archaic form of discussion such as a round table, and treat us to
> an important discussion of issues that I'm well informed about [?]

Gelber's question provokes laughter and serves as a healthy warning to intellectuals not to sink in the quicksand of theory but instead to go out into the
streets and face reality in its full complexity. Sergio agrees with Gelber, and
in the next shot he is literally out in the streets. But instead of confronting
reality, he becomes ever more reflexive:

I don't understand a thing. The American was right. Words devour words and
they leave you in the clouds or on the moon. A thousand miles away. How
does one get rid of underdevelopment? It marks everything. Everything. What
are you doing down there, Sergio? What does all this mean? You have nothing
to do with them. You're alone. In underdevelopment nothing has continuity,
everything is forgotten. People aren't consistent. But you remember many
things, you remember too much. Where's your family, your work, your wife?
You're nothing, you're dead. Now it begins, Sergio, your final destruction.

Intellectualism as underdevelopment? In a way, yes. Insofar as intellectuals
fail to progress from awareness to commitment and finally into action, they
will be inconsistent and therefore underdeveloped. For the second time in the
film (cf. sequence 12), the term "underdevelopment" is transformed from
economic descriptor to being a description of one's ability to connect things,
to show consistency between awareness and action.

This scene is a turning point for Sergio and the film. Recall the camerawork in sequence 2, when Sergio looks at the airplane taking off. In that shot,
the camera began with an almost subjective, over-the-shoulder shot behind
Sergio. It then tracked around him and ended with a frontal view of his face.
The shot was held as he whistled and watched the plane take off, so that the
viewer ended up looking *at* him as well as *with* him. Viewer identification
with Sergio was thus firmly established. In this sequence, on the other hand,
viewer identification with Sergio breaks almost completely. "What are you
doing down there?" Sergio asks as if he were looking at himself from above,
as if he and viewer shared the same point of view. But this identification
between Sergio and viewer via shared point of view rapidly deteriorates as
the extreme long shot from above zooms in until his image covers the entire
screen and becomes a meaningless blur. What had been clear is now blurred,
including, most importantly, the viewer's identification with the protagonist.

18. Letter from Mom

Back home, Sergio opens a letter from his mother: a note, a stick of chewing
gum, and a Gillette razor blade. "Every time my old lady writes it's the same
thing. She knows I don't chew gum and that I use an electric shaver." His
mother's intention may not be as innocent as it first appears. The note's illeg-
ibility may be her way of saying, "I have nothing to say to you"; the chewing
gum another way of saying, "Here's something for you to chew on, since
you're not doing anything productive"; and the razor blade, perhaps an
unconscious way of suggesting that he commit suicide.

19. Fifth Foray into the City (of Lost Love): Flashbacks to Hanna

The sidewalks are wet with a recent rain—or is it from Sergio's own tears of
grief?—and as he passes by the Lenin Special School, he has flashbacks of

Hanna, his only true love. "Why did I let her go?" he asks himself, and the answer comes in a series of shots from his days as owner of a furniture store, a gift from his father. A moving story, and one that endears the viewer to Sergio, just in case the previous sequences had made him too distanced. In real life, this story had a happy ending. Edmundo Desnoes, who based this part of the script on a personal experience, reunited with his "Hanna" in the United States many years later. Apparently she had seen the film and was moved to learn that Desnoes harbored such intense feelings for her. They met again, and today they live together in New York.[20]

20. Elena Comes Back; Sergio Does Not Let Her In

It's raining hard, only this time the rain doesn't reflect Sergio's sadness, but the storm that is about to unleash. He takes a cab home, and tells the cab driver to stop short of the entrance to the building. Elena is back, waiting for him in the lobby! Sergio takes the side entrance and makes it safely into his apartment. As he stands alone in the balcony, the doorbell rings loudly and persistently. It's Elena! Sergio hesitates before walking over to the door, but he can't get himself to open it. He walks back to the living room and adjusts the TV set, which shows documentary images of racial violence in the U.S. taken from Santiago Alvarez' documentary *"Now!"*

21. Urban Reform Surveyors

In October 1960 the Urban Reform Law was passed, expropriating all rental property and giving ex-owners compensation for their losses. Renters would make payments (adjusted to their income) to the state, and these payments would go toward the renters' eventual ownership of the unit. Just a month before the Urban Reform Law, the Committees for the Defense of the Revolution (CDR) had been established as a sort of thought police. Each city block would have its committee, made up of "voluntary" membership and entrusted with the "patriotic" duty of sniffing out real or imagined counter-revolutionaries. In this sequence members of the CDR visit Sergio in order to fill out forms that will help in the implementation of the Urban Reform Law. The line between public and private, between citizen and state agent, have become blurry, and neither the male surveyor nor Sergio are quite sure of what they're doing, what they're expected to do. The female surveyor, meanwhile, looks around judgmentally, but is unsure of what to make of Sergio's modern paintings and the apartment's surplus of toilets. The whole sequence is shot with the camera at eye level and with full frontal views of the surveyors, so that it feels as if the questions may be directed at us, the viewers. After the last question, the camera changes to show Sergio from the male surveyor's point of view. "And what's all this for?" Sergio asks. "We're just verifying, " comes the answer. "Yes, but . . .," says Sergio, visibly perplexed, and the next shot shows the picture of an eye such as one used for Santería practices and in the logo of the CDRs. Above the eye is the inscription: I AM HUNTING FOR YOU. In Santería such an eye symbolizes God's observance of all human actions. In the CDR logo, on the other hand, the eye may symbolize the Revolution's observance not only of actions, but of thoughts as well. Is Big Brother watching us? Alea's comments on the film's other intended audience comes to mind (see pages 22–23), especially in the case of the female surveyor.

22. Sixth Foray into the City (of Workers): May Day Demonstration,
Flashback to the Opening Sequence, and Photo-Essay of Sergio's
Family Life

The sequence opens with Sergio in a cab, a traffic policeman blocking the way. "Hey, wait! You can't turn there," says the policeman, as if commenting on Sergio's waywardness. Sergio decides to get off right there, and runs into a May Day demonstration. The demonstrators' mood is festive as they sing a rumba: "We are socialists / p'arriba, p'abajo / And whoever doesn't like us / Let them suffer and suffer." Sergio's mood, on the other hand, is somber, and as he walks in the opposite direction of the demonstrators, he says to himself: "Everything comes to me either too early or too late. In another time, I would've been able to understand what was going on here. Now, I can't." The transformation of the city is almost complete, and certainly beyond Sergio's recognition. No longer is Havana a city of markets (cf. sequence 4), of tourists (cf. sequence 7), of belle époque memories and sex-for-hire (cf. sequence 14). Havana is no longer a city of bourgeoisie, but a city of workers, and Sergio is clearly not keeping up with these changes. He's not even going in the same direction!

All this is too much for Sergio. The popular crowd around him provokes a flashback to the same night scene with which the film opened. Apparently Sergio was in that crowd, even though his mind was somewhere else, because in the flashback the music is no longer that of Pello el Afrokán, but rather a very dissonant arrangement by Leo Brouwer. The effect is that we see the same tumultuous scene through Sergio's eyes, and with a better appreciation of how much his inner world has distanced itself from outer reality. We also come to realize that the black woman's gaze at the beginning of the film was directed at Sergio. What was the nature of that gaze? Do we recall? Are we now in the same position as she was, looking at Sergio as one looks at a strange animal? Or are we still the object of her gaze, thrown off and even threatened by the new society that in so many ways she represents?

This flashback also complicates the reading of the film because it shows Noemi next to Sergio. What is she doing there? Did she go out with Sergio before his family's departure? Or is the opening sequence a flashforward to that night? Probably the second, especially given the fact that Sergio first noticed Noemi after his family had left for Miami. What seems to have happened is that the film began *in medias res*, went back in time to Sergio's family's departure, and has now caught up to where it began: after he dumps Elena, but before Elena's brother shows up at his apartment.

23. Seventh Foray into the City (of Nostalgia): Photo-Essay of Sergio's Family Life

At Havana's Central Park, a street photographer adjusts his camera to take Sergio's picture. The flash of the camera provokes a flashback of Sergio going through a pile of photographs in his apartment, which in turn explains the source of photographs in the photo-essay that follows: Sergio as a child, family pictures showing Sergio at various stages of his life, photographs of the store opening, and pictures of Laura, some with Sergio, at different places: a zoo, a public building in New York, a café, their wedding, and an amusement park. Toward the end of the photo-essay, Sergio comments: "I'm already an old man. In the whorehouses since I was thirteen. At fifteen I thought I was a genius. At twenty-five I owned a fashionable furniture store. And then Laura . . . . My life is like a monstrous and pulpy vegetable, with huge leaves and no fruit." These comments echo those he had made in sequence 7 regarding Cuban women, only this time he's the object of ridicule. Is Sergio becoming like the Laura of his mind—monstrous, pulpy, sterile? What seemed to be a moment of nostalgia for an idyllic past turns suddenly into a depressing assessment of his own failures. In the next shot Sergio stares at the passport photograph just taken. The contrast with the previous photographs is striking. He now looks depressed, and the light in his eyes is gone. "I believe that I project a certain dignity," he adds. The dignity of the defeated, perhaps. And just as we want to agree with him, he stops staring at the picture and looks directly at the camera, as if expecting a nod of agreement from us, our sympathy even. What comes to mind, however, is pity.

24. Elena's Brother Pays a Visit

Elena's brother shows up unexpectedly at Sergio's apartment in order to "make right" what Sergio made wrong. Elena's brother is clearly agitated by Sergio's taking advantage of his "innocent" little sister. Sergio tries to stay cool, but fear gets the better of him. "I didn't want any trouble with the police," he says in voice-over, explaining to himself and to the viewer why all of the sudden he's the willing victim of a manipulative lover.

25. Arguing with Elena's Family in Front of the Mannequin Display

Sergio meets with Elena and her family at a cafeteria. But instead of asking for Elena's hand in marriage, Sergio calls Elena's bluff. What follows is a heated discussion between Sergio and Elena's family in front of a shop window that displays wedding dresses (just in case we didn't know what everyone but Sergio was thinking). Sergio tentatively agrees to marry Elena, but then the mother says that Elena had come home from Sergio's apartment "with her underpants stained with blood." That does it for Sergio, who answers "That's not true, señora." Pandemonium reigns, Elena's family takes off in a taxi, and Sergio is left standing alone. "I was sure she was not a virgin," he says to himself.

26. At the Police Station

At a police station, a policeman types Sergio's deposition. "It isn't true," he says. "I have had relations with her, but they were voluntary. There was no abuse and certainly no rape. All that is a lie." A long shot of Elena's visibly stressed family on a bench is followed by a medium shot of Sergio sitting calmly in another room among other detainees. He takes out a cigarette pack, but by the time he gives cigarettes to everyone else in the room, he has none left for himself.

27. The Trial

During the cross-examinations Sergio is certain that he'll be found guilty: "I was the only one who spoke with some coherence. That finished me. They treated me as if I had cheated some unfortunate 'woman of the people.' Now everything is 'the people' . . . . Before I would have been the respectable one, and they the damned guilty ones." Sergio has not even heard the verdict, and he is already dismissing as unfair the new government's justice system. That's why it's somewhat surprising that Sergio does not look relieved when the bailiff pronounces him innocent of the rape charges. His thoughts as he leaves the courtroom may explain why: "It was a happy ending, as they say. For once justice triumphed. But was it really like that? There is something that leaves me in a bad position. I've seen too much to be innocent. They have too much darkness inside their heads to be guilty. I haven't seen them again. I hope they haven't locked her up."

What is that "something" that leaves him in a bad position? Maybe it's the knowledge that he can no longer act with impunity. Maybe he knows that from now on he will have to deal with women from a position of equals, and not from a position of power. And what is it that he has seen too much of to be innocent? Perhaps sleeping with Elena may have been a form of rape, perhaps sleeping with a sixteen-year-old adolescent who had confessed to taking medicine for her nerves is not the same as sleeping with a consenting adult.

28. At the Apartment with Newspaper and Noemi's Photos; Erotic Fantasies Interrupted

This sequence is almost entirely devoid of sound. Sergio is back in his apartment, reading the newspaper. Close-ups of the headlines:

MORE PLANES AND BATTLESHIPS TO FLORIDA

KENNEDY RETURNS SUDDENLY TO WASHINGTON

ATMOSPHERE OF WAR HYSTERIA GRIPS U.S. CAPITAL

YOUNG MOTHER GIVES BIRTH TO TRIPLETS

DOG WITH TWO HEARTS

TRADE UNIONS COMPETE TO GAIN RENOWN

BULLETIN BOARD MATERIAL. POST IT WHERE YOU WORK. CUT AND PASTE.

HOW TO PREVENT TETANUS. Anyone can become infected with the tetanus bacilus. Most cases are fatal. Vaccination is the only sure protection.

WORDS OF MAO TSE TUNG. Trying to solve ideological problems and the problem of what is right or wrong through administrative regulation or by repressive methods is not only useless but also harmful.

A fragment of a letter from a reader, complaining about the lack of attention on the part of the Institute of Urban Reform paid to the problem of masonry falling from the façades of buildings.

WORK WITH JOY AND . . .

As we read along with Sergio, we learn that there's a crisis looming, plus a few other facts, some significant, others not. We also try to make sense of Mao Tse Tung's words, but we can't. Maybe they have something to do with the earlier radio reports of guerilla activity in Venezuela, where Maoist guerillas, backed by Fidel Castro, were actively seeking to overthrow the government. Or maybe they have to do with the ideological battles between communists who supported Moscow's reformism and communists who supported Mao's revolutionism. In any case, the words are printed out of context, so what they may mean is a matter of speculation. As if to underscore Sergio's confusion, the camera pans across a newspaper comic strip by Chago titled "Salomón." In the first four panels a glum-looking figure is shown with a question mark suspended over his head. The question mark gets larger in each panel, until it comes crashing down on the figure's head in the fifth panel. A funny noise accompanies the crash, providing comic relief to a heavy atmosphere.

Sergio puts down the newspaper and begins to study some photographs of Noemi when she was baptized. "It wasn't like I thought it would be," he tells us. "The clothes didn't cling to her body. There were lots of people. I hadn't thought about them. Witnesses who are always everywhere." Sergio is now aware that the role of witness and witnessed have been reversed: He is no longer the judging spectator of a passive reality; rather, that reality is now the active spectator of Sergio's follies and inconsistencies. The urban reform surveyors, the justice system, and even the witnesses at Noemi's baptism impinge on Sergio's real and imagined worlds.

29. Reality Encroaches I (Intertitle: OCTOBER 22, 1962: KENNEDY SPEAKS)

Robbed even of the pleasure of imagining Noemi's baptism as he wants to, Sergio closes his eyes and imagines her in his arms, kissing passionately. A radio broadcast interrupts Sergio's daydream. He opens his eyes, and superimposed we read: OCTOBER 22, 1962 KENNEDY SPEAKS. A series of shots appear as Kennedy announces his ultimatum. After his last sentence ("I have directed the armed forces to prepare for any eventualities . . .") there is an aerial view of an atomic bomb explosion, followed by a series of shots of people and soldiers on the street in Havana during the missile crisis. "It makes no sense," Sergio says. "The people behave and talk as if war were a game."

The last shot of the sequence shows a man walking along a wall with the word DEATH painted on it. The audio that precedes this shot is taken from a Charles Mingus song that poignantly cries, "Oh Lord, don't let them drop that atomic bomb on me." With this very clever and timely audiovisual montage, Alea reminds us that Sergio's premonitions of death (the third one so far) are not only individual but potentially collective. Is this the price to be paid for Cuban independence? Since the triumph of the Revolution, the slogan "Patria o muerte" has adorned walls such as this one. Notice, however, that the word "patria" and half of the letter "o" is missing. Perhaps the message here is one of recognition of the painful truth of that slogan. The Cuban Missile Crisis, as this long shot suggests, came unbearably close to the point where the choice between homeland and death, "patria o muerte," was almost settled in favor of the latter.

30. Reality Encroaches II: Castro Answers; Sergio Increasingly Tense

This sequence serves as a counterpoint to the previous one. It begins with Sergio still tense and brooding over the uselessness of protesting, and ends with the broadcast of a TV speech by Castro. Unlike the previous sequence, where Kennedy was not shown as he spoke and the images that accompanied his speech underscored American belligerence, in this sequence we see Castro as he speaks, and the few images that do come up as he speaks underscore Cuba's defensive (and defensible) position:

> We know what we are doing and we know how to defend our integrity and we know how to defend our sovereignty. They threaten us by saying we'll

be nuclear targets. They don't scare us. We have to know how to live in the
age into which we are born, with the dignity with which we should know
how to live. All of us, men and women, young and old, are one in this hour
of danger! It is the same for all of us, revolutionaries and patriots, and victory will be ours! ¡Patria o muerte! We shall triumph!

Castro's use of "patria o muerte" in this sequence contrasts sharply with the
use of the same phrase in the last sequence. Whereas the phrase had an ironic
overtone before, it now sounds like the heroic battle cry of a people united in
their beliefs and determined to defend them with their lives.

31. Eighth (and Final) Foray into the City (of War): Malecón Scene, Pacing in the Apartment, Views of Havana

The final sequence takes full advantage of the tension that built up during the
last few minutes. It opens with Sergio walking by himself along the Malecón.
The high waves and strong wind come from the direction of the colossal
enemy, while the sea wall is as steadfast as the Cuban people in this hour of
danger. Sergio can't find neutral ground, and he seeks refuge in his apartment. Like a disenchanted romantic, Sergio aims his (telescopic) sight on the
stars and the moon. The next shots switch back and forth between images of
chronic indecision inside the apartment and collective determination outside.
Nelson Rodríguez's editing makes this one of the most memorable sequences
in the film. Here's how he described the process:

> In that final sequence in the apartment, when Sergio feels overwhelmed by
> the October Crisis, going in circles, doesn't know what to do, to the kitchen,
> to the bedroom, through the living room, looking out the window, back to
> thinking. He [Alea] didn't like too much the lighting work that Ramón
> Suárez had done in that sequence, done as it was with night illumination in
> the apartment. He was a bit bothered by the results, it seemed to him a bit
> false this illumination, especially since that it was the climactic moment for
> the character; and he considered that it wasn't a matter of whether the job
> was done correctly or not, but that the tone was not what that specific scene
> needed, it needed something else. And it occurred to us to use Godard, so I
> say to him "look, let's try to cut it: he comes this way, cut, and when he
> comes in the opposite direction, cut, comes in the opposite direction, cut,"
> so a situation of chaos is created in the character, based on a montage that
> can support all that confusion in the film, especially since what follows is
> that whole sequence in which one can see the whole city being mobilized
> by the militias and the military. And he said to me "look, let's try it, go
> ahead and do it, I'll leave and you show it to me tomorrow." He was doing
> that because that was the best thing to do, that was what had to be done, it
> was the best method with me, afterwards anything else could be fixed. Well,
> I did it that same day, I don't know, I said, "Well, Godard? . . . Godard?"
> and I remembered *Breathless* and *My Life to Live* and said to myself, "well,

let's see what happens." And it really worked out well, and we eliminated all that stuff that he didn't like."[21]

During this very intense sequence, several important clues to the film may escape the viewer. Two of them foreshadow Sergio's death: the glass rooster that he breaks and a drawing in which a figure holds a decapitated head by the hair. Why does Sergio not die? Why all the foreshadows of death and then no actual death? In the original script, *Memories of Underdevelopment* was going to be called *Pages from a Diary*, and it was going to begin with Sergio's suicide. Alea decided to keep Sergio alive in order to avoid closure and thus risk having a viewer who would leave the theater satisfied that justice had been done and so would not think about the issues the film raises beyond the four walls of the theater. This is what had happened with *Death of a Bureaucrat*, and Alea was smart enough not to repeat the same mistake twice. The other two clues have to do with Sergio's gaze. One of them is a drawing of a big eye on Sergio's wall. Like the eye at the end of the sequence with the Urban Reform surveyors, this eye serves to indicate that Sergio is no longer the observer, but the observed. And in this case, the viewer is clearly the one doing the observing, with eyes that in theory should also point back at himself or herself. The other clue as to why Sergio does not have to suffer a literal death is the fact that the final shots of the city of Havana show the telescope but not Sergio. Enrique Fernández explains:

> The final sequence ends with a shot of Sergio's telescope in the balcony followed by telephoto shots of the Havana city-scape. This syntagm retraces the montage that inscribed Sergio's position as spectator-in-the-text early in the film [cf. sequence 3], with one salient difference . . . Sergio has been deleted by the camera position, his diegetic presence or absence is irrelevant, he is out of the game.[22]

Indeed, Sergio is no longer in the frame, and as viewers we may ask ourselves, "As I look at the city-scape from Sergio's vantage point, will I remain a spectator like Sergio, or will I become a participant in the evolution from alienated individualism to committed socialism?" The very final shot is a zoom-in to the Malecón, a visual nod to the viewer that the only viable answer is to become a participant in that evolution.

The sequence-by-sequence analysis of *Memories of Underdevelopment* that I have just completed underscores the complexity of the film and the difficulties that viewers face when they attempt to formulate a coherent idea from such disparate and contradictory sequences. Alea recognized this difficulty, and, like Eisenstein, he developed a theory of film in order to address it. That is to say, just as Eisenstein wrote *Film Form* and *Film Sense* after he finished *Potemkin* in order to explain to himself and to others the new language he had developed with that masterpiece, Alea wrote *The Viewer's*

Dialectic after finishing *Memories of Underdevelopment* in order to explain to himself and to others the complexity of ideas that make *Memories* an enduring classic. It is to this book that I now turn my attention.

The Viewer's Dialectic

"What is your position with regards to cinema?" In an interview in 1964 Alea was not sure what his answer to that question was:

> These days, that's a question I frequently ask myself. I don't think I can give a definite answer . . . . I always have to start by recognizing that I'm not a theorist, and that I think that the best answer will be found through the films I may make. In other words, the question makes me uneasy, the answer I give myself does not convince me, I throw myself on a film project, and only afterwards do I analyze the work.[23]

Thirteen years later (1977) he was still thinking about the question, but by now he was also seriously thinking about writing about it:

> [Besides working on my own films and helping younger filmmakers], I am also extremely interested in improving the level of our theoretical activity. This is one of the things that concerns us most, because now, at this particular stage of our development, we have come to realize that we have to dedicate a lot more of our attention to theoretical work, to formulating our preoccupations at a much deeper level. We have to analyze everything we have done so far in order to plan for the future with a greater awareness, instead of leaving everything up to spontaneous solutions, which is more or less what we've been doing up to now. I should clarify that our work was never completely improvised; there have always been theoretical investigations, but never with the degree of discipline or insistence that we are now capable of attaining.[24]

The fruit of these deliberations is *La dialéctica del espectador* (*The Viewer's Dialectic*, 1982), a collection of six essays on film, plus an introduction and an appendix. The book is part film history, part film theory, and part manifesto. In the introduction, Alea gives a definite answer to the question posed in 1964, "What is your position with regards to cinema?" He is in favor of a socially productive cinema that also entertains: "We understand what cinema's social function should be in Cuba in these times: It should contribute in the most effective way possible to elevating viewers' revolutionary consciousness and . . . it should also contribute to their enjoyment of life" (18). This is the "what" part of the answer as articulated in *The Viewer's Dialectic*, that film should be both entertaining and a tool for raising viewers' revolutionary consciousness: not entertaining and pedagogic nor entertaining and ideologically correct, but, rather, entertaining and provocative in a productive way, in a way that raises revolutionary consciousness. The "how" part of the answer is more difficult to declare with the same assertiveness because "the expressive possibilities of the cinematic show are inexhaustible" (19). And in any case, he writes, that is not the "how" he is interested in here. Rather, the book will try to answer another "how": the "how" of the relationship between show and spectator, that is, the viewer's dialectic:

> The expressive possibilities of the cinematic show are inexhaustible; to find them and produce them is a poet's task. But on that point, for the time being, this analysis can go no further, for I am not focusing on film's purely aesthetic aspects but, rather, trying to discover in the relation which film establishes over and over again between the show and the spectator, the laws which govern this relation, and the possibilities within those laws for developing a socially productive cinema. (19)

Having stated his position and aims, Alea begins with a brief history of film, continues with a discussion of what kinds of viewers have emerged from that history, follows with a discussion on how to change things, and closes with a case study of *Memories of Underdevelopment* as a good model to follow. However, before reviewing Alea's own explanation of *Memories*, it will help to discuss the three main parts of the book in more detail.

The book is not divided into three "parts" per se, but this division helps me conceptualize what would otherwise remain a loose collection of six essays. In any case, each "part" contains two essays that say similar things in different ways. In the following synopsis I discuss what connects the two essays of each part and summarize each essay separately.

On the History of Film Production: From Show to Ideas

This part provides a historical background to the discussions that follow. First Alea discusses the bourgeois origins of cinema and how the profit motive fueled subsequent developments of genres. The result in many cases was that quality of product was sacrificed for quantity of tickets that could be sold. This overarching trend has been resisted here and there by filmmakers who aim to promote the interests of the majority of the people by raising their consciousness of the social, political, and economic forces that rule their lives.

Essay #1: " 'Popular' Film and People's Film" Film was born when capitalism was entering its imperialist phase. Investors therefore looked for products that could attract a heterogeneous public, that could sell in Paris as well as in Patagonia. In the 1920s, the European avant garde expanded the range of expressive possibilities available to film, but it failed to rescue film "from the vulgarity to which commercialism had condemned it" (22). With Soviet cinema, film became a tool for expressing the interests, aspirations, and values of the popular masses, and its influence on future generations of filmmakers has been deep. The coming of sound coincided with the capitalist economic crisis of 1929. People wanted to see movies that would ease their suffering, and U.S. producers, who took advantage of the crisis to consolidate and globalize the industry, were more than willing to oblige. Despite this, the U.S. film industry produced a few works "which spoke about social conflicts afflicting everyone" (22). Toward the end of World War II, Italian neorealism pointed the way to an authentically popular cinema, a lead followed in postwar France by a "new wave" of young directors who "took Brecht as their point of departure—and the New Left as their point of arrival" (23). Godard, the great destroyer of bourgeois cinema, "managed to make anti-bourgeois cinema but he could not make people's cinema" (23).

In general, then, the movie-viewing public has been conditioned by film language, formulae, and genres that "have almost always responded better to capitalism's interests than to socialism's, . . . to a consumer society's interests more than to a revolutionary society's interests, . . . to hypocrisy and lies more than to the profound truth" (24). And yet this "popular" cinema has been extremely successful at gaining mass acceptance. The same cannot be said for people's cinema, that is, cinema that has as its final objective "transforming reality and bettering humankind" (24).

Essay #2: "From Film Show in Its Purest Sense to the 'Cinema of Ideas' " In Cuba, normal movie theater programming consists of a newsreel, a short documentary (or reportage), and a fiction feature. Alea touches briefly on the first two and then focuses on the feature fiction film. He begins this part of the essay by making clear that he does not agree with the thesis that for a film to be revolutionary it has to introduce social content in an attractive form. "This attitude considers the spectator a passive entity, . . . and can only lead to the bureaucratization of artistic activity" (28). Instead, Alea proposes that a film be judged effective to the extent that it helps spectators discover *for themselves* some aspect of reality. On the other hand, he says, if a film "neglects to fulfill its function as show and appeals exclusively to reason (to the viewers' intellectual efforts) it noticeably reduces its effectiveness because it disregards one of its essential aspects: enjoyment" (30). By now it is clear that Alea thinks in terms of both theory and praxis.

On Film Reception: From Escapism and Engagement

In this second part Alea proposes that film should take advantage of its extraordinariness in order to help viewers make the kinds of generalizations about reality that are necessary before taking consequential action.

Essay #3: "Show and Reality: The Extraordinary and the Everyday" A show is by definition extraordinary; otherwise it would be a reproduction of everyday reality. Fictional films are shows in this regard; they capture bits of reality, and in the process of putting them together in a narrative, these bits take on a new meaning, an extraordinary meaning. At their best, films can reveal "through associations and connections between various isolated aspects of reality . . . deeper, more essential layers of reality itself" (33). The trick is to lay down a bridge to reality so that viewers can return to reality and apply their discoveries to their everyday lives. That is, cinema should not be escapist, but rather "should propitiate the viewers' return to the other [everyday] reality, . . . stimulated and armed for practical action" (36).

Essay #4: "The Contemplative and the Active Spectator" When viewing a film, one's attention will oscillate between passive contemplation and active interiorization, depending on the viewer's social and historical locus and the film's ability to provide a stimulus "for unleashing in the viewers a consequential action *beyond* the show" (38, my emphasis). In capitalist societies, where films tend to have a happy ending, the spectator leaves with a feeling that all is well, that there is no need to change anything. The solution is not simply to have a tragic or open ending, because this by itself will not provoke in the spectator a response that is consequential. The solution is to make films that pose problems and at the same time "show viewers the road they ought to take in order to *discover for themselves* a higher level of discernment" (41, my emphasis). That is, film should not give ready-made answers to problems because all this does is encourage a contemplative attitude. Films should instead push viewers to actively discover for themselves the adequate responses to the problems of social reality. "What this is about, then, is stimulating and channeling spectators to act in the direction of historical movement, along the path of society's development" (40).

On How to Make Films for an Active Spectator: The Dialectics between Identification and Alienation

Essay #5: "Identification and Distancing: Aristotle and Brecht" The key to this essay is the conjunction "and" in the title. What Alea proposes here is a theory and praxis of film that includes *both* identification *and* distancing. Alea opens the essay with the example of a Tarzan movie, in which the mechanism of identification has been made into an absolute, so that even black and female audiences cheer as the animals in the jungle heed Tarzan's call to help him rescue Jane from a group of black savages. What happens in such cases is that the mechanism of identification has been made into an absolute, thus putting the spectator in a position in which the only thing he or she can distinguish are "good guys" and "bad guys." This is *not* what Alea has in mind when he argues for the use of identification in film. Nor is it a matter of "openly proclaiming a kind of 'prohibition' [on the use of identification] whose effect would be to deprive the theater of a resource which has had such sustained acceptance" (44). "Not even Brecht," writes Alea, "with his lucid, consistent, and necessary emphasis on rationality, thought that . . . those resources capable of provoking a state of fascination—especially psychological identification—ought to be tossed aside" (50). Instead, Alea advocates the use of Brecht's *Verfremdungseffekte* as a tool in helping achieve the goal set forth in part two of the book; that is, to help viewers "*discover for themselves* a higher level of discernment" (41, my emphasis):

> Some have understood this estrangement effect as a simple cooling of the emotional process [of identification] that takes place during the show. But . . . the emotional process should break off in such a way that it obliges spectators to seek compensation also in the emotional plane. The estrangement effect must replace any emotion with the specific emotion of discovering something, of finding a truth which has previously been obscured by accommodation to daily life. (45)

This description fits perfectly with what happens vis-à-vis Sergio in *Memories of Underdevelopment*. First, viewers identify emotionally with him (in sequence 2, but in subsequent sequences as well). Slowly, this identification begins to wear off (as early as sequence 3), and we compensate for this loss by discovering Sergio's contradictions, contradictions that had "previously been obscured by accommodation to daily life." The fact that we made the discovery is itself an emotional experience, greater even than our initial emotional experience of identifying with the intelligent and goodlooking character whose position as spectator-in-the-text in the opening sequences closely corresponded with our own position as spectator-of-the-text. As the case of Sergio shows, the rupture of identification through distantiation need not be an emotional turn-off because distantiation leads back to identification—only this time the identification is not with a character, but with the discovery of a higher level of discernment.[25]

Essay #6: "Rapture and Rupture: Eisenstein and Brecht" This is the longest essay in the book, and in many ways the most important one. So far, Alea has established his position regarding cinema as one that has as its final objective transforming reality and bettering humankind. Film can do this because of its potential to help us attain a higher level of discernment, the first step in effecting a mental transformation, and a necessary condition for transforming reality itself. Finally, in the essay on Aristotle and Brecht, Alea suggests that the most effective way of transforming viewers' level of discernment is to guide them so that they discover this higher level of discernment by themselves. How? By using *both* identification *and* alienation in a way that promotes the creation of a viewer's dialectic.

Alea believes in the effectiveness of the *Verfremdungseffekte*, that is, of rupture within the *process* of identification, not of rupture with identification itself. And yet, this process as described by Brecht (with its emphasis on the alienation half of the identification-alienation dialectic) does not travel well to film because film deals primarily with images, and images are better suited for communicating at the level of emotions, not the intellect. This essay is therefore an attempt to elaborate, starting with Eisenstein, a suitable equivalent of the estrangement effect for the medium of film.

The essay begins with a comparison of Eisenstein and Brecht. Both were born in 1898, both became known in the 1920s with their early works—*Battleship Potemkin* (1925) and *The Three Penny Opera* (1928)—both worked "to promote reasoning as a weapon in the spectator," and both "based themselves on dialectical materialism in their aesthetic pursuits" (52). Nevertheless, in the identification-alienation dialectic, Eisenstein emphasized identification while Brecht emphasized alienation, "one wanted spectators *committed emotionally* to the show, the other wanted them to be *separate*, distant, analytical and rational" (53 emphasis in original). "For Eisenstein," Alea continues, "the moment in which spectators become *alienated from themselves*, stop being themselves so as to live within an other—in the character—was of particular interest insofar as it constitutes the premise of a desirable change. And for Eisenstein, this change occurs—or at least originates —in the ambit of feeling, emotion, ecstasy" (54, my emphasis). By identifying with a character, viewers became alienated from themselves. For Brecht, on the other hand, alienation ought to come "not from themselves but *from the characters* (or, in a broader sense, from the dramatic situation unfolding before them, the show, the fiction . . .)" (54, my emphasis).

Alea points out the importance of biography in explaining how two men with similar social and political agendas arrived at such different conclusions on how art should achieve similar goals. On the one hand, Eisenstein was most productive during the early years of the Bolshevik Revolution, at a time of relative intellectual freedom and experimentation. Eisenstein was only nineteen years old when the Bolsheviks assumed power, so the enthusiasm of these years and Eisenstein's own success as a director explains much of the enthusiasm and positive force of his theory of transformation through emotional identification. Brecht, on the other hand, was a German and a pacifist, a combination that brought him into constant conflict with authorities who promoted the Horatian dictum "Dulce et decorum est pro patria mori." The skepticism, detachment, and lucidity extolled by Brecht in his theoretical writings were clearly influenced by his mistrust of authority as he had experienced it.

What about Alea? How does his involvement in the Cuban Revolution inform his theory? On the one hand, Alea always welcomed the changes brought about by the Revolution, especially in terms of ending North American dominance of the Cuban economy and politics. On the other hand, as a member of the urban opposition to Batista, Alea shared in this group's skepticism toward "the boys from the jungle," as members of the July 26 Movement were derisively called. In effect, Alea felt both emotionally identified with the Revolution and at the same time distanced from its guerrilla roots. This may help to explain why Alea gave equal weight to both identification and alienation in his own theory. To Alea these were not mutually exclusive processes, but different sides of the same process whereby the viewer attains a greater understanding of reality.

The differences between Eisenstein and Brecht become less pronounced when one considers their later works. For "certainly, if at first Eisenstein devoted all his energy toward directing viewer's sentiments in a specific sense (political agitation, propaganda . . .), . . . [his] predominant role drifts little by little toward other mechanisms which lead him to stir up 'contradictions in the spectators' minds' " (59). On the other hand, and "starting with *Mother Courage*, Brecht made room in his works for other traditional theatrical elements, which he could now manipulate with a complete mastery of measure" (63). That is, Brecht accepted the importance of entertaining viewers, and Eisenstein was forced by circumstance to make films of more intellectual complexity, films such as *Ivan the Terrible* and *Alexander Nevski*. "The divergence between both," Alea concludes,

> can be logically surpassed only if we consider Eisenstein's *pathos* and Brecht's *estrangement* as two moments of the same dialectical process . . . from which each artist isolated and emphasized a different phase. The new rules of the game, under which that relationship takes place, make it possible for the spectator not only to enrich himself spiritually and to further his knowledge of reality on the basis of an aesthetic experience, but they also propitiate in him a critical attitude toward the reality encompassing him. Spectators will cease to be spectators vis-a-vis reality and will face it not as something given but as a process in whose unfolding they are involved." (64–66, emphasis in original)

This is, in many words, the viewer's dialectic.

Appendix: "Memories of Memories . . ."

The appendix opens like this chapter—with a sketch of the reception history of *Memories*. Alea then picks one critique (that of Andrew Sarris) and deconstructs it until it is clear that it is "consistent with a whole way of thinking prevalent in the United States and with a way of defining self-interests which are not . . . those of the Revolution" (71). *Memories*, says Alea, should not be judged by these liberal standards, that is, by the degree to which it is contentious or countercultural. This would miss the point that *Memories* is a militant cinema produced in a country where the Revolution is in power. Rather, it should be judged by the degree to which it promotes and develops people's critical sense while at the same time strengthening the reality of the Revolution and promoting its collective goals.

The rest of the essay is an explanation of how *Memories* succeeds on both counts. Alea begins by pointing out the four instances of double-repetitions in the film: (1) the popular dance (sequences 1 and 22), (2) the parting scenes at the airport (both in sequence 2), (3) Sergio's tape-recorded argument with Laura (sequences 3 and 11), and (4) the hidden camera shots of people in the streets (sequences 4 and 30). In this last case (as in all four cases), "the truth does not lie in the first sequence of faces, nor in the second, nor in the sum of both, but rather in the *confrontation* between both and the main character, and what that *suggests* to the spectator within the general context of the film" (81, my emphasis). The apparent ambivalence of the film is no such thing, but rather the "expression of contradictions whose purpose in the film is none other than to contribute to the concerns and impulses for action which we wish to awaken in the spectator" (81). In each of these double repetitions, the first sequence serves to help the viewer identify with Sergio, while the repetition serves to help the viewer break off that identification and replace it with a critical attitude toward Sergio. What happened with critics like Sarris is that they performed only half of the viewer's dialectic (that of identification) and ignored the other half (that of alienation); without their confrontation, the resulting interpretation is partial.

The alternation of documentary images with explicitly fictional images also serves to set up a dialectic, this one between Sergio's subjective viewpoint and the documentary shots' more objective viewpoint. Again, the first part of this dialectic serves to help the viewer identify with Sergio, but then the second half, the documentary footage, helps the viewer to take a critical stance toward Sergio. And again, the truth is not in *either* the subjective *or* the objective viewpoints, but rather in the confrontation between *both*, in what that suggests to the spectator within the general context of the film. That is to say, the truth lies in the viewer's dialectic (see Figure 1), in that

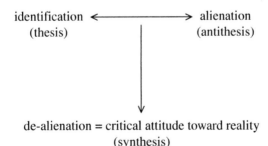

Figure 1. The viewer's dialectic.

come and go between identification and alienation that results in de-alienation, a synthesis where the viewer stands at a distance from both Sergio's subjective viewpoint and the filmmaker's "objective" one.

Memories will have succeeded if it helps the viewer perform this dialectic; that is, if the film helps the viewer to take a critical attitude toward *both* Sergio's subjective reality *and* the filmmaker's more objective one. This of course requires a very active spectator, one who actively engages with the film at all levels. In the best of cases, this ideal viewer will also be consistent enough to interiorize that critical attitude and apply it to the realities outside the theater, to his own subjective reality as well as to the objective reality surrounding him.

On a broader level—that is, on a level that applies to both fictional characters and to viewers outside the theater—the viewer's dialectic may be defined as one between individual and society (see Figure 2). In this dialectic of humankind, the interaction between the two poles will determine the extent to which a productive synthesis is reached, a synthesis in which social commitment is balanced by personal growth and society and the individual develop together.

Each side of the dialectic has its potential advantages and disadvantages. Placing emphasis on the interests of the individual is desirable and healthy insofar as it promotes personal development, but too much emphasis on this pole runs the risk of one's alienation by defining "self-interest" too narrowly. On the other hand, placing emphasis on the interests of society will be beneficial insofar as this promotes solidarity and the creation of a community in which individuals may flourish as interconnected beings. At the same time, placing too much emphasis on this aspect of the dialectic runs the risk of stunting personal development, of annulling the individual. Clearly, the ideal would be one in which a balance is struck between the needs of the individual and his or her duty to society, for, ultimately, the separation between individual and society is an illusory one: Personal development is unattainable without social commitment, and social development cannot advance much farther than the average individual's level of personal development.

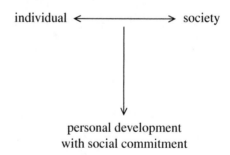

Figure 2. The human dialectic.

Most of the main characters in Alea's films struggle with this dialectic between individual and society. Sometimes the character struggles with the moral dimension of the dialectic, sometimes with the economic, sometimes with the spiritual, and, in the more complex cases, with a combination of two or more of these dimensions. In all cases, however, the trajectory that the character follows may be explained as the move toward the synthesis of personal development with social commitment, or as the move away from it, as the case may be. Sergio, for example, moved a little bit toward the synthesis by deciding to stay in Cuba. Unlike Pablo, who leaves so that he won't have to deal with redefining his very narrow definition of "self" as white male–apolitical consumer, Sergio puts himself to the test, attempts to recover his own humanity. The problem with Sergio is that his only previous taste of authentic humanity, with the synthesis of the human dialectic, was through love with a European woman, and he incorrectly believes that the only way to experience that authentic humanity again is to reproduce as much as possible the externals of that experience. His definition of self is so narrowly defined as "white Euro-Americanized bourgeois" that he cannot see himself in Laura or Elena as he had once seen himself in Hanna, or, from another perspective, he can't see in Laura or Elena the authentic humanity he detects in himself. He is afraid to discard his old definition of self, even though he recognizes that it is too narrow and that it will ultimately bring about his downfall. That is, his old self-definition no longer works to his advantage, either politically (because the bourgeoisie is no longer in power) or ethically (because that self-definition is impeding his personal development). He tries to discard the old self, but fails. However, in the process of trying, he makes some very sharp observations about Cuban society, and this sharpness of mind, this ability to see some things clearly, is what the viewer can rescue from an otherwise disdainful character.

Film as Tragedy

Like Sergei Eisenstein's *Potemkin*, *Memories of Underdevelopment* has been called the film of the Revolution.[26] In very different ways, both of these films address the process of mental change away from a colonized state and toward true freedom, from alienation to de-alienation. In *Potemkin*, the collective protagonist succeeds in finalizing this process into action, and the film's end is a celebration of an important precedent to the October Revolution. In *Memories*, on the other hand, the highly individualized protagonist cannot or will not take the necessary actions to finalize a different kind of colonization, the cultural colonization of his own class. Notwithstanding these important differences, there are striking parallels between the two films. In a memorable article on the "Organic Unity and Pathos in the Composition of *Potemkin*," Eisenstein discusses the unity of the film's composition:

Outwardly, *Potemkin* is a chronicle of events but it impresses the spectator
as a drama. The secret of this effect lies in the plot, which is built up in
accordance with the laws of austere composition of tragedy in its traditional
five-act form. The events, first taken as unembellished facts, are divided
into five tragic acts, the facts themselves so arranged as to form a consecu-
tive whole, closely conforming to the requirements of classical tragedy: a
third act distinct from the second, a fifth distinct from the first, and so on.[27]

This description could very well apply to the structure of *Memories*,
insofar as each intertitled "act"—"Havana 1961," "Pablo," "Noemi,"
"Elena," "A Tropical Adventure," and "October 22, 1962/Kennedy
Speaks"—is distinct from each other yet "permeated and cemented, as it
were, by the method of double repetition."[28] We've already seen how double
repetition works in the film, but here I would like to focus on the idea that
each part (Pablo, Elena, Hemingway and his attendant, Noemi, and Laura) is
a small tragedy within the larger tragedy of Sergio. That is, I will read *Memories* as a tragedy.

Memories is formally what Northrop Frye called "tragic irony," the
study of tragic isolation as such, which thereby drops out the element of special case.[29] Sergio is not a tragic hero like Oedipus, whom we see from below
as a larger-than-life figure, or like Othello, whom we see as our equal.[30]
Instead, we see Sergio from above, in the sense that we look down upon a life
full of absurdities and follies. By the end of the film, there is no identification
between the spectator and Sergio because Sergio is not a special case, but
rather quite mundane. His isolation from others within the film reinforces his
isolation from the spectator, as is evident from the repetition of the airport
scene from his point of view. Moreover, his status as an intellectual, which in
a capitalist society would set him apart as a special person, does not (in theory) confer any special status in a revolutionary society. In Cuban social theory, intellectuals are simply mental workers, an element among the many that
will coalesce to form the new society. Mario Benedetti, the official voice of
the revolutionary intellectual, said as much during the 1968 Cultural Congress of Havana. His talk, aptly titled "The Intellectual and the Fight for Liberation of the People of the Third World," emphasized the need for the
intellectual to "take on a role like that of a technician, the teacher or even the
athlete, a person with particular skills all of which are needed in the effort to
create a new kind of human being, a job just like any other."[31]

Coincidentally, this historical congress took place the same year as the
screening of *Memories*. Nineteen sixty-eight was a year of turbulence
throughout the world—student demonstrations in Paris and Manila, the civil
rights movement in the United States, the massacre at Tlatelolco, Prague
Spring, to name a few. The role of the traditional intellectual amidst so much
turbulence is questionable and put to the test. It was not a year to vacillate,

but rather a year to act and to effect concrete and immediate changes. Insofar as Sergio represents the traditional bourgeois intellectual who vacillates and who hides his prejudices behind the veil of objectivity, the film postulates the death of traditional bourgeois intellectuality. Alea's own commitment to the Revolution, on the other hand, serves as an alternative course to Sergio's death by irrelevance. Nineteen sixty-eight is like 1962 in the sense that it is a time of taking sides. Sergio's inability to take sides at the height of the 1962 Cuban Missile Crisis is his undoing, as will be for those intellectuals in 1968 Paris, Manila, Prague, and Mexico City who ignore the changes around them. Perhaps this is the real reason for the film's censorship in the United States; at a time of virulent polarization stemming from the Vietnam War and the civil rights movement, the film shows a Cuba whose military is used for defensive purposes, not for killing innocent people, and where racial harmony seems to be a fait accompli.

The dilemma confronting Sergio is similar to the dilemma faced by most Latin American intellectuals in the 1960s. The Cuban Revolution marked a whole generation that came of age under the influence of its leaders and ideals, most notably Ernesto "Che" Guevara and his call for a New Man and social justice. Outside Cuba, many intellectuals were forced to question their own relationship to states that served the interests of a few instead of the necessities of the vast majority of the population. Inside Cuba, where the Revolution quickly became identified with the state, intellectuals had to go beyond the posing of questions and actually take a position one way or another. By 1968 the situation in Cuba had stabilized and the Revolution had been secured, so Sergio's political dilemma was in many ways dated when the film was released. Outside of Cuba, however, Latin America seemed poised to follow the path of socialism, even if not by the same means as in Cuba. Panama, Argentina, Brazil, and Chile are the best examples of countries with strong leftist movements in the 1960s whose success was dependent on convincing people like Sergio of the need for structural changes of the kind undertaken in Cuba. In this sense, the audience of *Memories* was truly pan-American at the time of its release, and its ideology was clearly pro-Revolution.

But going back to the reading of *Memories* as a tragedy, we may conclude that the film is a tragic irony, its (anti)hero an intellectual who does not take the leap of faith from the individual to the collective. The most obvious example of Sergio's failure to go beyond himself is his relationship with women. From his first love Hanna to his last object of affection, Noemi, Sergio never takes the crucial step, the one that will take him out of himself and into a broader social reality. Each of the women in Sergio's life represents an aborted attempt to integrate into a different social reality. With Hanna, it would have been the reality of a bohemian; with Laura, the reality of the petit bourgeoisie; with Elena, the reality of the working class; and with Noemi, the reality of an idealized Revolution. Clearly, each of these four women represents more than individuals. Yet the metaphor woman-Cuba, which is as old as Cuban nationalism[32], applies to *Memories* in subtle and somewhat problematic ways. The case of Laura seems obvious: She represents the bourgeoisie that flees, leaving behind what she sees as the filth, the sweat, and the *chusma* of Cuba. But does she really? Judging from her quarrel with Sergio in their bedroom (cf. sequence 11), she seems to flee Sergio's machinations as much as the Revolution. Elena, on the other hand, represents the popular masses in whose interest the Revolution was ostensibly fought. Yet she still lives by the rules and appearances of the pre-Revolution petit bourgeoisie, as when she accuses Sergio of raping her so that he will marry her (cf. sequence 25). Finally, Noemi represents the hopes and aspirations of the Revolution, the woman who may yet save Sergio from himself. Unlike Laura and Elena, Sergio is attracted to Noemi as much by her beauty as by her innocence, an innocence signified by her baptism, and in no small degree associated with the early years of the Revolution. Like Cuba after 1959, Noemi after her baptism is the embodiment of hope and the possibility of a new beginning for Sergio. This new beginning actually takes place, when Sergio takes Noemi out on a date (cf. sequence 22). In fact, this sequence, halfway into the film, continues the film's opening sequence, with the difference that in the continuation, the music has changed from the original Mozambique (a type of Afro-Cuban song) to a dissonant, vanguardist music that reflects Sergio's alienation from Noemi and from the crowd. Insofar as the crowd represents the Revolution, and given that Sergio's alienation applies to both Noemi and the crowd, the resulting parallelism between Noemi and the Revolution reveals that the fight for socialism is inseparable from the fight for equality between the sexes. If Sergio cannot treat women as his equals, neither can he forgo his individuality for the sake of the supra-individual, and in this way end his alienation.

In *The Birth of Tragedy*, Friedrich Nietzsche defines tragedy as a conflict between the Apollonian ideal of order, lucidity, and individuation on the one hand and the Dionysian vortex of confusion, ecstasy, and collective transubstantiation on the other. The opening sequence shows the Dionysian tumult from an insider's perspective. In the repetition, on the other hand, the perspective is that of Sergio, distant and self-centered. His perspective corresponds to that of Apollo, but the correspondence is distorted by Sergio's confusion. The Dionysian perspective, on the other hand, belongs to the crowd. If one considers the sequence immediately preceding the repetition, the identification of Dionysian frenzy with the Revolution becomes clear. In sequence 22, Sergio walks alone in the streets of Havana, and a demonstration of mostly black people march in the opposite direction. It is daylight. The demonstrators chant slogans in support of socialism. The contrast between Sergio's unfocused brooding and the crowd's directed enthusiasm could hardly be stronger, as it is underscored by their racial and class differences, their opposite directions, and Sergio's interior monologue: "Everything comes too early or too late. In another time perhaps I would have been able to understand what is going on here. Today I can't." His lack of understanding is the underlying cause of his alienation. In the shot that follows we see Sergio with Noemi, and the crowd's racial and class composition harks back to the daylight demonstrators, so that the two crowds are identified through both metaphor (one crowd is like the other) and metonym (one shot follows the other). In both cases Sergio fails to integrate into the Dionysian frenzy, and this is precisely what makes *Memories* a tragedy: its hero's inability to integrate into the collectivity, the realm of Dionysus, the Revolution.

In classic Greek tragedies, the satyr embodies the tension between mind and body, between Apollo and Dionysus. In *Memories* there are of course no satyrs. Yet like a satyr, Sergio is torn between two opposing and seemingly irreconcilable forces. Before the Revolution, his desire to be a bohemian writer and live with Hanna in New York clashed with his family's demands for him to settle down into a life of work and responsibility as a furniture store owner. Sergio grudgingly chooses the latter and settles for Laura, whom he tries to mold into the Hanna of his dreams. But Laura is not Hanna, which is like saying Cuba is not Europe. All the make-up in the world will not change that, and Sergio knows it.

After his family's departure to Miami, Sergio gets an unexpected chance to redeem himself. He tries, unsuccessfully, to find a new Hanna and to live the life of a bohemian writer, but fails on both counts. Sergio's ideal of feminine beauty and sophistication is not to be found in Cuba, and even if he did find it, it is doubtful that Sergio would meet his end of the bargain: to treat her as an equal subject rather than as an object of desire. His treatment of Laura and of Elena suggests as much. The second possibility of redemption—becoming a bohemian writer—also falls short of expectations. Sergio lacks the discipline and talent to be successful on this account, but even if he did have these two requirements for a successful career as a writer, his isolation from the Revolution and its cultural industry signals his failure in advance.

Before his family's departure, then, Sergio was half-integrated into his social class. He loathed its shallowness and consumerism, yet grudgingly participated in them. After his family leaves for Miami, Sergio follows the same pattern of behavior: He loathes the Revolution's populism and the physical deterioration that accompanies it, yet grudgingly participates in them. The result of this lack of integration into society is alienation, a feeling visually captured in the famous shot of Sergio looking down on Havana through a telescope.

The original script of the film called for Sergio's death by suicide, the logical outcome given his role as a tragic hero who cannot overcome his alienation. Many scenes throughout the film prepare the viewer for this eventuality—for example, the caged birds in his balcony. The cage represents his marriage to Laura, and the death of one of the pair signals Laura's departure. Yet the other bird, the one that would represent Sergio, remains caged, locked up as if its fate will also be that of its ex-companion. Another foreshadowing of death comes right before his trial, when he tells himself that he has decided to let himself be carried by the tide of events. Sergio's premonitions of death culminate in this scene, where he says to himself: "You are nothing. Nothing. You are dead. Now, Sergio, begins your final destruction." The shot is taken from above, thus underscoring the earlier observation that the film functions as an ironic tragedy because we see Sergio from above. Moreover, Sergio walks alone and crosses the lanes diagonally, two visual cues that again underscore his lack of direction and his alienation. Finally, and as if to leave no doubt about what will (or should) happen to Sergio, toward the end of the film a shot shows a man walking in front of a wall with "MUERTE" written in huge letters (see discussion of sequence 28).

Against all expectations, however, Sergio does not die, and the film is open-ended. The death in the opening sequence may be seen as Sergio's own death deflected, projected onto another individual. Yet this is no substitute for the hero's death. Certainly it does not give a sense of closure, let alone produce a catharsis. Sergio's survival suggests two possibilities (discarding, of course, the option of exile): Either he will continue down the road of ambiguity, which would exacerbate his alienation and thus precipitate his death by suicide (literally) or by sacrifice (figuratively), or he will confront the cause of his alienation and attempt to overcome it. The concern with alienation in 1960s Cuba was so central to intellectual discourse that its cure even had a technical term: *desgarramiento*. Literally, the word means to tear, rip, or rent, as one would with a piece of cloth. Figuratively, it means to shatter, to crush. Both definitions underscore the destruction of something, in this case the pre-Revolution consciousness.

Memories leaves open the possibility of Sergio's integration to the revolutionary process through a *desgarramiento*. But it is not enough for Sergio to become aware of his false consciousness. This he does partially, as when he reads from Leo Rozitchner's book or when he expresses disbelief at his five-year friendship with Pablo. The step Sergio has yet to take is to translate his inchoate awareness of a false consciousness into a truly liberated practice. Otherwise, his *desgarramiento* will be incomplete: He will still manipulate women, live off the work of others, criticize without attempting to effect changes in the situation he criticizes, or, worse still, not apply to himself the criticism he hurls against others.

Notwithstanding the possibility of Sergio's *desgarramiento*, this change does not take place within the film. The most one can say with certainty is that

Sergio is suspended between integration to the new order (which is still in its embryonic stages) and his alienation from others, both at the individual level (Laura, Elena, Noemi) and at the collective level. For Sergio, the personal informs the political, so that his incapacity to love any of these three women parallels his incapacity to love Cuba and, by extension, the Revolution.

Sergio's death, whether literal or through a *desgarramiento* whereby Sergio becomes a New Man, is made desirable because of all the negative things Sergio represents: racial prejudice, class privilege, compulsory heterosexuality, and the reification of metropolitan values at the expense of local culture. At the same time, Sergio's self-critical attitude constitutes a practice without which the Revolution runs the risk of fossilization. Perhaps this is Sergio's saving grace and the reason why Alea chose to keep him alive despite all expectations to the contrary.

In *Memories*, Alea tackles the very real and critical issue of how the Revolution has fared in its attempt to get rid of bourgeois patterns of thought and action. In doing so, he steers clear of simplistic representations of the new society and, at the same time, avoids the categorical dismissal of the old. Instead, Alea sets in motion a dialectic between Sergio's limited individual subjectivity and a broader collective subjectivity presented through documentary footage and through the eyes of other characters. The confrontation between these two subjectivities defines the dynamics of the film. In the end, Alea's criticisms of these two subjectivities are constructive rather than corrosive, and his method one of suggestion rather than prescriptive solutions. In short, Alea poses difficult questions and then leaves it up to the viewer to formulate answers from the evidence given. This is quite remarkable considering the Manichaeism that has plagued debates on the Revolution's achievements and shortcomings. It is a balancing act that few people inside or outside Cuba have achieved, yet one that Alea maintains throughout the film.

Postmodern Postscript

The film's irresolution and above all Sergio's political ambivalence give *Memories* a postmodernist feel in the Baudrillardian sense of the word, a postmodernism that, in contrast to previous metaphysical theories, "is ironic rather than serious, fragmentary rather than systematic, and abandons the belief in an objective, representational reality."[33] In this transpolitical world, simulacra have more value than reality, and political strategies lack effectiveness. I personally see Baudrillard's position as extreme, but it helps to explain Sergio's political apathy. *Memories* is by no means a transpolitical film, nor does it refute the possibility of a political strategy. On the contrary. It asks the spectator to take a position, one way or the other. Yet the film's main character, like Baudrillard, seems to value images more than reality, and also disavows the potency of any political strategy. Sergio, for example, values women to the extent that they resemble images, be they Botticelli's *Venus*, Manet's *Olympia*, or Brigitte Bardot. And on the question of political strategy, he confesses in the last sequence that "It's no use protesting. I'll die like the rest." Sergio's fatalism translates into apathy and a disavowal of any political strategy, a position similar to that of Baudrillard.

At the same time, postmodernism may also be seen in a more positive light, as a set of discourses that pushes the limits of the modern project by looking beyond class to a closer analysis of gender, race, popular culture, and political plurality. In this sense, Sergio's *desgarramiento* would have to assimilate all of these realities in order for it to be complete. In this second (and more productive) reading of postmodernism, postmodernism becomes an attack against the binarisms associated with modernism and the Cold War, a point that gives the film an unexpected meaning. As I write these lines in 2001, Cuba stands out as a political and economic anachronism, trapped by an unfair U.S. blockade as much as by a narrow version of modernity that justifies the ruling party's monopoly over politics. Thirty years after the film's release, Sergio's inability to integrate into the Revolution may be read as an ill-fated strategy of resistance—resistance to think in slogans and resistance to accept a revolutionary master narrative that justifies the exile of one-tenth of the Cuban population and the state's monopoly of knowledge. Sadly, Alea's fears of a fossilized Revolution have become a reality, a fact caused as much by external factors as by Castro's insistence that political pluralism is somehow separate from the Revolution's project of social and economic justice.

4
The Search for Cuba's "Intra-Historia"

After completing *Memories of Underdevelopment*, Alea finally felt that he was ready to tackle the twice-postponed project of adapting Fernando Ortiz's *A Cuban Fight against Demons*. The mastery of *Memories* dispelled any lingering doubts he may have had about his own and his coworkers' readiness, both technical and formal, to embark on this ambitious project. Moreover, the favorable reception of that film convinced Alea that the public was ready for an even more complex one. *A Cuban Fight against Demons* is, in effect, Alea's most complex and brilliant film in terms of form, but it is also the most difficult to follow. People simply did not understand what was going on, and Alea realized that, at least on this count, the film had failed.

> [What I like least about *A Cuban Fight* . . .] is that people ask me the meanings of the film because they can't figure out its purpose, its general super-objective. That leaves me very frustrated and puts me in the position of having to explain the film—which is something I detest—because if the film does not effectively speak for itself, there's nothing to be done. *A Cuban Fight* . . . fails in the communication of a clear idea, it suffers from a problem of cinematographic narration.[1]

This may explain why his next film, *The Last Supper*, is so simple in terms of form and so clear in its presentation of ideas. Alea wanted above all to communicate with the Cuban public, and if pushing the limits of filmic expression to their limits meant losing his viewers, then it was clear to him that he had to leave the formal experimentation to others. The strategy paid off. *The Last Supper* became Cuba's first international box office success, and critics are in general agreement on what the film means.

After working on these two very somber films, Alea was ready for something lighter. The result was *The Survivors*, a black comedy that postulates the possibility of historical regression. History, in fact, had been the main concern at ICAIC throughout the seventies, and by making a film about historical regression when everybody else (including himself) had been making films about historical progression, Alea effectively closed that chapter in the history of ICAIC.

There are two interrelated reasons for ICAIC's focus on history throughout the seventies. On the one hand, the First National Congress on Culture and Education (1971) revealed the low educational level of the population at large, despite the dramatic success of the literacy campaign. Artists were called upon to help in the task of education, and Alea responded with enthusiasm:

> As far as we are concerned, the development of a didactic cinema is one of the consequences of [the First National Congress on Culture and Education . . .], not only as filmmakers, but as professors; that is, as people who now have something to give to others through film. . . . Not with any paternalistic posture, but simply because of the need to give of what one knows instead of keeping it to oneself. . . . Film in this sense is easier: the material is there, one becomes aware of it, and the films are made.[2]

Unlike the earlier literacy campaign, where the goals were to bring the average level of education to the third grade in reading, writing, and arithmetic, the Congress on Culture and Education focused on the more difficult goal of ensuring a minimum of social awareness. In many ways, Alea and others at ICAIC were already doing this before the congress. The difference now was that the favored means for achieving this was through a rewriting of history, a rewriting that would replace bourgeois historiography with a materialist historiography:

> Our historical films are needed particularly because the vision that exists of the past has been systematically distorted by bourgeois historiography. Fortunately, we've also had a few historians who have dedicated their lives to the study of our past with a distinct optic—including some who have used a decidedly Marxist optic—and their studies sometimes were genuine acts of rebellion in the midst of a reactionary and racist society that was subjected to the interests of capitalism. . . .
>
> Needless to say, given our ideological position, the criteria for making historical films cannot be reduced to a desire to reconstruct particular moments of the past. The importance of this kind of cinema is, for us, directly related to the repercussions that a correct (scientific) interpretation of historical facts may have in the present, and by the degree to which this interpretation helps viewers to understand and affirm the revolutionary development of our present.[3]

Alea's historical films are therefore part of a larger project to understand the material basis of contemporary society. But Alea was also aware of other components in the formation of the current national consciousness, particularly the African element in Cuban consciousness and the predominant religion in the island, Christianity. Of the African presence, Alea was not the first or the only director to study this heritage through film, but *The Last Supper* was and still remains one of the best attempts to construct an Afro-Cuban subaltern perspective on slavery and to dramatize the process of syncretism between African pantheism and Christian hagiography. Moreover, all of Alea's historical films deal directly with Christianity, but in ways that avoid Marx's dismissal of religion as the opiate of the masses. Instead, Alea recognized, from early on in life, that Christianity and Marxism were similar in more ways than one:

> [As a teenager] I began to read Marxist literature. How can I explain the change that took place within me in the way of looking at things? The idea of communism seemed to me very similar to the idea of paradise. The only difference was that in Marxism, paradise presented itself as the logical and rational consequence of humanity's development, and as something that should be reached in this life. It was no longer a matter of "good guys" versus "bad guys", but rather about the fact that there existed specific laws of development that manifested themselves in individuals as well as in history. Also, it was no longer about preaching Christ's virtues in order to improve mankind and eliminate social injustices, but rather a matter of admitting that men are motivated by their interests and that the economic factor is in the end determinant. That is to say, it was not about expecting men to become angels in order to enter paradise, but rather that men would better themselves in that long and arduous process of constructing paradise. That's how I went from Christian preaching to revolutionary practice.[4]

This very personal conflation of Marxism and Christianity can be seen in many of Alea's films and is a topic I develop in the Conclusions Chapter. For now, suffice it to say that for Alea, the attempt to achieve paradise on Earth is a very noble human aspiration that can easily get deformed by greed, zealousness, and lust for power. By pointing out how these all too human motivations deform nominally Christian characters like Father Manuel in *A Cuban Fight against Demons* and the Count in *The Last Supper*, Alea indirectly pointed to a similar process of deformation in nominally Marxist state officials whose policies and actions were inhibiting instead of aiding Cuba's development.

> The fundamental objective of the Revolution is Man, the improvement of Man, the perfectionability of the human condition. Or, as has been said so many times, the creation of a New Man who is more humane, who can live in a more just society, conscious of his social responsibility. Because of a legitimate zeal for social justice, for ideological purity, the Revolution almost got to the point of ignoring the personal interests of Man, his

individual necessities. . . . From that point on I felt that something very
valuable was being lost, and that the Revolution was dangerously close to
resembling the caricature that her enemies made her out to be.[5]

This last reference to the Revolution as a caricature of its former self
brings me to the other reason for ICAIC's focus on historical films during the
seventies, and that is the atmosphere of oppression that hung over artists and
intellectuals. The storm was foreshadowed by Cuba's support of the Soviet
invasion of Czechoslovakia in 1968, precipitated by the 1970 sugar harvest,
and fueled by a series of scandals in 1971: the "Padilla affair," the closing
down of the Department of Philosophy at the University of Havana, the shut-
ting down of the aptly named magazine *Pensamiento Crítico* (and its replacement with the aptly named *Revolución y Cultura* the following year), and,
close to home, the censure of Humberto Solás' *A Day in November.* The
result of these and other government clampdowns was the so-called *quinque-
nio gris*, a period of five "gray" years during which Cuban art lost much of
the freshness and vitality that characterized it during the 1960s. Under these
circumstances, it is not too surprising that filmmakers would choose historical subjects over contemporary ones. This way they could denounce the
excesses of these gray years by drawing parallels between the past and the
present, while at the same time contributing to the pedagogic and historio-
graphic project outlined in the declaration of the First National Congress on
Cultural Education. Alea and other filmmakers at ICAIC during the seventies
sought answers to an immediate crisis by searching for Cuba's "intra-
historia," a term coined by Miguel de Unamuno in his volume *En torno al
casticismo*: "The intra-historic life, silent and continuous like the very depths
of the sea, is the substance of progress, the true tradition, not the false tradition that is usually sought in a past buried in books and papers and monu-
ments and stones."[6] In Spain at the end of Empire as in Cuba during the gray
years, the noble hope was that such an understanding of the past would help
people overcome the crisis of the present, and in turn face the future with
renewed confidence.

A Cuban Fight against Demons

A Cuban Fight against Demons is an adaptation of Fernando Ortiz's book of
the same title. In that book, the renowned Cuban cultural anthropologist
recounts the story of a priest who in 1672 tried to move a whole coastal village inland, to an area where he owned a large hacienda. His first justification
for such a radical move was to protect the inhabitants from pirate attacks and
from contact with Protestant heretics. After that failed to convince the local
authorities, he got himself a notary who actually wrote down that Lucifer,
speaking through a black woman, was announcing the town's doom. When

that also failed, the priest appealed to a higher authority—God himself—and asked that God transubstantiate Himself into the eucharistic Host so that through the priest, He could manifest His divine will on the matter. The notary duly wrote down God's will as spoken by the priest, but not even God's words convinced the local authorities. The priest's last recourse was to appeal to the King of Spain (Charles II), who was himself a believer in the power of demons. With the king's support secured, the priest ordered that the coastal town of San Juan de los Remedios del Cayo be destroyed "by blood and fire."

Up to here the story and the historical facts speak of the seventeenth century's obscurantism (the priest withholds his material motives for the move) and occultism (the priest converses with both God and Lucifer). But what happens next speaks of a new emerging political consciousness that is distinctly Cuban, not Spanish; local, not metropolitan; pragmatic, not dogmatic. When the priest began to destroy the town, some people supported him, but many more resisted. This challenge to Spanish control of the island is one of the first recorded attempts by Cubans to assert their sovereignty, and as such is an early precursor of the Revolution itself. The film privileges this particular interpretation by moving the date of the events from 1672 to 1659 (exactly three hundred years before the Revolution) and by including stills of José Martí, Fidel Castro, the Sierra Maestra, and Che Guevara.

In his book, Fernando Ortiz focuses on the material and economic motivations of the priest. In the film, on the other hand, the stress falls on the spiritual motivations behind such aberrant behavior. Asked why he made these radical changes, Alea replied:

> Well, that's something I ask myself even today, but at the time it seemed to us too obvious to criticize the priest only for his material interests. It is also true that in all our history demons have played an important role, revealing the extent of fanaticism, and the contradictions between those who did not let themselves be scared by them, and those who . . . feared falling into heresies. We thought that some of the problems in our history would become clearer in light of this confrontation.[7]

Alea, it seems, was interested in going beyond the "obvious" materialist explanation of history to an exploration of deeper human motivations such as fear and love. In the film, these primal forces (or "idea-forces," as Ortiz called them) are embodied in the two main characters, the priest (Father Manuel) and the town smuggler (Juan Contreras).

The film begins with black-on-white credits shown against a background of convent music that has somehow been distorted, so that the feeling from the very beginning is one of confusion and dissonance. The first sequence shows Father Manuel blessing Juan Contreras' new sugar mill, followed by the festivities of such an occasion. All of the town's regents—Evaristo, the mayor, and Juan Contreras, among others—are having a good time when all of the sudden pirates attack and burn down Contreras' property. The camera follows Evaristo's wife Laura and her black female slave as they flee the scene and find their way to the coast. The slave finds refuge in a cave, but two of the pirates catch up with Laura and rape her.

In the next sequence Father Manuel is sermonizing from his pulpit in the church, when Laura stands up and acts as if possessed by the devil. In fact, she's been traumatized by the rape to the point of insanity. Father Manuel tries to exorcise her, but succeeds only in calming her down. Throughout this sequence, and in others like it later in the film, a cock's constant crowing in the background foreshadows Father Manuel's eventual betrayal of Christ's message of love and his replacement of that message with a message of fear, superstition, and obscurantism.

During a regents' meeting, everyone except Evaristo expresses their unwillingness to go along with Father Manuel's plans to move the town inland. At the local pub, Contreras conspires with the pub's owner (the "Portuguese") and one of Evaristo's peons to steal some of Evaristo's cattle. When Evaristo confronts the peon, his excuse for having opened the gates was that the devil possessed him. All of these goings-on deeply affect Evaristo. Not only has the devil possessed his wife, but now his peons are also victims of the creatures of Father Manuel's imagination. Is he next? With this worry in mind, Evaristo visits the priest at the local madhouse, and the only coherent thought to come out of Evaristo's mouth is that he's afraid, he's afraid, he's afraid.

Father Manuel's exorcism of Laura did not work well, and in the next sequence we see Laura's slave performing an African ritual on Laura, followed by an abortion and a ceremonial bath in the river. The slave then takes the aborted fetus to the cave where Laura was raped and throws it into the abyss. Laura then visits the church to be baptized by the priest, but the priest is overcome with lust for Laura and succumbs to the temptation. His remorse and self-flagellation afterward is but a small price to pay for the crime just committed, especially when compared to the price Laura has had to pay (and will continue to pay) as a victim of rape, first by pirates and now by the priest.

Next, the town crier announces the arrival from Havana of some judges who are to decide on the fate of the town, whether it will be moved inland or stay where it is. At the pub, a local gives an impromptu performance of *décimas* with the refrain "y que en el camino, el demonio acabe con ellos [los jueces]," that is, that on their way back to Havana, may the devil destroy the judges who have come to dictate the fate of the town. The locals clearly don't want to move anywhere, and Juan Contreras quickly seizes on this feeling to incite them to rebellion with cries of "¡Que se vayan!"—a sort of precursor to future cries of "Yankee go home!" Meanwhile, back in the regents' meeting room, Evaristo reads a document written by Father Manuel, in which he explains his reasons for wanting to move the town inland, among them the fact that a shower of stars was followed by a terrible drought that shows no signs of abating after two years and that he's had to struggle with over 800,000 spirits just to keep the town afloat. Contreras makes a grand entrance at the end of Evaristo's lecture and proceeds to give convincing reasons for not moving inland, uppermost among them the fact that the supposed benefits to be gained by such a move do not outweigh all the sacrifices that would have to be made. The priest, visibly disturbed by the mayhem among the people of the town, confronts them in the town plaza and controls them using fear tactics. But as soon as the town crier announces that the judges are going back to Havana effective immediately, the townspeoples' defiant mood reigns again, this time with the added pleasure of having just won a victory for themselves.

Having secured a victory for himself, Juan Contreras is free to engage in his smuggling activities. To celebrate his newfound wealth, Contreras has another party at his place, where he makes fun of Father Manuel by saying that he too has had revelations. His smuggling partners shortly arrive with several prostitutes, and the civilized atmosphere that opened the party turns into debauchery. Contreras welcomes the change with a toast: "Let us establish Paradise right here, in the middle of this pigsty!" All of the sudden, Contreras turns serious and takes off on his white horse. He encounters Laura close to a promontory by the sea and follows her into the jungle, where they begin to kiss until Laura all of the sudden flees because she has a vision of Contreras destroying the altar at the local church. Contreras, unlike the priest, does not take advantage of Laura, and instead begins a mythic journey to the depths of his being. First he pays a ferryman to take him across the river. The parallel with Charon and the River Styx immediately comes to mind. Once on the other side, Contreras enters a house of prostitutes, one of whom introduces herself as love incarnate. She tells Contreras that he'll see and cry because he's been born too early, and this vision is followed by a vision of Cuba's history as a struggle for liberty and a search for Paradise on Earth, a struggle that began with the arrival of the first Spaniards in the fifteenth century and will culminate three centuries later with the Cuban Revolution. After the vision, the scene cuts to Contreras emerging from beneath the waters of a flowing river, thus underscoring the mythical dimensions of Contreras' vision and transformation.

Back in the church, Father Manuel has had a revelation of another sort, one that seals his transformation from a seeker of salvation to the enemy of Christ. The stage is thus set for the head-on confrontation between Father Manuel and Contreras, which is indeed what happens next. First, the governor's decision to move the town inland is announced. At that moment, Juan Contreras rides into town and warns the regents against Father Manuel's fear-based motives. Father Manuel can't take it anymore from Contreras, and he tries to convince the governor's representative to get rid of him. The representative ignores Father Manuel, whereupon he goes to Evaristo and coaxes him to go kill Contreras. That night, dressed in Inquisition regalia, Evaristo shows up with a group of followers in front of the mayor's house. Contreras, somehow aware of what was going to happen, appears dressed like Evaristo, stabs him to death, and flees. Laura arrives with her attendant slave and seems undisturbed (and almost content) by her husband's death. Finally, Father Manuel appears at the scene and proceeds to give a sermon about devils. In an amazing display of acuity, Laura's attendant calls the priest's lies for what they are, whereupon the priest's followers seize her and take her to the church. Once there, and with the excuse that he's exorcising her, Father Manuel gets away with murdering her by making her fall off his pulpit.

The next day the whole town is enveloped by paranoia, and when Father Manuel appears in front of the church with the chalice, the Eucharist, and other paraphernalia, most of the townspeople are there waiting for him, and they willingly follow him as he leads the way inland. Before taking off, however, Father Manuel had opened the doors of the madhouse, and after he leaves, the town truly seems to be inhabited by possessed beings. Contreras arrives into the half-empty town and decides to celebrate with his smuggling friends at the local pub. All of the sudden he turns serious, walks to the center of the plaza, and is shot to death right then and there. A group of English-speaking pirates has invaded the town and proceeds to kill almost everyone in the pub. One of the pirates announces from the church's bell tower that he sees a column of people advancing toward town, and they all decide to flee. Father Manuel, it turns out, has decided to return to town in order to destroy what's left. When he sees Contreras dead in the middle of the plaza, he slowly approaches with sword in hand and, with a very ceremonious gesture, buries it in Contreras' prostrate body. Father Manuel then starts a bonfire and begins to set the town ablaze. After these ultimate forms of exorcism, Father Manuel goes completely mad and throws himself into the abyss of the cave where Laura had been raped. The film ends with the Portuguese (who had been miraculously revived by the town idiot) taking the sword and the dagger from Contreras and brandishing them in the air as if possessed by the devil.

A materialist reading of the film can explain Father Manuel's move inland as signaling the economic suicide of the town, whereas Juan Contreras' smuggling can be seen as a means of satisfying a number of vital necessities. The problem with this kind of reading is that we may conclude that the priest's search for salvation is fully explainable in terms of his material motivations or that Juan Contreras' debauchery is fully explainable in terms of his smuggling activity. And yet this is not the case. Rather, Father Manuel's search for salvation is a legitimate human aspiration that has been deformed by his material motives, while Juan Contreras' utilitarian pragmatism is a legitimate form of social commitment that has temporarily degenerated into debauchery.

If we take the idea of the human dialectic developed in the last chapter and apply it to Father Manuel (see Figure 3), it is evident that he has fallen victim to his own narrow interests and that because of this he is moving away from the desired synthesis of personal development and social commitment. In his case, the immediate causes of the deformation may have been material (in Ortiz's version) or psychological (in Alea's version), but that does not take away from the legitimacy of his spiritual aspirations to help others and himself overcome irrational fears. The results—fanaticism at the individual level and a repression made possible by the power structures of the time—are both counterproductive and lamentable in that they take Father Manuel further away from his goal, which is spiritual salvation.

Similarly, in the case of Juan Contreras, the immediate causes of his debauchery may have been material, but again, that does not take away from the legitimacy of smuggling as a way of promoting the best interests of his society, especially at a time when commerce was unfairly monopolized to protect the interests of a few individuals at the expense of the vast majority of people. Another dimension to Contreras' character that escapes any predominantly materialist interpretation is his search for Paradise on Earth. On this point he and Father Manuel share a common spiritual quest. But whereas for Father Manuel this quest degenerated into fanaticism and culminated in his own sterile death by suicide, for Juan Contreras the search for Paradise on Earth ended with the realization that Paradise is not something to be *found* but something to be *made* or, more specifically, not something to be *bought from* others but something to be *made with* others.[8] In terms of the human

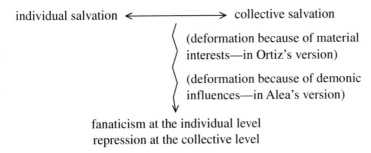

individual salvation ⟵⟶ collective salvation

(deformation because of material interests—in Ortiz's version)

(deformation because of demonic influences—in Alea's version)

fanaticism at the individual level
repression at the collective level

Figure 3. Father Manuel's deformed dialectic.

dialectic, Contreras develops as a person, from a hedonist to a socially committed individual (see Figure 4).

At first, Contreras' quest degenerated into debauchery not because hedonism or smuggling are bad in and of themselves, but because Contreras defined himself too narrowly: His hedonism was childishly egocentric (based on the incorrect belief that he could find his little individual Paradise independently of social commitment), and his smuggling was politically unstable because it lacked ideological justification. But seeing that this road led to a dead end, he traveled, like a mythic hero, to the depths of his being. Out of this experience, which is symbolized by his trip to the brothel, he emerged transformed and revitalized "by a new force, destructive insofar as it breaks old patterns of thought, tears down masks, and aspires to the truth, and constructive insofar as it affirms living authentically."[9] The resulting synthesis is one where Contreras will continue his smuggling activity, but with the understanding that smuggling is part of a broader search for happiness that includes the interests of the townspeople as much as his own. He now will fight Father Manuel and his allies thinking not only of himself, but also realizing that his destiny is tied to the destiny of those under Father Manuel's repressive yoke. Contreras' eventual death, unlike that of Father Manuel, is not the sacrifice of a man who let fear rule his life, but the creative act of a life-affirming individual who realized that his destiny was the destiny of his people, the people of San Juan de los Remedios del Cayo.

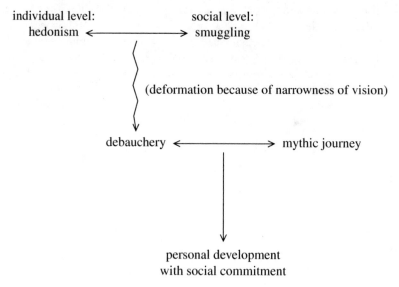

Figure 4. Juan Contreras' dialectic: From hedonism to heroism.

Insofar as Father Manuel's manipulation of Christianity is a process that deforms and devalues a powerful emancipatory discourse, the film also becomes a commentary on the process of deformation that Marxism, another powerful emancipatory discourse, was undergoing in Cuba during the late 1960s and early 1970s. In the introduction to this chapter, I pointed out how the cultural atmosphere in Cuba deteriorated during the so-called "five gray years" between 1971 and 1976. In each of the cases I cited as examples of state repression, Marxist ideas regarding the social aims of art were manipulated to justify unnecessary clampdowns on freedom of expression. But Marxism was manipulated in other ways in order to justify the creation of a statist economy in the late 1960s. Cuba in 1971 had just given up on a four-year experiment called the "moral economy." The goals of the experiment were, like Father Manuel's calls for spiritual salvation, praiseworthy: Material stimuli would be replaced by moral incentives, free distribution of basic services would be provided, money would be abolished, and the wealth of the land would be a common good. But the process by which those results were to be achieved were, like Father Manuel's methods, somewhat repressive and, worst of all, oblivious to basic human nature: Preference in placements and promotions was given for revolutionary loyalty over technical knowledge and administrative expertise, economic policymaking and organization were militarized through the imposition of order and discipline in productive tasks, and every economic sector—including small businesses and most small farms—was collectivized.[10]

José Antonio Evora has called *A Cuban Fight against Demons* "a vindication of utilitarianism,"[11] and Alea himself has pointed out that the film should help people understand "that it is *sometimes* he who seems to think only of himself who can actually do something to help others" (emphasis mine).[12] Fortunately, many counterproductive aspects of the "moral economy" were abandoned in 1970 after it became evident that the economy was in shambles and the people were displeased with the results. But many other aspects of the experiment, and above all its legacy of ideological fanaticism, continued throughout the seventies, and Alea felt that he needed to make the same points he made in *A Cuban Fight against Demons* again in *The Last Supper*, only this time much more clearly.

A Cuban Fight . . . strikes one as a seamless succession of images, stylized by the fluidity of Mario García Joya's camerawork and by the exaggerated gestures of the actors. So fluid is the movement of the camera throughout the film, and so stylized the acting, that even the still images of José Martí, Fidel Castro, and Che Guevara during Contreras' vision in the brothel somehow fit in, at least formally. Thematically, however, the film would have gained in suggestibility without them, and it is surprising that Alea did not learn this particular lesson from Glauber Rocha's *Black God, White Devil*, the film that is in many ways the direct precedent to *A Cuban Fight against Demons*.

The Last Supper: Marxism Meets Christianity

Film as Historical Drama

The Last Supper is based on a real-life incident that took place sometime in the 1780s and is recorded in a footnote to Manuel Moreno Fraginals' *The Sugarmill*, a classic of postrevolutionary historiography:

> His Excellency the Count of the House of Bayona, in an act of profound Christian fervor, decided to humble himself in front of his slaves. And following the example of Christ, on a Maundy Thursday he washed the feet of twelve Blacks, sat them at his table, and served them his food. As things turned out, the slaves, whose theological knowledge was not very profound, did not behave like the Apostles. Instead, and encouraged by the prestige they had acquired in the eyes of the other slaves, they rebelled and burned the sugar mill. The Count's overseers finished off this most Christian act by hunting down the runaway slaves, and then displaying on top of twelve spears the decapitated heads of the slaves for whom the Most Excellent Count of the House of Bayona had humbled himself.[13]

The irony of this passage notwithstanding, Fraginals' *The Sugar Mill* was and still is the most objective study of the origins and development of the sugar industry in Cuba, an industry that has defined, for better and for worse, the course of Cuban history after the independence of Haiti. The purpose of the book, published in 1964, was to provide a Marxist interpretation of Cuban history by highlighting the sugar industry's role in defining class relationships: "We were absolutely certain that if we could clarify these aspects [of the sugar industry] in different critical junctures in our history (1760, 1992, 1814, 1832, 1848, 1884, and 1895), we would tear off the thick veil that hides the true history of Cuba."[14] What Fraginals means by "the thick veil" is the kind of interpretation of Cuban history exemplified by Francisco Arango y Parreño's *Discurso sobre la Agricultura en La Habana*. Arango, the sugar barons' most articulate spokesperson, refers to the ten-month occupation of Havana by the British in 1762 as *la época feliz*—the happy interlude—because with that occupation the fortunes of the emerging bourgeoisie improved dramatically. What Arango does not consider, and what Fraginals takes pain to demonstrate, is the fact that with this brief occupation began the increasing brutalization of slaves because of the concomitant shift from small sugar estates to larger semiplantations modeled on those in Jamaica and Haiti. In choosing to re-create the incident narrated in Fraginals' book, Alea aligns himself with Fraginals' project of reinterpreting Cuban history by including in that history the previously ignored perspective of the working masses. But Alea goes beyond Fraginals' Marxist interpretation by re-creating the world of black slaves from their perspective, something that

Fraginals does not attempt. In this sense, *The Last Supper* belongs to the parallel project of national awareness and recognition for the history and culture of Afro-Cubans, a project with a long and venerable history that includes such luminaries as Cirilo Villaverde, Lydia Cabrera, Fernando Ortiz, and Sara Gómez.[15]

Fraginals uses the incident at the sugar mill owned by the Count of the House of Bayona to illustrate, in a section of his book subtitled "The Church and the Sugar Mill," the tensions between Catholic doctrines and economic imperatives during the 1780s. In the film, however, the action is moved forward to the 1790s, after the slave uprising in the neighboring French colony of Saint Domingue. Before the Haitian revolution, the economy in Cuba was based not on sugar but on trade. The Port of Havana served as the gateway for the Spanish empire in the Americas, and tobacco, cattle, coffee, and shipbuilding were as important as sugar. When the French were forced out of Saint Domingue (as they called Haiti before its independence) the ex-colony changed from being the number one exporter of sugar in the world to economic insignificance. Many of the French landowners who left Haiti—perhaps as many as 30,000—moved to the eastern provinces of Cuba and transplanted their way of life, slaves and all, to their adopted homeland. Most importantly, however, they brought to Cuba the knowledge needed to run a large-scale sugar operation. While in Haiti, the French had developed a very profitable way of producing sugar using large plantations, a system that took root in Cuba with incredible speed. The economy of Cuba changed accordingly from one of trade centered on Havana to one of cash crop exports consisting mostly of sugar. It is no coincidence that the engineer in *The Last Supper* has a French surname (Ducle), as this symbolizes the role played by the new French arrivals in the technical development of the sugar industry in Cuba.

The film makes reference to at least three stages of the technological evolution transforming the sugar industry at the time: the old-fashioned *trapiche*, a mill powered by animals and adapted for relatively small plantations of about three hundred acres; the *ingenio*, or steam-powered sugar mill popularized by the French; and the parallel presses that were to be imported from Britain. Interestingly, the word *ingenio* can mean both the mill itself or the sugar plantation that included cane fields, mill, estate, chapel, and slave quarters. In any case, the socioeconomic changes brought about by the new technology were astounding:

> The size of the average sugar plantation in 1762 [which used animal-powered *trapiches*] was 320 acres worked by six to eight slaves. Thirty years later [after the introduction of steam-powered *trapiches*] the average had increased to 700 acres worked by almost one hundred slaves. The acreage devoted to sugar cane increased in spectacular fashion—from 10,000 acres in 1762 to 160,000 in 1792.[16]

The sugar mill owned by the Count of the House of Bayona is one of these new midsize semiplantations, with an average of "700 acres worked by almost one hundred slaves." Each of the technological changes mentioned—the animal-powered *trapiche*, the steam-powered one, and the parallel presses—increased the amount of sugar cane that could be processed, but none of them increased the amount of cane available. The cheapest way to go about increasing that amount was the exploitation of unpaid labor. And so it should not come as a surprise that the black population in Cuba increased dramatically at the turn of the century: "During the previous 250 years of Spanish rule between 1512 and 1763, an estimated total of 60,000 slaves had been introduced into Cuba. This rate changed dramatically, and between 1764 and 1790, the number of slaves imported into Cuba surpassed the 50,000 mark, averaging approximately 2,000 slaves a year."[17]

It is within this context of demographic change brought about by technological advancements that the action in *The Last Supper* takes place. The context, finally, must include reference to the increase in the number of black slaves, which was expected once the technology of parallel presses was installed. This increase actually took place in the first half of the nineteenth century, with the number of slaves jumping from roughly 40,000 in 1791 to almost 400,000 by 1862.[18] When, ten minutes into the film, Monsieur Ducle warns the Count of the danger inherent in switching to parallel presses, he is thinking of and anticipating this demographic revolution, a revolution that is central in explaining the history of nineteenth-century Cuba.

The film has three parts: The first sets the stage, the second shows the supper sequence itself, and the third plays out the consequences of what happened during the dinner. Moreover, the narrative structure is classical, with the tension increasing until reaching a climax at the end of the second part, and then working out the consequences of that climax in the remainder of the film, with the killing of eleven of the twelve slaves who had dined with the Count. The first part of the film, then, sets the stage but does not add much to the contributions made by historians to our understanding of the slave economy in Cuba. Likewise, the execution of the slaves at the end of the film is not surprising given the historical fact that all slave rebellions in Cuba during this period were brutally and thoroughly crushed. The supper sequence, however, provides a brilliant exploration into the mind of a sensitive if hypocritical slave owner and the contradictions in behavior and thought that result from the distortion of Christian values by material interests.

In the opening sequence, the camera moves slowly and deliberately to show us close-ups of faded baroque frescoes depicting an angel and a chain. As the camera draws back, the chain becomes a rosary and a scene of the Easter passion is revealed. The background sound is also religious, something like a Gregorian chant, and the feeling one gets is of being inside a convent; the only sensory stimuli missing is a little bit of incense or myrrh. The next sequence shatters this conventlike peace. Two *rancheadores* are looking for a missing slave. The bright outdoor light contrasts sharply with the interior light of the previous sequence. A few shots into the sequence we are inside a slave barracks, with its extremely dark interior and crammed quarters, and just as suddenly we are back outside again, in the intense light of the tropics. The slave has run away.

In the following sequence the Count arrives from Havana. He has come to inspect his mill, his slaves, and his conscience (it is, after all, Holy Week). Everyone who is anyone greets his arrival with much courtesy and respect. Only Don Manuel, the slaves' overseer, arrives late, with the news that a slave has run away. The Count won't let that or anything else detract him from the spiritual purpose of his visit. Inside his hacienda, he takes a bath-cum-baptism in preparation for the mission ahead, while the priest updates him on the slow progress of the evangelization of the slaves. "Oh, c'mon, you know very well why I have come," says the Count, referring to his plan for reincarnating the Last Supper with twelve slaves. After the bath, he meets with Don Manuel, who is indignant at the priest's meddling with his workforce. The Count tells Don Manuel that one has to obey the rules of Holy Week and give God His due.

The counterpoint between the priest and the overseer is repeated visually in the very next sequence, as they all head together to the sugar mill. The positioning of the characters is not accidental, as Don Manuel (to the right of the Count) represents the material interests of the Count, while the priest (to the left of the Count) represents his spiritual aspirations. Once at the mill, Monsieur Ducle explains how he has come up with a new way of fueling the mill now that most of the surrounding forests have been cut down. He will use the pressed sugar cane husks and mix them with a magic ingredient, which turns out to be none other than chicken shit. He also explains the process whereby sugar is refined until it is completely white. But not all sugar will become white, he says, one implication being that miscegenation in Cuba will not produce a white race, as some abolitionists were arguing at the time. After this tour of the mill, the *rancheadores* bring the runaway slave, Sebastián, to the Count's presence, cut his ear off, and feed it to the dogs. The Count is visibly repulsed, but does not protest the brutal tactics being used to keep the slaves in a subjugated position. Next comes the inspection of the slaves and the selection of twelve of them for the Count's dinner the following day. He washes and kisses their feet, and the priest prepares them for the occasion. The Count, explains the priest, is like Jesus Christ, merciful and compassionate, and Don Manuel, well, Don Manuel is like the Father of the Old Testament, vengeful but just.

The dinner sequence lasts an astonishing fifty-five minutes, almost half of the film's duration. The mise en scene is modeled after Leonardo da Vinci's *The Last Supper*, thus underscoring the Count's identification with

Christ. At the same time, however, the intertextuality with Buñuel's *Viridiana* is all too obvious. In Buñuel's film, beggars from the town where Viridiana's uncle lives break into his estate and stage a riotous feast. The feast ends in a frenzied orgy accompanied by the strains of Handel's *Messiah*, and when Viridiana returns from town, she is all but raped by a leper, her spiritual pride shattered forever. Blasphemous and ironic, Buñuel's masterpiece is the ultimate insult to Christian hypocrisy, and while Alea never reached such extremes, the intertextuality clearly points to their common practice of using religious history to highlight practices and aspects of consciousness unchanged since the eighteenth century or earlier.[19]

Absent the apparatus of control that the priest and the overseer represent, the Count is figuratively naked during the supper. With the aid of wine, the artificial differences between master and slaves that exist at the beginning of the supper gradually blur and give way to a more fraternal and truly Christian gathering of equals. However, the Count's interpretation of equality is that of the eighteenth-century Enlightenment, in which equality meant parity among male property-owners of the nobility. When he takes off his wig the next day, he is symbolically acknowledging the central contradiction in Enlightenment thought. And yet he couldn't do the same with Christianity, not because Christianity was any more compatible with slavery, but because it was a lot easier to discard a young set of ideas that never took root in the Spanish Empire than it was to ignore a centuries-old set of beliefs that had in any case already been distorted to serve his material interests.

Some of the Count's other distortions of Christianity during the supper are from sources closer in space and time than the Enlightenment. In 1797, for example, the priest Antonio Nicolás Duque de Estrada published a book of sermons for preaching to black slaves titled *Explicación de la doctrina cristiana acomodada a la capacidad de los negros bozales* (*Explanation of Christian Doctrine, Adapted to the Capacity of Newly Arrived Blacks*). In that book the author recommends that priests in *ingenios* never side with the blacks, but should rather say to them, "You yourselves are to blame because not all of you fulfill your obligations; you are many; overseer only one; today one is missing, tomorrow another one, today one does a naughty thing, tomorrow someone else does it: every day overseer must put up with this: every day the same story, but he doesn't like it; of course, he gets mad."[20] Compare this with the Count's sermon after Sebastián is seated to his right:

> You see, Sebastian, where pride has led you! [Turning to the other slaves] Negro doesn't learn, he is stubborn. Overseer, say what he say, Negro must close his mouth and obey. Negro don't answer back to overseer. Don Manuel is the overseer and you don't complain when he orders you to work. Negro suffers because he is ignorant. Then don Manuel is right to get

rough. Negro takes off to the hills, overseer catches him and then has to punish him real hard, so that Negro does not do it again.[21]

The similarities are clear enough, both in the use of Creole and in the paraphrasing of the argument that force is justified to subdue the slaves. More importantly, however, is the fact that the Cuban Catholic Church, by promoting priests like the Duque de Estrada, sanctioned this kind of discourse, a discourse that distorts the spirit of Christianity for the purposes of justifying and perpetuating the interdependent systems of slavery, aristocracy, and capitalism.

It would be unfair to suppose that aristocratic Cubans were not aware of the contradictions between the Christian message and the local church's teachings. In all probability, they were painfully aware of them, as the following report from the insular government's Junta de Información makes clear:

> "[It is essential] for us to instill, not only in slaves, but also in free men, the religious spirit; because that is the only way of helping him to overcome his situation with resignation, and for him to be humble, hard-working, and respectful." Nicolás Azcárate opposed this special religious concept and affirmed that if evangelization were to be carried out according to the principles of Jesus Christ, it would cry out against slavery, and stir thoughts of freedom. Pastor agreed with him and concluded that slavery was opposed to Christianity, and therefore should not be taught at the plantations. Last but not least, San Martín presented the opposite view, saying that there was no opposition between slavery and Christianity. He said: "Give to Caesar what is Caesar's. Knowledge of Christian doctrine makes slaves more submissive."[22]

This extensive citation lays out clearly the main function of the supper sequence: to dramatize how material interests can deform and eventually turn against noble and legitimate human aspirations such as humility and brotherly love. The results of the Count's deformations of emancipatory Christianity into dogmatic Catholicism are, at best, schizophrenia, at worst, hypocrisy. On the morning of Good Friday the Count flees the *ingenio* because he understands that if he were to be confronted by his slaves, he would have to either face up to his own hypocrisy, or else violate the social and economic system on which his wealth and privilege depend.

The other function of the supper sequence is to dramatize the transculturation between Europe and Africa as it played itself out in Cuba. Here Alea met with the sad fact that, compared to the amount of historical information available to accurately reconstruct the worldview, gestures, and speech of the Count, there existed almost no information on how slaves in eighteenth century Cuba thought, talked, or acted. Luckily, Alea was able to enlist the help of Tomás González and María Eugenia Haya, who contributed immensely to the film's veracity and complexity by researching and integrating into the script important aspects of African folklore and mythology. The result of this collaborative effort was the creation of twelve sketchy yet distinct African and Afro-Cuban characters who don't fall into the easy stereotypes of brute or superhero. Instead, the slaves' plurality of voices provides a heterogeneous Afro-Cuban perspective on European notions of equality, slavery, freedom, and the European religion par excellence, Catholicism.

Bangoché, for example, accepts slavery as natural, but unlike the Count, interprets equality from a positional perspective. When the Count asks Bangoché whether he prefers Africa or the *ingenio*, Bangoché, who claims to have been a king in Africa, answers adroitly: "Bangoché is a slave." For Bangoché, roles may change, but the very notion of slavery is not questioned. The same may be said of Ambrosio and Antonio, although they have internalized their subordinate status to the point of not considering the possibility of being something other than slaves. The case of Old Pascual is revealing. He exemplifies the chasm that exists between formal and substantive rights. Yes, Pascual has the formal right of freedom granted by the Count, but he lacks the substantive rights of education and material resources to give that freedom any real meaning. Finally, Sebastián's view of slavery is the most modern (or perhaps most ancient?), since he sees it as inherently wrong. His uncompromising position sets him apart from the other slaves, as when he describes Oloffi's creation of the world:

> Oloffi made the World, he made all of it; he made day, he made night; he made good thing, he made bad thing; he also made pretty thing and ugly thing too. Oloffi made good everything in the world: he made Truth, and he made False too. Truth came out pretty. False came out not good: she was ugly and skinny like a stick, like a sick person. Oloffi felt pity of her and gave her a sharp machete to defend herself. Time passed and everyone always wanted to be with Truth. Nobody, I mean nobody, wanted to be with False . . . . One day Truth and False met in the woods, and since they are enemies, they fight each other. Truth is more strong than False; but False had the sharp machete that Oloffi gave her. When Truth look the other way, False—chaz!—and cuts off the head of Truth. Truth now don't have no eyes and she starts to touch everything to find her head. [Sebastián imitates Truth by closing his eyes and feeling the table.] She looks and she looks with her hands until she finds the head of False and—wham!—she rips the head off False and puts it on where her head was before. And from that day she goes around and around, fooling everybody with the body of Truth and the head of False.[23]

The most immediate meaning of the parable, given the context of the discussion, is that the Count's use of Christianity to justify slavery is nothing but a crass deformation of a noble Truth that speaks of love and freedom, not fear and bondage. El Negro Conguito makes a similar point after the Count admonishes the Old Man Pascual for not knowing what to do with the freedom the Count has just granted him. Slavery, El Negro Conguito explains in a *mucanda* (a kind of storytelling that combines dance and song), is not about people not knowing what to do with freedom, as the Count implies, but rather about the erroneous belief that a man may own, sell, or buy another man.

> The slave is cursed by God, born to suffer. When you see a black man laughing, ask him, "Who's crying?" If a slave's singing, ask him, "Who's crying?" [repeat several times, singing] In Africa, when black man hungry for many days, he not hungry just one day, he hungry many days and his whole family hungry. Once upon a time a good father did not have no food to bring to family. He called his best son, the one he loved most and said, "My son, tomorrow we go get food." Early in the morning . . . [singing] Morning star! We travel far! The father wanted to look back to see the face of his son, but he couldn't because he would then feel like crying. [Singing] He walked and cried, walked and walked, cried . . . . But when he was about to reach . . . what's that called, where the sand is together with the sea? [*off*: "The beach!"] That's it! When they were about to reach the beach, the son asked the father, "Father, why you crying and crying while you walking?" "Oh, my son! Your father crying because father has to sell son to get food for the house." And walk and walk, and when they get to the beach, where blacks and whites do their business, the son speak first and sell the father right then and there. [*off*: Sighs of disapproval] Then he bought food for the family! [Laughs]
>
> But the story's not finished yet! When the family, hmm!, saw the son and not the father, they asked, "Son, where your father?" "Here's the food" [says the son]. And for selling his father, the family took him to the authorities and they put him on trial. And you know what was the punishment? They sold him to a white man! Ay! And with the money, the family ate twice! [Singing] Morning star . . . The blacks are crying . . . Don't know why . . . [repeat several times] Only those who ain't no black slaves . . . don't know why!

In this *mucanda*, as in Sebastián's parable, one sees the outlines of a subaltern Afro-Cuban perspective that is oral, playfully subversive, and democratic, as opposed a European cultural tradition that is written, overserious, and paternalistic.

This brings me to a final observation about the supper sequence. In the Gospels (Matthew), Jesus is the messenger who brings the Truth, Judas Iscariot the opportunistic traitor who betrays his teacher and his teachings. In *The Last Supper*, however, these functions have been inverted. The Count, who pretends to be Jesus during the supper, betrays the teachings of Christ and even dares to compare the Overseer's death with Christ's sacrifice on the cross. On the other hand, Sebastián, who the Count accused of being like Judas, assumes the role of the Messiah by escaping death and slavery with the aid of miraculous powers. Insofar as the supper sequence breaks the traditional roles of the Count and his slaves (as in the example of Judas/Jesus), the supper functions as a carnival in the Bakhtinian sense of the word: "In all genres of the serio-comical, to be sure, there is a strong rhetorical element, but in the atmosphere of *joyful relativity* characteristic of a carnival sense of the world this element is fundamentally changed: there is a weakening of its one-sided rhetorical seriousness, its rationality, its singular meaning, its dogmatism."[24] If nothing else, the supper creates an atmosphere of wine-induced joyful relativity in which the one-sided rhetorical seriousness of the Count is weakened by the playful storytelling of El Conguito, the purposeful naiveté of Ambrosio, the ridiculous pride of Bangoché, the pathetic Uncle Tomism of Antonio, and the powerfully vital seriousness of Sebastián. Within the logic of the carnival, the subversive and emancipatory qualities of Christianity are personified in Sebastián, and are therefore preserved and even celebrated in his final escape, while the Count's distortions of Christianity are revealed as hypocritical and opportunistic.

Besides Sebastián's powerful parable of Truth and Falseness, another major clue to interpreting the supper sequence may be Bertolt Brecht's *Mr. Puntila and His Man Matti* (1940). In this play, a hard-drinking Finnish landowner (Mr. Puntila) suffers from a divided personality—when drunk he is human and humane; when sober, surly and self-centered. Oscillating unsteadily between these two poles, he plays havoc with his workmen, his women, his daughter's marital arrangements, and the loyalty of his sardonic chauffeur, Matti. At the end of the play, Matti leaves the master no longer the servant, but master of himself:

> *The hour for taking leave has struck*
> *So, Puntila, I wish you luck.*
> *I've known them worse than you and twice as tough:*
> *You're halfway human when you've drunk enough.*
> *But comradeship dissolves in boozer's gloom.*
> *It's back to normal, and the old "Who whom?"*
> *Sad as I am to find out in the end*
> *That oil and water cannot ever blend*
> *It's not much help, there's nothing I can do:*
> *So—time your servants turned their backs on you.*
> *They'll find a decent master pretty fast*
> *Once they've become the masters here at last.*[25]

In both Alea's film and Brecht's play, the master becomes more human with the aid of alcohol. As they say, *in vino veritas*, and what both Brecht and

Alea may be getting at is the idea that human nature is basically good and that Mr. Puntila and the Count are also victims of an unfair economic super-structure because it distorts their basic humanity. The suffering of the work-ers and the slaves may be more graphic, more obvious, but in the case of the masters, their very humanity suffers a deformation. Dennis West has pointed out the Hegelian roots of this idea and how it applies to *The Last Supper*:

> In *The Phenomenology of Mind*, Hegel's notion of recognition means that the master depends on his bondmen for acknowledgment of his power, indeed, for assurance of his very selfhood. As the count reiterates his order that Sebastián recognize him, the camera emphatically dollies on their jux-taposed faces, and a tense silence reigns. The slave's eventual answer is to spit in the master's face—a brutal refusal to recognize the other's lord-ship and the graphic expression of the birth of the bondman's true self-consciousness: in spite of his actual bondage, the slave's mind is his own.[26]

But whereas this explanation leaves one with the uncomfortable feeling that the slave's suffering is justified because through it, the slave molds and validates his own humanity, in Alea's film and in Brecht's play there is no sense of justification for either the master's privileges or the slaves' suffer-ings. That is, the slave does not win in humanity what the master loses in selfhood. Rather, both master and slave lose out because in unfair economic systems such as slavery and feudalism, it is almost impossible for either mas-ters or slaves to recognize themselves in the other. Not only do these systems create such deformations of humans as "masters" and "slaves," but by reduc-ing the definition of "self" so drastically, they impede personal development and solidarity with one's fellow humans. The saddest thing of all is that the obstacles that stand in the way of these two goals—personal development and solidarity—are artificial and historically specific creations: social class in Brecht's play and racial, cultural, and class differences in Alea's film.

Wine chips away at these differences during the supper, so that toward the end of the sequence there is a mood of joyful relativity, of a fraternal community of (almost) equals. And yet, Sebastián knows that the solidarity just experienced is as artificial as the relationships that rule outside the dining room. When the Count falls asleep, he points this out to the other slaves with the story of the creation of the world and its parable of Truth and Falseness. Besides the already mentioned interpretation of Truth-as-equality, another possible interpretation of the parable may be one where Truth stands for love of oneself and of one's fellow humans and greed stands for Falseness, so that when the two are put together, what one gets is a deformation of a legitimate and noble human aspiration because of material motivations. With this para-ble Sebastián recognizes the Count's Christian teachings as deformed Truth and indirectly acknowledges his enemy's humanity. Clearly, Sebastián is the most developed person in the whole group, and this makes him worthy of salvation in the end. The only thing he lacks is the ability to transform his love of self and his desire for freedom into a productive social practice in which he recognizes his own fate in the fate of the other slaves and mobilizes others to work together for the common goal of affirming and practicing their sacred humanity.

Even though the hero of the film is Sebastián, the main character is the Count. The situation is akin to that of *Memories of Underdevelopment*, in which the Cuban people were the collective hero and Sergio a tragic character torn by opposing forces: on the one hand, his desire to become more authentically human, and on the other, the baggage of a petite-bourgeois background that put too much emphasis on differences (of race, class, gender, or nation) and not enough on promoting solidarity. In *The Last Supper*, a similar process takes place in the Count. On the one hand, he sincerely wants to become more authentically Christian, but the vanity and self-righteousness of his class, both of which he has internalized, are obstacles to that end. In the human dialectic between individual and society, Sergio and the Count share a common deformation based on the mistaken notion that culture and class are insurmountable obstacles to the solidarity among human beings of different classes and cultures.

The same dialectic between individual and society is played out in the Count on two other levels: the spiritual and the material (see Figure 5). In this the Count has much more in common with Father Manuel than with Sergio. In *A Cuban Fight against Demons*, Alea decided to isolate the spiritual by deleting from the film the important fact that Father Manuel owned vast tracks of land where he wanted to move the town. In *The Last Supper*, however, the spiritual and the material are both present, so that the causes for the deformation of the Count's spiritual quest are clearly material, instead of psychological, as was the case with Father Manuel. Like Father Manuel, the

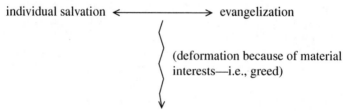

individual salvation ⟷ evangelization

(deformation because of material interests—i.e., greed)

at the individual level: hypocrisy (calls "spiritual salvation" what is really an attempt to clear his guilty conscience)

at the collective level: paternalism–during the supper
repression–after the supper

Figure 5. The Count's dialectic.

Count feels a need to purify his soul, to end his spiritual suffering. And like Father Manuel, he feels compelled to do the same with others, as if acknowledging that his own individual salvation depends on the salvation of the collective. In practice, however, their legitimate and noble aspirations are deformed by fear (in Father Manuel's case) and by greed (in the case of the Count). Greed, the deformation of an otherwise healthy desire to have things that make life easier and more enjoyable, becomes for the Count the obstacle in his quest for salvation, so much so that it deforms the Christian teachings he wishes to emulate. Instead of seeing greed as un-Christian, the Count ends up deforming Christianity to justify his greed and any economic and social arrangements that help to satisfy that greed, however un-Christian they may be. This deformation of Christianity can be sustained because the Count holds all the power in his hands, and any contradictory views are either dismissed with the affected sympathy of one who believes that might makes right or else crushed with brute force, in the case someone protests. At the individual level, the result of this deformation of Christianity is hypocrisy: The Count pretends he seeks spiritual salvation, when in fact what he's doing is trying to clear his guilty conscience. At the collective level, the results are more marked because of the power the Count has to enforce his views. During the supper sequence, the Count's hypocrisy manifested itself as paternalism, and this seemingly benign attitude transformed itself all too easily into brutal repression the following day.

The images of eleven decapitated heads as the Count finishes delivering his sermon in the second to last sequence highlights once again the degree of distortion and deformation that Christianity has undergone at the hands of someone who let material rewards get in the way of spiritual growth. In the specific case of the Count, such spiritual growth could have been attained through solidarity with his fellow human beings, the slaves. Like Sergio in *Memories of Underdevelopment* and Father Manuel in *A Cuban Fight against Demons*, the Count in *The Last Supper* tried to become more authentically human but failed. His failure is as much personal as social, for even if he would have chosen the path to freedom for his slaves and for himself, the society to which he belonged would still have had a long way to go before reaching that synthesis of the human dialectic where personal and social development go hand in hand, reinforcing each other in a virtuous cycle in which limited ways of thinking are continuously destroyed while new life-affirming acts broaden the possibilities for personal and social development.

Film as Allegory of Contemporary Events

The reconstruction of history implies its correction. In the case of *The Sugarmill*, Fraginals achieved this correction through a Marxist interpretation of

Cuban history between 1760 and 1860. Alea's contribution to that interpretation lies in the dramatization of an anecdote from that book and in the exploration of the subjectivity of its historical actors. But the reconstruction of history also implies a comment on contemporary events. Consider the following two citations:

> [The sugar harvest] was characterized by the abandonment, to incredible limits, of all activities that did not affect, directly or indirectly, sugar production.[27]

> [The sugar harvest was] achieved by depleting resources from other sectors of the economy, which in turn suffered output declines offsetting the increase in sugar output.[28]

The first, taken from Fraginals' *The Sugarmill*, refers to the first sugar boom in Cuba's history in 1792, the time frame of the film. The second comes from Carmelo Mesa-Lago's *Cuba in the 1970s* and refers to the ten million–ton harvest of 1970. Their dates could be switched and they still would remain valid.

In the early years of the Revolution the main goal of economic planners had been the reduction of Cuba's historic dependence on sugar. Two parallel strategies were to achieve this goal: industrialization and agricultural diversification. By 1964 these progressive efforts were abandoned as output in all sectors declined to unacceptable levels, whereupon sugar once again became the primary target of agricultural planning.[29] Two factors spoke in favor of this reversal: the rise in 1963 of the commodity's price and the realization that sugar offered "an obvious and relatively cost-effective method of reversing the mounting balance of trade deficits by mobilizing efforts around a sector in which Cuba possessed adequate personnel and sufficient experience."[30] In March 1968 Fidel Castro proclaimed that

> The question of a sugar harvest of 10 million tons [for the 1970 harvest] has become something more than an economic goal; it is something that has been converted into a point of honor for this Revolution, it has become a yardstick by which to judge the capability of the Revolution . . . and if a yardstick is put up to the Revolution, there is no doubt about the Revolution meeting the mark.[31]

The sugar harvest was to be the basis for Cuba's great leap forward into the developed world. As in China, this economic leap was to be achieved with a parallel shift in subjective consciousness, a veritable cultural revolution. The blueprint for this new "moral economy" is spelled out in Che Guevara's essay "The New Man":

The resulting [economic] theory will unfailingly give preeminence to the two pillars of the construction [of a moral economy]: the formation of the new man, and the development of technical knowledge. Much remains to be done on both counts, but the backwardness in science is less excusable, because in this respect it is not a matter of walking blindly, but of following for a good stretch of the way the path opened by the most advanced nations of the world. [Our youth] is the malleable clay with which we must build the new man. . . . We will make a new man for the twenty-first century. We will forge ourselves in daily action, and create a new man with a new science.[32]

The essay's messianic tone—not to mention its author's own heroic example—set the tone for Sino-Guevarism, a fusion of Maoist ideological purity with Guevara's charismatic zeal and humanistic ideals. Like Christianity in the 1790s, Sino-Guevarism was a powerful emancipatory discourse in the 1960s. The main features of the New Man were discipline, selfless motivation, and a strong work ethic, the combination of which would purge persisting bourgeois sins. Similarly, the Count in the supper sequence lectured his slaves on the virtues of selfless suffering and obedience as a means of purging their sins and thus entering the Kingdom of Heaven. In the Cuba of the late 1960s the equivalent to the Kingdom of Heaven was the Worker's Paradise, and the road to that paradise was the "moral economy" that lasted for four years, from 1966 to 1970.

Many of the features of this moral economy enhanced the quality of life of Cubans and convinced many of them of the possibility of erasing the distinction between formal and substantive rights. The 1970 sugar harvest, a massive and collective undertaking aimed at the production of a record ten million tons of sugar, was to secure these advances by providing the state with the necessary capital for a second and final shot at industrialization and diversification of the economy. Two events in 1968, however, did not bode well for the future. One was the nationalization of all small businesses; the other was Castro's approval of the Soviet invasion of Czechoslovakia. Beginning in 1970 the Cuban state gained increasing control over more aspects of Cuban life than ever before, a state of affairs achieved at the expense of the openness, freshness, and promise that characterized the 1960s. After the failure of the ten million–ton sugar harvest, disappointment set in and cynicism grew. Just as importantly, Cuba's attempt to finance its own way out of sugar dependence by means of a massive sugar harvest ended up costing the country dearly. Instead of shaking off the monoculture economy, Cuba became even more defined by it.

The parallelisms with Cuba's first sugar boom in 1792 cannot have escaped Alea, especially since the effect of the 1970 harvest on Cuban Marxism was similar to the effect of the 1792 harvest on Cuban Christianity: In each case, a potentially liberating message degenerated into stultifying dogma. The sugar economy of the late eighteenth and early nineteenth centuries differed in many important ways from the Cuban moral economy of 1966–1970. The differences are especially marked in matters of intentions and proclaimed goals. However, one cannot help but note that these two widely divergent economic models, which differed so much in professed ends and actual practice, shared many outward features. Both concentrated economic decisions in the hands of a few. Both treated workers paternalistically, tying them to their masters through "free" services. Both minimized material stimuli in their compensation of workers. Both responded to the attendant decrease in production by militarizing the workplace. And finally, both contributed to the deformation of legitimate and noble human aspirations—Christianity in the 1790s, Marxism in the 1970s.

The last aspect of *The Last Supper* as allegory that stands out is the role of the intellectual. As a filmmaker working for the state, but acutely aware of that state's increasing control of all aspects of civil life, Alea occupies a similar position as that of Monsieur Ducle in the film. That is, both Monsieur Ducle and Alea acknowledge that the most they can do is point out the distortions of enlightened ideals. In the Case of Monsieur Ducle, the distortion of Enlightenment ideals—the very ones that had swept France just a few years before—would be exacerbated by the plan to import more slaves, since such a move would entail the increased use of brutal force against human beings. In the case of Alea, on the other hand, the distortion of Marxism would be exacerbated by the continued institutionalization and bureaucratization of all aspects of Cuban life. Like Monsieur Ducle, Alea and other Cuban intellectuals in the 1970s were in the uncomfortable position of risking their livelihood if speaking out against a growing and increasingly authoritarian state apparatus. Many, like Monsieur Ducle, chose voluntary silence; a few, like Sebastián, simply fled; and still others, like Alea, found oblique ways of expressing their concerns without losing sight of the final objectives of the Revolution.

The Survivors

The Survivors is a black comedy about a bourgeois family that decides to stay in Cuba after the Revolution. They lock themselves up in their mansion, convinced that the Revolution will soon pass, but as the years go by and their supplies dwindle, they regress in from capitalism to feudalism, slavery, primitive community, and, finally, savagery. Before the Revolution catches the Orozco family by surprise, they were part of the island's industrial bourgeoisie. After the Revolution, Vicente Cuervo's marriage into the family symbolizes their "descent" into the merchant bourgeoisie. As time goes by, the supplies are not enough to sustain the family, and they decide to parcel out the estate's gardens to the servants in exchange for a part of their production. The living conditions continue to deteriorate and some servants, inspired by what they hear is going on outside the walls of the mansion, try to escape. Only forced labor will ensure continued production, but even that doesn't last, as Julio, the family's only lucid observer but a feeble alcoholic, stages a furtive and festive coup against the more reactionary forces in the family. After he and the rest of the servants are killed, the few survivors are faced with the reality of having to work in order to survive. One commits suicide, two are killed as they try to escape, and one dies of exposure. The film closes with the last two of the Orozcos facing each other at the dining table, ready to eat their aunt, who had been conveniently "cooked" by a lightning strike.

As in many of his previous films, Alea's goal is to denounce the survival of bourgeois habits of mind and behavior that stand in the way of a truly socialist practice: "If we really trust in man's potential transformation, our activity should aim to transform the circumstances in which we are developing, so that one may produce within oneself a real transformation, one's own personal revolution. . . . The spirit of the petit-bourgeois can act from within the Revolution, and in this way contribute to deform its final objectives."[33] Many of the superficial bourgeois habits, such as the obsession with keeping appearances and the idea that work is degrading, may have been largely overcome, but others, such as paternalism and empty ceremony, have simply changed garb to show up in the most unexpected places. In one of the opening scenes, for example, the family patriarch talks about the need to keep the young people in the family busy with sports events and other ceremonial activities:

SEBASTIÁN: We were talking about the need to organize a series of recreational and educational activities, something to keep the spirits high and to strengthen our beliefs, our convictions, and to prevent any contamination.

PRIEST: And boredom, Don Sebastián, especially among the youngest ones. Leisure is the mother of all vice.

UNCLE: To fill their minds with loftier and healthier ideas!

SEBASTIÁN: The mind and the body! *Mens sana en corpore sano*, as the classics would say. One must be concerned with these things. We must organize competitions, give out prizes. Don't you agree, Vicente?

VICENTE: Oh, yes, yes, of course! One has to think of everything. But one also has to be up to date with what is going on outside.

The allusion to contemporary practices inside Cuba is hard to miss, as is the central argument that history is not always unidirectional. By 1979, the year the film was made, the Cuban economy was deteriorating and even

regressing in ways not unlike those of the Orozco family. But more omi-
nously, the Orozco family's isolation and patriarchism spoke of the Cuban
state's own growing isolation from the rest of the world, its own paternalism
when addressing and administering the country's increasing problems, and
the empty ceremonies with which it hoped to keep young minds from
rebelling. *The Survivors* is a pessimistic film that postulates the transforma-
bility of man, but in reverse. It's almost a thought experiment, a way of showing what could happen during an ever-worsening economic crisis if a
community does not have the awareness, solidarity, and courage to break old
destructive habits that impede the development of the individual and the
community.

5

Up to a Certain Point:
Turning the Lens on Himself

Upon finishing *Memories of Underdevelopment*, Alea approached Sergio Corrieri (the actor who had played Sergio) with the idea of doing a film whose main character would be a committed intellectual, as opposed to a voyeur. Corrieri declined, in part because at the time he was working as director of the experimental Theater Group Escambray and in part because he did not want to play another brooding intellectual and run the risk of being pigeonholed into that kind of role.[1] Alea then turned his attention to other projects, but after three historical films, he was ready to pick up where he left off and face the present in all its complexity. The result was *Up to a Certain Point*, a film whose theme picks up where *Memories* left off and whose form comes from Sara Gómez' *One Way or Another*.

Up to a Certain Point is a love story between a middle-class intellectual and a working-class single mother. It begins with a project: to make a documentary film about machismo in the docks of Havana. Arturo, the director of the film, enlists Oscar, a playwright, to write the script. Oscar is the perfect choice: a revolutionary intellectual who has achieved some success with a play about machismo, the ending of which we see performed in the film.[2] But Arturo has preconceived ideas about his film and won't listen to Oscar's suggestions that they make Lina—an exemplary dock worker he's falling in love with—the model for the film. When Arturo leaves Cuba on some business-related travel, the film effectively ceases to be about Arturo's authoritarianism, and becomes instead a film about the clash between Oscar's machismo and Lina's liberated spirit.

The film's theme song summarizes Oscar's dilemma: "If I wanted to, I could cut her wings and then she'd be mine. But then she couldn't fly and what I love is the bird in flight." In the end, we see Lina boarding a plane to Santiago, where a better job and her mother await her. The camera moves as it did when

Sergio's family left for Miami, so that first we see the plane leaving and then we see Oscar watching the plane leaving. But unlike *Memories*, in which the plane's take-off signaled the protagonist's release from an undesirable woman, in *Up to a Certain Point* the plane's take-off signals Lina's freely chosen liberation from a sensitive but undesirable man. Like the play-within-the-film, where the lead character tears up the script and throws it at the audience, Lina takes off, leaving behind Oscar's script and keeping her own choices open.

With this film, Alea seems to have turned the telescope in Sergio's balcony around, so that the object of observation is no longer the outside world, but instead an intellectual like himself: his aspirations and his achievements, but also his contradictions and prejudices. To convey more clearly the ideas developed in *The Viewer's Dialectic*, Alea created two characters, each of whom personifies a pole of the dialectic between individual and society.[3] Arturo, the director who wants to use reality to make his fictional film, represents a thesis of egocentrism, while Oscar, the scriptwriter who wants to use film in order to better understand reality, represents an antithesis of social commitment. This approach did not work well. Arturo became a stereotype of the power-hungry bureaucrat, while Oscar's character withered away in endless uncertainty, a Cuban Hamlet who loses his Ophelia because he can't defend his own truth against the manipulations and prejudices of Arturo or against those of his own wife.

At the same time, even though Arturo is a stereotype, the stereotype seems to have hit a nerve, for the film was cut from an original eighty-some minutes to the final sixty-eight. In a telling review published in *El Caimán Barbudo*, a Cuban magazine that follows the government's official line, we learn that "the plot could not be more simple: in eighty-some minutes [Alea] tells us the story of a film director and a playwright who want to make a film about the problems faced by the dock workers."[4] There is of course the possibility that the reviewer was mistaken about the length of the film. However, given his description of the film as centering on Arturo and Oscar (as opposed to Lina and Oscar), and given Alea's comments about how the film was censored (discussed later), it is quite possible that the reviewer saw an uncensored version of the film that lasted, as he states, eighty-some minutes.

One possible explanation for Arturo's diminished role in the final version of the film may be the one given by Alea, that the actor who played Arturo did not live up to expectations.[5] Rumor has it, however, that in those "missing" minutes, Arturo makes gestures and comments that parody Fidel Castro, in which case the reasons for editing out those parts would be obvious. Asked who has the right to a film's final cut, Alea responded:

> In principle, that right belongs to the director. But because the films are produced by the Cuban Film Institute [ICAIC], the Institute reserves that right, especially when it comes to political and ideological matters. That is to say,

that's where censorship takes place. It's a right that the Institute has, and which it has used emphatically on only a few occasions. . . . I can tell you that in my case I've only had conflicts of that kind only one time. It was with *Up to a Certain Point*, and I believe it was reasonable that there was a conflict in that case. I was trying to discuss in that film the paternalism of the State, . . . but the truth is I had not done it in a manner that was sufficiently solid and consistent so as to direct the discussion in a way that would be the most advantageous for my point of view. So, I realized that I could not insist on that, even though I was right in my theoretical approach.[6]

Whatever the exact reasons for the censorship of *Up to a Certain Point*, Alea tells us that the film ceased to be about a kind of paternalism Cubans call *machismo-leninismo* and became instead a film focused on the problem of machismo as it manifests itself in male-female relationships:

As it is, the film focuses on the machismo problem. I wanted originally to use that as a point of departure, to look at machismo not only as a relationship between men and women, but as an attitude that pervades social relations—an authoritarianism. Machismo is an attitude towards life which I would qualify more generally as paternalism. The attitude of the macho vis à vis the female is one of paternalism.[7]

The film's original purpose, then, was to show how a supposedly enlightened intellectual could act with an attitude of "father knows best," with a paternalism that pervades the political culture of Cuba and to which ICAIC was not immune.

The final product, however, can be better explained as part of a tradition of feminist features that includes Humberto Solás' *Lucia* (1968), Sara Gómez's *One Way or Another* (1974), and Pastor Vega's *Retrato de Teresa* (1979). All of these films deal explicitly with "the twin thematics of feminism of the late 1960s and 1970s in Cuba: the centrality of women within the revolutionary activity of the nation, and the rebuke of persistent machismo."[8] These themes enjoyed the prestige of official support, as evidenced by the formulation of the Family Code in 1975. The code recognized the pervasiveness of the "double shift" among Cuban women—working outside the home during the day and tending to domestic chores in the evenings and weekends—and exhorted men to share domestic tasks with their partners. In *Up to a Certain Point*, the problem of the double shift does not enter the picture, as it does in *Retrato de Teresa*, but the two central concerns of Cuban feminism mentioned here do: Lina is the embodiment of revolutionary consciousness (she actively participates in workers' meetings, where she stresses the values of dedication and vigilance within the revolutionary community), and she also rebukes the persistent machismo of Cuban men, first by divorcing the possessive father of her child, and later, by leaving Oscar behind when she sees that he won't measure up to her standards. Unlike the Lucías in Humberto Solás' masterpiece, Pastor Vega's *Teresa*, or Sara Gómez's Yolanda, Lina's goings-on are not determined by the men in her life, and her identity is certainly not dependent on a relationship—or lack thereof—with a man. This is a new development in the representation of women in Cuban film, and even though *Up to a Point* does not measure up to these other films in terms of character depth, plot development, or entertainment value, the fact that Lina does not need a man to make her life complete or even valuable in and of itself ensures that Alea's film will occupy an important place in the history of Cuban film.

Memories of Underdevelopment is an important precursor to *Up to a Certain Point*. Nevertheless, Sara Gómez's *One Way or Another* is its most direct precedent; in *Up to a Certain Point*, Alea sought to emulate what he saw as Gómez's genuineness and authenticity. Here's how Alea described *Up to a Certain Point*:

> It deals with the "población," a group of people in Havana, in a district which had been a slum before the Revolution. After the Revolution, they built new houses for themselves, since they had been living in cardboard houses like the "favelas." . . . In other words, after the Revolution there are no more slums in the strict sense of the word, . . . so everything would make one suppose that this had completely changed the mentality of the "pobladores." Fifteen years after the change, however, the film shows that the transformation on the level of awareness has not taken place at the same rate as that of the economic base of the group. . . . The film analyzes this phenomenon in a very penetrating and effective manner. It was a polemical film and provoked many discussions among the public. . . . Also, in terms of style, even though it is a first film, and has a certain, let's say, untidy style, it is so genuine that it wins you over in spite of its formal defects.[9]

Not only did Alea try to emulate this genuineness and authenticity in *Up to a Certain Point*, but he also incorporated Gomez's formal experimentation with, for example, interviews that would be incorporated into the plot and the use of characters who would play themselves in stories they themselves make up.

The plot of *One Way or Another*, however, is much more developed, more dramatic. It tells the story of a middle class teacher (Yolanda) who goes to teach in the *población* and falls in love with a worker who lives there (Mario). She is a light mulatto woman and he is a dark mulatto man. He belongs to an Afro-Cuban cult that perpetuates machismo, and she is steeped in the modernist project of liberation through education. Both believe in the Revolution, but they define it differently, especially when it comes to domestic life. Slowly but surely, Yolanda makes Mario see that his idea of the Revolution is passe and ultimately counterproductive. The climax of the film comes when Mario betrays a friend who had asked him to cover for him at work. The film actually opens with this climactic scene, with Mario confronting his friend at a workers' meeting. At first Mario seems to be falsely accusing his friend. Toward the end of the film, after we learn how things got to that point and how they had precipitated a break-up between Mario and Yolanda, the scene is repeated. We now understand that Mario was framed by his supposed friend and that Mario's accusations are legitimate. The film closes with a long shot of Mario and Yolanda together again, talking as they enter the *población*—the city of the future, the modern world—in a brilliantly conceived dramatization of the dialectical process whereby both grow individually and as a couple.

The parallels between characters in *Up to a Point* and characters in *Memories* and *One Way or Another* provide clues to the relationship between Oscar and Lina.

Memories	*Up to a Certain Point*	*One Way or Another*
Sergio ←——(1)——→	Oscar ←——(2)——→	Yolanda
Noemi ←——(3)——→	Lina ←——(4)——→	Mario

Oscar shares with Sergio (1) the privileged status of a white, middle-class, male intellectual, and àwith Yolanda (2) the political commitment to a revolutionary process. Lina, on the other hand, shares with Noemi (3) and with Mario (4) the status of working class, and with Noemi (3) the added qualifier of being a female object of desire for a male intellectual. The difference between Noemi and Lina is similar to the difference between Sergio and Oscar, in that the characters in *Up to a Certain Point* are politically committed to the Revolution, whereas Sergio and Noemi were not there yet. Twenty-five years after the triumph of the Revolution, Alea takes stock of the advancements, and these are indeed substantial.

However, as *One Way or Another* makes clear, there are as many internal obstacles to liberation as external ones. In Sara Gómez's film, the blame for Cuban machismo is placed squarely on the Efik belief that casts women in the role of archetypal traitor for having revealed the secret of creation[10] and on the Andalusian tradition of Don Juanism. Mario's relationship with Yolanda is a process whereby he leaves behind these foundational fictions and instead begins the difficult process of embracing new foundational fictions that go beyond even the founding fictions of the Revolution. Catherine Davies describes Mario's difficulties in this process of radical change as stemming from his fear of castration, a fear that indicates "not only a potential loss of belief in male adequacy but also in the dominant 'national' fiction."[11] The dominant national fiction in 1974, when the film was made, was already the Revolution. The film makes this clear in a scene in which Mario and his friend are standing in the Plaza de la Revolución under the statue of General Maceo, whose horse is attributed with enormous balls. Here Mario exclaims, "Men made the Revolution, *coño!*"[12] The machismo inherent in this popular understanding of the Revolution is something Mario must transcend before he can truly love Yolanda, the representative of a newer, more far-reaching revolution in consciousness.

Oscar undergoes a similar process of questioning in *Up to a Certain Point*, even though he does not grow as Mario did. When Arturo explains the film project to Oscar's wife Marian, he tells her that she'll play a female dock worker in love with a macho boyfriend, not a "wimp [*maricón*] like him," pointing to Oscar. Marian asks if Arturo intends to castrate the macho worker, and Arturo replies that he'll only criticize him. The parallels between Oscar and Mario are clear. As was the case with Mario, Oscar's machismo (not to mention Arturo's) reveals a fear of castration that in turn indicates, per Davies, "not only a potential loss of belief in male adequacy but also in the dominant 'national' fiction." The twist in Alea's retelling of the story is that in *Up to a Point*, the macho is not a conventional working-class male, but rather a sensitive intellectual, precisely the kind of person that should have overcome machismo but hasn't. Oscar's machismo, although far less virulent than Arturo's brand of machismo, still costs him dearly. That is, even though Oscar does not suffer from Arturo's *machismo-leninismo*, he still suffers from a more subtle form of machismo, a machismo that distorts his relationship with Lina by turning her into an object of study and desire instead of celebrating her as a subject worthy of love. This is Oscar's undoing, and in losing Lina, he also loses the possibility of developing into a more authentic human being.

From the perspective of this film, women and workers are generally more advanced in their revolutionary consciousness and practice than their intellectual male counterparts, a sobering thought for Alea and others at ICAIC and a factor that may have influenced Alea's choices of intellectual characters in the future: a homosexual artist in *Strawberry and Chocolate* and a female economist in *Guantanamera*.

6
Melodrama and the Crisis of the Revolution

Up to a Point marked the end of Alea's Brechtianism. In *The Viewer's Dialectic*, Alea made clear that in the process toward de-alienation, both identification and distancing must be present. Beginning with *Memories* and ending with *Up to a Point*, Alea, like Brecht, put the accent on distancing. But after finishing *Up to a Certain Point*, Alea seems to have "rediscovered" the power and efficacy of emotions as a legitimate tool for mobilizing the viewer's dialectic. I put the word "rediscover" in quotation marks because Alea had already discussed the important role of emotions in *The Viewer's Dialectic* and, even before that, in an interview published in 1977:

> One of those unforgettable moments which helped determine my vocation as a film director was my first encounter with *Film Sense*, by Sergei M. Eisenstein. This happened around 1948 or 1949. . . . It was for me a decisive book, even when the result of that initial reading and of the discussions it provoked among my friends was a serious indigestion of confused theories about montage, audiovisual counterpoint, film and dialectics, et cetera. A period of maturation and settling was necessary for those ideas to be fully assimilated and for them to flourish in practice. . . . But certainly, those initial worries have never abandoned me, that enthusiasm for the discovery of something new, those ideas that the brilliant teacher set forth. Eisenstein was not only a great artist, but also a revolutionary, and both in his films and in his writings he always sought to communicate his concerns, to arouse the viewer's sensibility and activate his intellect, so that he could not remain passive, complacent, or drugged, but ratter active, restless, lucid, and armed with a more profound vision and understanding of the reality in which he must struggle. This is for me the ideal of all truly revolutionary art, and it was in Eisenstein's work that I first fully witnessed it.[1]

After watching *Letters from the Park*, this ideal of revolutionary art may seem an inappropriate description of the film, but what this small gem of a film represents in Alea's oeuvre is a swing of the pendulum in a filmography that had put too much emphasis on the intellectual at the expense of the emotional. *Letters from the Park* is a simple love story, a moving if predictable version of the Cyrano de Bergerac story. It's not political, and there are no political meanings attachable to it. But it marks the first time Alea succeeded in telling a love story convincingly and movingly—from the heart, instead of from the mind, as in *Cumbite, Memories,* or *Up to a Point.* There are two reasons for this shift, for this move from intellect to emotions. On the one hand, ICAIC was extremely short on cash, and filmmakers began to work in international coproductions in order to work at all. *Letters from the Park, Strawberry and Chocolate,* and *Guantanamera* were all international coproductions between ICAIC and other producers from Latin America and Europe. This change in production partly dictated the choice of subject matter and form; experimentation and alienation techniques simply do not sell very well in the international market of heterogeneous moviemakers. Second, and perhaps more important in explaining the shift from alienation to identification, is the fact Alea underwent a period of emotional and political changes during the mid-eighties, first because of his relationship with Mirta Ibarra and second because of a polemic he sustained with Néstor Almendros over Almendros' documentary *Improper Conduct.*

On the subject of love, both Ibarra and Alea have talked about how *Up to a Point* helped to deepen their relationship, how working as equal partners at a professional level made their personal relationship deepen and blossom. Ibarra has been most eloquent in describing this change in language that is direct and precise:

> We had been together for ten years when we began working on the film *Up to a Point.* That film has a special significance for me, because as of that film, he discovered that with me he could have both a compañera and actress, as well as a collaborator and accomplice in his projects. Domestic life moved to a higher level, since artistic work became the center of our daily life together, where his intolerance for work badly done, his stubbornness, and his keen sense of humor were our daily bread. . . . It was a miracle that our relationship grew wings with time, like the words in the Basque song that was the theme of *Up to a Point:* "If I wanted I could clip her wings and she would be mine, but then she couldn't fly, and what I love is the bird." That's how I felt at his side, a free bird, loved and protected.[2]

Alea has been more poetic in describing his love story in terms of a mythical journey:

> Fiction allows you to go deeper into reality in an analytical way. In fiction one uses certain aspects of reality to try to show more general aspects. You

can abstract certain facts from reality and draw more general conclusions, reflect on them, and later return to reality, enriched by this emotional involvement. I'm writing something on this process now, in fact, which I call "Ariadne's Thread" because it's based on the story of Theseus from Greek mythology. There are many different interpretations of this myth, but there's one that I especially like. Theseus, as you know, has to get to the center of the labyrinth and confront the minotaur, a monster which eats people. It's possible to get to the center of the labyrinth but then it's difficult to get out. In the best of cases you enter the labyrinth, get to the center, and beat the monster. In other words, you enter into an abstraction and have a moment of revelation, you are able to conquer or understand something, but you can't always return to reality. That's something that happens very often. Theseus manages to get out, however, because Ariadne gave him a thread to follow. That's another very lovely aspect of this myth—Ariadne gave Theseus the thread because she was in love with him. Love is what makes it possible for one to come back to reality after having conquered the minotaur, conquered the most negative forces within oneself. For me, then, this is a myth about the possibility to grow, to develop, to understand the world better.[3]

This citation, taken from an interview conducted in 1985, is full of suggestions. First, it partly explains *Up to a Point*. That film was originally going to be called *Labyrinth*, and it was going to deal with a theater director who was committed to the Revolution and whose successes and failures in integrating into the Revolution would be reflected in his love life. On another level, the myth explains Alea's own struggle with himself, a struggle to defeat the most negative force within himself and within Cuban society: the minotaur called intolerance.

It was relatively easy and defensible to denounce people like Jorge Mas Canosa, the leader of the ultra-right Cuban American National Foundation, but it was something else to be intolerant of a close, albeit estranged, friend like Néstor Almendros. In early 1984, Almendros and Orlando Jiménez Leal (of *P.M.* fame) made a scathing documentary about the repression of gays in Cuba. They titled it *Mauvaise conduite (Improper Conduct)*, a reference to the Cuban penal code that made long hair, make-up, and public lasciviousness (in men) a punishable offense. In three short articles published in New York's *The Village Voice*, Alea and Almendros sustained a public debate over Almendros' documentary that spilled over from the political to the personal. In the first of the three articles, a gem of a piece, Richard Goldstein contextualizes the documentary's reception in both the United States and in Cuba; of the latter he writes:

> The silence persists, with *Granma* [the official newspaper in Cuba] asserting that "the writers and artists of this country are not prepared to become ensnared in a gross controversy promoted and encouraged by the United States." But last month, Cuba's greatest resident filmmaker, Tomás Gutiér-

rez Alea, was passing through New York, and we asked for his response. Alea's most renowned film, *Memories of Underdevelopment*, poses some of the same questions that *Improper Conduct* does about individual alienation in a revolutionary society. For Alea, such alienation is at heart an aspect of class privilege, but at least he acknowledges the tension between self-consciousness and social solidarity.

Alea is hardly a surrogate for Fidel Castro. In agreeing to answer questions about *Improper Conduct*, he may have been taking a risk, professionally and personally. The personal seemed to weigh on his mind as he approached the tape recorder. Almendros had been a friend in Cuba; now they are politically estranged. And Alea has a daughter living in exile in New York. To watch him reenter that broken circle is to comprehend the pain that persists in Cuban intellectual life.

"I tell you, honestly, I think this is a very superficial film," Alea began. "It is a type of propaganda based on testimonies that might be proven to a point. I can make maybe 10 or 20 films like that, but if you don't put them in a context, you are distorting reality because reality is much more complex."[4]

Almendros lashed back with an article of his own in the same newspaper, where he "corrected" the problem of contextualization in *Improper Conduct* and added more fuel to the fire:

There have been four major periods of repression of gays in Cuba in the 25 years of this so-called "revolutionary" power. The first, in 1961, was called "Operation 'P' "—it consisted of street raids and the victims were sent to camps in the Guanahacabibes peninsula. The second, from 1964 to 1969, is the period of the UMAP camps, and this is the period best documented in our film. The third period began in the 1970s, after the Congress of Education and Culture, with new harsh legislation, more street raids, and "rehabilitation" camps. The fourth period, in 1980, was a kind of Cuban "final solution" of the gay "problem"—the deportation of about 20,000 homosexuals from the port of Mariel to Florida. It was well known then that the best way to get an exit permit from Cuban authorities was a declaration of homosexuality. . . .

When Alea declares that "in the middle of a battle you can't discuss aesthetics or homosexuality or *anything*, you have to pick up your gun and receive orders," one can hear an updated echo of the Stalinist rhetoric of the '40s. No Marxist intellectual in the West today would dare to sustain such worn-out principles. . . . Discuss aesthetics, discuss homosexuality.[5]

Two months later, *The Village Voice* published the last article in the series, with the following remarks by Alea:

Why has Almendros, after so many years (he emigrated in 1961) and after traveling a road full of professional successes, lent himself to a dirty game of such dimensions? It's significant that at this very moment, coinciding with an aggressive policy by the U.S. administration toward our country, some intellectuals (and some who can barely boast of this distinction) have thrown themselves into a "cultural" offensive against Cuba, in which great economic resources of strange origin come into play. It's obvious that most of these people have nothing better to sell and that they try to make a career out of their anti-Cubanism. This is not exactly Almendros' case—he has already made a career and is legitimately well-placed in that world. However, in his film, almost all these characters are gathered, this time focusing their attacks against Cuba on the theme of homosexuality. Everything very well prepared. And very opportune for satisfying the needs of the master who has received them "with open arms" but who, at the same time, demands loyalty in exchange for a good reward.[6]

That was the last article in the series. Either Almendros decided not to reply, or *The Village Voice* realized that this was all turning into a personal diatribe under the guise of a political debate.

In Alea's telling of the minotaur myth, Theseus kills the darkest forces within him and is then saved from alienation by Ariadne's love. After the polemic over *Improper Conduct* was over, Alea may have realized that the accusations he hurled against Almendros were coming from the minotaur of intolerance inside of him and that it was time to find and kill that minotaur. More specifically, Alea's recognition that he had been intolerant with Almendros, a homosexual exile, explains the combination of these themes (homosexuality, exile and intolerance) in *Strawberry and Chocolate*:

> [*Strawberry and Chocolate*] is a way of continuing the polemic [over *Improper Conduct*], but through other means. That seems to me the most just thing to do: to treat the problem of homosexuality with sincerity and to show that in our country we're struggling to resolve it. . . .
>
> Néstor was not a friend like many others, he was a friend in a very particular way. When he arrived in Cuba [from Barcelona], at a moment when I had already defined my vocation for cinema, he had a kind of viewer's fanaticism. He wanted to see every film—something that never happened to me—and he dragged me along, made me discover things I had never seen before, opened new vistas for me. I remember we went together to the movies all the time and we had to seat in the first rows because . . . he had to fill himself completely with the screen. That was a very important stage in my artistic and political development. It may seem contradictory, but the first person who talked to me about Marxism as something that had to be assumed was Néstor. . . .
>
> When I found out about Néstor's death, I must confess that it affected me. It affected me because, in spite of the discussion over *Improper Conduct* and of everything else, it's impossible to break affective ties that existed 30 or 40 years ago. I would have loved him to see this film . . ., perhaps to continue the discussion . . . . But he was a special addressee of this film.[7]

With this in mind, the final embrace between Diego and David in *Strawberry and Chocolate* takes on a very personal meaning, for that embrace fictional-izes a reconciliation that never took place in real life between Almendros and Alea. David, the younger, heterosexual, and more militant of the two friends, in many ways represents Alea, while Diego, the gay intellectual and artist, represents Almendros. In this reading, Alea's naively idealistic alter ego chooses to stay in Cuba, desperately wanting to believe in the attainment of an idealized Revolution, while Almendros' alter ego, disillusioned yet assertive, chooses exile.

The fact that Alea's last three films lack the corrosive irony and black humor that had been his trademark since *Death of a Bureaucrat* indicates that something fundamental had changed. And at the same time, the fact that love triumphs in all three films reflects a newfound vision of love as salvation, a vision in which Ibarra must have played the part of Ariadne to Alea's role of Theseus. In effect, what these last three films reveal is a shift in Alea's films from tragic to the melodramatic. In *The Melodramatic Imagination*, Peter Brooks defines melodrama as an

> emotional drama [that] needs the desemanticized language of music, its evocation of the "ineffable," its tones and registers. . . . [Its origins] can be accurately located within the context of the French Revolution and its after-math, . . . [and it represents] a response to the loss of the tragic vision. It comes into being in a world where the traditional imperatives of truth and ethics have been violently thrown into question, yet where the promulga-tion of truth and ethics, their instauration as a way of life, is of immediate daily, political concern."[8]

After 1985 (when Castro announced his rectification campaign), but especially after the collapse of the Soviet Union (when subsidies ended and the economy collapsed) traditional imperatives of truth and ethics were vio-lently thrown into question in Cuba. Alea's shift to melodrama may be a reflection of that crisis, of the loss of the tragic vision that sustained the rhetoric and praxis of the Revolution for over three decades. Most of Alea's films before *Letters from the Park* have characters with a tragic dilemma, characters torn between two or more competing and conflicting priorities. Sergio in *Memories*, Juan Contreras in *A Cuban Fight*, the Count in *The Last Supper*, Julio in *The Survivors*, and Oscar in *Up to a Point*—are all tragic or at least semitragic characters torn by an internal conflict that they never quite resolve. In Alea's last three films, on the other hand, the conflicts no longer persist inside the characters, but are instead resolved by circum-stances outside of them. Thus externalized, the tragic conflict becomes a melodramatic solution. Pedro in *Letters from the Park*, Diego in *Strawberry and Chocolate*, and Gina in *Guantanamera* are all clear about who they are and what they want. Even Gina, torn between the traditional conception of being a wife and her desire to love Mariano, does not have to make the decision herself. Rather, Adolfo thrusts it upon her when he hits her for wearing a sexy dress. It's as if the demands of a dire reality had become so imposing that there was no longer any room for internal conflicts. Mirta Ibarra summed up this feeling for many: "We always thought that ideology was more important than the economy, and now [1995] we see that the economy is what ends up stamping the ideology."[9] Alea's characters previous to *Letters from the Park* live in a world where they have the relative freedom to worry about ideological conflicts. After the economic collapse of 1991, however, this freedom is a privilege that few in Cuba can relate to, either in daily life or in films.

Theoretically, this shift from the tragic to the melodramatic (or sentimental, in the case of *Letters from the Park*) marks a move away from the attitude of alienation to an attitude of identification, from an attitude that privileged Brechtian rupture to an Eisenstenian attitude that takes advantage of the powers of pleasure and identification. Asked how *Strawberry and Chocolate* would be when finished, Alea answered as if paraphrasing Eisenstein: "The first word that comes to my mind is that it should be moving, that through sentiments and emotions, the film touch on a number of problems; and from here, that it encourage and stimulate the viewer to reflect and think about the problems that the characters face. The film will be—I would like it to be—a very moving event, charged with humor and emotion."[10] The viewer's dialectic does not have to begin and end with alienation, Alea seems to be saying. It may be more effective, thirty years into the Revolution, and especially during the Special Period,[11] to use the technique of identification with more freedom so that the film is not only more pleasurable but also more communicative of ideas. *Strawberry and Chocolate* and *Guantanamera* may not be as cutting-edge as *Memories of Underdevelopment*, or as ideologically complex as *The Last Supper*, but they are more effective in terms of achieving the synthesis between "film show" and "cinema of ideas" that Alea postulated in *The Viewer's Dialectic*. And what better form to achieve this than through melodrama? Alea may have come late to the realization that melodrama is Latin America's preferred form of spectacle, but luckily that did not stop him from making two melodramas and one sentimental comedy that move us like the best of them do. There are, to be sure, limits that come with the melodramatic form, such as a loss of complexity for which tragedies are better suited. Alea consciously accepted these limitations and focused instead on melodrama's power to reach a broad audience without having to sacrifice much in terms of the ideas he wanted to discuss. In *Strawberry and Chocolate* and less subtly in *Guantanamera*, these ideas were the deterioration of civility because of economic survivalism, political intolerance and dogmatism, and love as the ultimate redeemer of humanity.

Letters from the Park

In 1985 the New Latin American Cinema Foundation was created in Cuba, with Gabriel García Márquez as its founding president. Like Alea, García Márquez had studied at the Centro Sperimentale in Rome and had always harbored a love of cinema, to the point that *One Hundred Years of Solitude* was a reaction to his frustrated attempts at scriptwriting.[12] One of the first projects García Márquez promoted through the foundation was a series of six ninety-minute films collectively called *Amores difíciles* (*Difficult Loves*), produced by Spanish Television in collaboration with the International Network Group. *Letters from the Park* was the fifth and best film in the series.

Before *Letters from the Park*, Alea had already approached Márquez with the idea of making a film based on *Crónica de una muerte anunciada*, and also one based on an episode from *Love in the Time of Cholera*. Neither proposal was accepted at the time, but when Márquez contacted Alea some years later to ask him to direct one of the films in the *Difficult Loves* series, Alea chose to adapt an episode from *Love in the Time of Cholera*:

> In the novel there were many episodes that could be developed by themselves, independently from the others. The main character is a man who grows old and never stops loving a woman who's married. In order to relieve his feelings of love, he goes to the park and begins to offer his services as a writer of love letters. One day, a young woman approaches him because she wants to respond to a love letter she received from a young would-be lover. From that moment one, a dialogue develops between the young man and woman, and it culminates with their marriage. This episode caught my attention above the others. I selected this idea and we developed a story that has nothing to do with that ending. . . . I worked with Eliseo Alberto Diego. . . . He presented a developed story to García Márquez and I, so that we only had to add a few things.[13]

In the film, the letter-writer is the one who ends up with the girl (María), and the setting is a small town in Cuba instead of a small town in Colombia. Otherwise, the atmosphere and themes are the same.

Unlike Alea's other films, *Letters from the Park* is an overtly readerly[14] film that explicitly tells the viewer how to interpret the plot through intertitles and through the codified language of handkerchiefs and flowers that Pedro teaches to Juan and María. The interpretation that emerges is so utterly romantic and nostalgic that the question arises: What do this nostalgia and this romanticism mean? Traditionally, nostalgia in Romantic art has been interpreted as a symptom of the artist's disillusionment with an earlier idealism, as a defensive move whereby the artist recedes into an interior world because that's the only place where he or she can still be free and creative.

There is something of this in *Letters from the Park*, but it's not something that Alea sustains in his next films. Rather, *Letters from the Park* and its companion piece, *Contigo en la distancia* (*With You in the Distance*, 1991, a twenty-seven-minute melodrama made for Mexican television), gave Alea a break from the making a cinema of ideas:

> *With You in the Distance* is really a prolongation of *Letters from the Park*. They both have the same tone, and both are a sort of exorcism. I've never forgotten my responsibility as creator of something that—this is the case of a film—can influence so many people, and that feeling of responsibility, more than burdensome, can become paralyzing. As Babel said: "My respect for the people has made me mute." It takes a lot to push that compromise aside and make something simply because you want to. That's why making two purely sentimental films, with no political commitment, was for me liberating. For me they were two very positive experiences, very refreshing.[15]

Pedro's yearning for María's innocence may reflect a general nostalgia for an earlier innocence in the wider political sphere, but *Letters from the Park* is, and remains, a simple love story, "so simple," the first intertitle tells us, "that the names of the protagonists are Pedro, Juan, and María."

Strawberry and Chocolate: Homosexuality, Marxism-Leninism, and Exile

In 1991, Ediciones Era, a left-of-center publishing house in Mexico City, published "El lobo, el bosque y el hombre nuevo," Senel Paz's short story on which *Strawberry and Chocolate* is based. The publication of the story came after it was awarded the prestigious Juan Rulfo Prize in 1990. But the story had been known for some time, both as a manuscript and through theatrical adaptations in Havana, Puerto Rico, Brazil, and Mexico. After the Rulfo Prize, many more theatrical adaptations were made, and Alea asked Paz to write a script based on it. The script for *Strawberry and Chocolate*, credited to Paz but written in collaboration with Alea, won the Coral Prize[16] for best unfilmed script at the Havana Film Festival, a prize that provided close to $150,000 for its production. If nothing else, the fact that the story won the Rulfo Prize and the script won the Coral Prize facilitated the production of the film, for without the recognition bestowed by these prizes, it is unlikely that ICAIC would have been able to secure additional funding from Mexico's INCINE or Spain's Telemadrid.

In the short story version, a middle-age intellectual falls for an attractive university student. The intellectual's homosexuality is at first an impediment to their friendship, but after some time they become friends and confidants, although not lovers. The story explains some things that are not explicit in the film, specifically Diego's typology of homosexuals in Cuba and the story of how Diego became aware of his homosexuality. Moreover, the film adds two important features to the original story: (1) the character of Nancy, based on a character of the same name from Gerardo Chijona's film *Adorable Lies* (1990), and (2) the content of Germán's exhibition. The film, then, complicates the plot of its literary source, but retains the short story's simplicity in terms of narrative strategies: Both story and the film are linear narrations with strong and well-rounded main characters. The film version is also more dramatic, even melodramatic, with character development centered on action and conflict as opposed to the internal monologues of the original story.

Strawberry and Chocolate is set in 1979, and begins with David ready to lose his virginity with Vivian, his upwardly mobile girlfriend. They go to a *posada*, where people pay by the hour for the privilege of a little privacy they can't get at home because of Havana's housing shortage. But even here the private is public. When David looks out of the window he sees a billboard of the CDR, the Committees for the Defense of the Revolution, and then turns his attention to the room next door, where a woman is making love to a man—that is, the man is lying passively on his back while the woman "rides" on top of him. Already two of the central themes of the film are presented— first, the fact that one's sexual life is a matter of concern to the Revolution, and second, the subversion of traditional male sexuality as active and female sexuality as passive. These two themes combine in the third sequence, when Diego tries to pick up David. In this sequence, David feels threatened by Diego's unorthodox sexuality as much as by his unorthodox politics. Diego senses this and is smart enough to lure him to his apartment by other means, namely, with a set of photographs of David playing Torvaldo in a student production of Ibsen's *A Doll House*.

Their sexual preferences aside, David and Diego develop their friendship because they share a common understanding of the Revolution as the continuation of José Martí's project for Cuban sovereignty. Sexual attraction on Diego's part is certainly important in starting the friendship, but without common ground in other areas, plus a healthy dose of tolerance, that potential friendship would have faltered after their first encounter. At the same time, had David and Diego actually slept together, the film ran the risk of alienating many potential viewers, of being censored, and of becoming a film centered more on sexuality than the political statement that Alea makes of it. This is not to say that sexuality and politics can or should be separated. Foucault has taught us otherwise. But to conflate the two would be a mistake in this case. Therefore, to avoid a reductionist analysis of sexuality in *Strawberry and Chocolate*, one must contextualize that sexuality within the larger picture of Cuban history and culture.

The First Congress on Education and Culture (1971) is illustrative in this regard. The congress was part of a wider institutionalization process that began in the aftermath of the failed ten million–ton sugar harvest in 1970; the declaration that came out of the congress literally emphasized the "need to maintain our people's ideologically monolithic unity and combat any form of deviation among young people."[17] The declaration also functioned as a programmatic manifesto that set very strict limits to what may be considered revolutionary art and who may be considered a revolutionary artist:

> The cultural sectors shall not be used as a means of proliferation for false intellectuals who pretend to transform snobbism, extravagance, homosexuality, and other social aberrations, into expressions of revolutionary art. . . .
>
> The ideological formation of young writers and artists is a central task of the Revolution. It is our duty to educate them in Marxism-Leninism, to steep them in the ideas of the Revolution, and to empower them technically.[18]

These excerpts from the declaration are textbook examples of what Foucault called "discourse," in the sense that the implementation of the policies outlined in them had the effect of closing off alternative ways of speaking and thinking. In the case of *Strawberry and Chocolate*, these alternative ways correspond to an understanding of homosexuality as a valid form of desire (not as the social aberration that the declaration makes it out to be), and to the separation of the idea of "Revolution" from "Marxism-Leninism." In effect, *Strawberry and Chocolate* may be understood as an attempt to correct these two "mistakes" of the Revolution by singling them out as unnecessary and inauthentic deviations from the true master narrative of the Revolution, which should instead be identified with the life and teachings of José Martí.

The film does this by portraying a homosexual artist and educator who is not, as the Declaration would have us believe, a "false intellectual." On the contrary; Diego is shown in a positive light as an heir to Martí: a very authentic artist with high moral standards and unquestionable revolutionary credentials. David, on the other hand, is an intelligent if naive university student who has been so successfully indoctrinated into Marxism-Leninism that when Diego confesses that he believes in God, David answers, "And I am a dialectic materialist," as if Marxism and Christianity were on equal epistemological footing. In a way they are, as both aim to emancipate mankind from the shackles of slavery and both ask for sacrifices to be made in the name of that goal. But the main point of this brief exchange between David and Diego is that in Cuba's restricted political and educational system, Diego represents an alternative source of knowledge for David, a gnosis that discredits parts of the hegemonic discourse taught through official channels while reinforcing others. As I will demonstrate, the parts that are discredited are those that have to do with Marxism-Leninism, while the parts that are reinforced are based on José Martí's ideas on Cuban nationalism.

Most spectators of the film identify more readily with Diego than with David. This identification, based on Diego's looks, sophistication, good humor, sensibility, and intelligence, belies the fact that David is the main character in the plot. It is David, after all, who changes most radically, from initially being a "new man," to being a "patriot" as defined by José Martí. For even though David insists on being a dialectical materialist, this gives way in the film to another discourse based less on Marxism-Leninism than on Martí's three pillars of Cuban nationalism: patriotism, anti-imperialism, and pan-Americanism. In the end, both David and the spectator are convinced of Diego's particular interpretation of these foundational pillars of Cuban nationalism as compatible with his sexuality but incompatible with Marxism-Leninism. In the following sections I will develop each of these two hypotheses separately and will follow with a discussion of the politics of exile, as this is inseparable from the Cuban experience of both homosexuality and Marxism-Leninism.

Homosexuality

Machismo is a phenomenon older than the Revolution, and one that is not limited to Cuba. The military origins of the Revolution and the subsequent militarization of the state, however, promoted an identification of heterosexual virility with progressive politics that had existed before, but never in such extremes. The image of strong, bearded men in military fatigues, carrying rifles and smoking cigars—phallic symbols if there ever were any—turned into a symbol of discipline, leadership, and the will to effect strong and decisive changes to the conditions in prerevolutionary Cuba. Even the subsequent adoption of Marxism-Leninism, with its emphasis on the active and privileged role of a vanguard party, fit perfectly into the revolutionaries' phallocentric understanding of their recent victories. No doubt the guerrilla origins of the Revolution had a direct effect on the subsequent official discourse on sexuality. Heterosexual male desire—the kind that emanated from the images of the guerrillas and that included not only desire toward women but also social bonding with other men—became the norm from which issued a number of prescriptive laws, decrees, and cultural pronouncements dealing with sexuality. Intimately related to the prescriptive view of male heterosexuality was the proscriptive view of deviations from that norm, most notably homosexuality and prostitution. In the Manichaean discourse of the Revolution, one could either be with the Revolution or against it, with little or no space for conditional approval or critical appraisal. Not surprisingly, official discourse flatly rejected homosexuality and prostitution and simultaneously associated them with a picture of the Batista regime as "a combination of the poverty of Haiti, the barbaric gangsterism of the Chicago of the 1930s, and the corruption and prostitution of Shanghai."[19] Moreover, since the Batista regime had been a puppet state of the United States, it was relatively easy to conclude that homosexuality and prostitution were outward signs of North American decadence (in the case of homosexuality) and exploitation (in the case of prostitution). Finally, homosexuality and prostitution had the common stigma of being unproductive and unreproductive activities. This, in a society that put a premium on quantitative measures of well-being, amounted to sinful, illegal, and counterrevolutionary behavior.

These are some of the prejudices that David has to overcome to become a true revolutionary in Diego's book. When David first encounters Diego at Coppelia, he sees not just an individual who acts with effeminacy, but, worse, an individual who, because effeminacy is an outward sign of homosexuality (with all the reactionary, decadent, and immoral connotations of that label) is therefore prejudged to be counterrevolutionary, morally weak, and even abnormal in the added sense that he does not conform or aspire to the guerrilla-inspired ideal of the new man. Add to this the fact that Diego carries around a novel by Mario Vargas Llosa (*Conversación en la catedral*, 1971) and a travel account by Juan Goytisolo (*Campos de Níjar*, 1960), and David's request that they not be seen together becomes understandable. After all, Vargas Llosa and Goytisolo were both considered *personae non gratae* during the 1970s in Cuba, Vargas Llosa because of his well-publicized anti-Castro position and Goytisolo for his celebration of homosexual love and for another not-so-flattering travel account (*Pueblo en marcha*, 1962), in which he describes his experiences in Cuba right after the Revolution. In this regard, Diego's invitation to David to read Vargas Llosa and Goytisolo points to his subversiveness, even though it is a subversiveness that is qualified and problematized by the specifics of the texts involved. In the case of Vargas Llosa, Diego's subversiveness is problematized because of the rampant homophobia in *Conversación en la catedral*, while the potential subversiveness of reading a text like *Campos de Níjar*, a travel account that highlights the conflict between aesthetic delight and the depressing reality of life, is mitigated by Goytisolo's subsequent project of creating a private and quasi-spiritual world interested more in aesthetics and eroticism than in politics.[20] Clearly, Diego is not a schematic character, but rather a very complex one, full of nuances and contradictions. In this respect, Diego is like Sergio in *Memories of Underdevelopment*, and it is precisely this complexity of character that makes *Strawberry and Chocolate* a polyvalent film, a film that can elicit multiple and sometimes contradictory responses from its viewers.

After this revealing scene, the film goes on to show that just because David's request is understandable does not mean it is justified. As Diego vehemently points out, the state never compensated homosexuals who were stigmatized or punished for their homosexuality, nor were any officials punished for having committed these crimes. Moreover, by calling them "mistakes," the state simply domesticated and decriminalized its own excesses without having to change any of the structures that permitted and even promoted such excesses. Notwithstanding Diego's strong condemnations of state abuses, however, the central political message of the film is summed up by David's assertion that the prosecution of homosexuals and other injustices of the state are "those parts of the Revolution that are not part of the Revolution." As far as the Revolution is concerned, then, *Strawberry and Chocolate* is corrective and didactic, but not subversive. That is to say, *Strawberry and Chocolate* does not advocate the abandonment of the ideals of the Revolution. Rather, the film points out past and current deviations from these ideals so that with this heightened awareness, viewers may leave the theater with the desire to effect the changes needed for the rescue and recovery of abandoned or distorted revolutionary ideals.

This kind of complexity of thought was probably a determining factor in Senel Paz's wish to have his script filmed by Alea. It is a complexity demanded by the original story, as is evidenced by Diego's quasicomic classification of homosexuals in "El lobo, el bosque y el hombre nuevo":

> We homosexuals fall into an even more interesting category than the one I explained to you the other day. That is, *homosexuals* properly speaking—I repeat the term because the word preserves, even in the worst of circumstances, a certain degree of restraint—; the *maricones*—ay, I also repeat it—, and the *locas*, the lowest of which are called *locas de carroza*, old queens. The scale is determined by the subject's disposition towards social commitment, or dirty tricks. When the scale tilts towards social commitment, you are in the presence of a homosexual . . . . Just like the heroes or the political activists, we place Duty before Sex . . . . The *maricones* don't deserve their own explanation, like everything that's left hanging between one thing and the other . . . [and] the *locas*, who are very easy to conceptualize, walk around all day and all night with a phallus firmly fixed in their heads; everything they do is for its sake.[21]

In a society that tended to lump all homosexuals into a single and all-encompassing pigeonhole, this typology attempts to make distinctions more subtle, even as it perpetuates old stereotypes. Further into this monologue, Diego even attempts to normalize homosexuality by projecting the same hierarchy onto heterosexuals:

> This typology is applicable to heterosexuals of either sex. In the case of men, the lowest rung, the one that corresponds to old queens and is marked by perpetual procrastination and the perpetual desire to fornicate, is occupied by the *picha-dulce* . . . . Among women the scale naturally ends with prostitutes, but not the ones that swarm in hotels hunting tourists, or any of the others who do it out of necessity, of which we have few, as official propaganda rightly claims, but rather those who give themselves freely and out of sheer pleasure.[22]

Diego's tactic in this second part of the monologue is one of legitimizing homosexual desire by demonstrating its similarities with the normative heterosexual desire. What strikes me beyond Diego's very clever tactic is the fact that in both cases—homosexual and heterosexual—the typology in effect takes for granted and even reproduces the tripartite division of people according to their commitment to the Revolution. That is to say, good homosexuals and good heterosexuals make good revolutionaries because they all have in common a keenly developed sense of social duty. Bad homosexuals or bad heterosexuals, on the other hand, require altogether different and derogatory terms—*locas* or *picha-dulces*—much like counterrevolutionaries require an altogether different and derogatory term: *gusanos*. Most people occupy a position somewhere between these extremes, yet neither official discourse nor its counterpart in exile promote an open discussion that might explore the variety and complexity of this huge middle ground in the political or cultural spheres. Diego's relegation of those who attempt to strike a balance between duty and pleasure to a category of people who "don't deserve their own explanation" strikes me as an unwitting reproduction of the Manichaeism that has plagued the Cuban experience since 1959.

In the film, however, the previous correlation between libido and social consciousness (i.e., the higher the libido, the lower one's revolutionary consciousness, and vice versa) gives way to a separation of the two. Diego, responding to David's questions as to why Diego became a homosexual, responds, "It's very simple. You like women. I like men." The implication is that a person's sexual preferences are no guide to their political or ethical views. Sexual preference is not a political, ethical, or, as David suggests, endocrinal issue, but rather a matter of taste. Sexual practices may be another matter, but preferences are as far as the film pushes the issue. David accepts Diego's homosexuality as one among his many identity markers, one that does not define him. At the end of the film the spectator, like David, would probably define Diego as an intellectual who happens to be homosexual and effeminate, not as an effeminate homosexual who is also an intellectual. These are the terms for David's acceptance of Diego's friendship and tutelage.

The film, then, ostensibly privileges a reading of David's conversion as one centered on the mind. For example, David's two unexpected returns to Diego's apartment are intellectually motivated: the first to get a book by Vargas Llosa and the second to show Diego a manuscript. We as spectators know that David has additional reasons for these visits—in the first case, to fulfill the "mission" of finding out more about the possible subversive activities of a dissatisfied homosexual, and in the second case, to ameliorate his own remorse for having falsely accused a respected friend. Yet in neither case are David's visits explained in terms that may be called "sexually motivated." Friendships, however, are very complex emotional affairs, and to exclude the possibility of an unmanifested homosexual desire on David's part would close off one possible interpretation of David's motivations.[23] As the film stands, however, the friendship between David and Diego and David's conversion from a naive revolutionary to a critical revolutionary are satisfactorily explained without recourse to explicitly sexual motives. What one cannot ignore is the politics (sexual and otherwise) surrounding that friendship, a topic I take up next.

Marxism-Leninism

Diego and David, two individuals who do not share the same sexuality, can nevertheless find common ground in other areas. As the film develops, it becomes clear that the common ground is an understanding of the Revolution as a worthy humanistic and Martían project whose embrace of Marxism-Leninism goes against its enduring and endearing qualities. The idea that Marxism-Leninism is alien to the Revolution may strike one as crude, given the Cuban state's three-decades-long identification with Marxism-Leninism. It is to this apparent paradox that I now turn my attention.

Since the French Revolution of 1789, the word "revolution" has signified a potent mixture of progressive politics with violence. Revolutions differ from reformist changes in government (which also promote progressive politics) in their suddenness and in the use of force. The distinction between revolution and reform is especially important in Latin America, where forced changes in government are often reactionary, and where reformist social programs are usually too little, too late. Examples of what would qualify as "revolution" in Latin America abound: the Mexican Revolution of 1910, the Guatemalan reformist measures of 1954 (violence came afterwards, with CIA intervention), the military revolution of 1968 in Peru, the Nicaraguan Revolution of 1979, and the most famous of all, the Cuban Revolution of 1959. What all of these revolutions have in common, to a lesser or greater extent, is a humanistic heritage that argues for the development of society's potential, but as defined in nationalistic terms. That is to say, each of these revolutions had a distinct nationalistic signature. In the case of Cuba, the life and writing of José Martí provided that signature. His teachings have been so imbedded into twentieth-century Cuban nationalism that the things he stood for—patriotism, anti-imperialism, and pan-Americanism—have become part of what Unamuno would call "intra-historia," the historical undercurrents that define the essence of a people beyond the turbulence of current events. These three ideas, more than Marxism or Leninism, are the ideological base of the Cuban Revolution. The proof of this is the fact that even after the collapse of the Soviet Union and the abrupt suspension of subsidies to the island, there is still in Cuba a strong sense of patriotism, anti-imperialism, and pan-Americanism that even the crudest cynics have not abandoned. Very few, on the other hand, still swear by the ideas of Marx, Lenin, or even Guevara.

Unamuno's idea of "intra-historia" is a powerful metaphor, but one that I will not develop here because it is impossible to predict how Martí's ideas will fare in the age of globalization and interdependence. In a well-documented and superbly argued book titled *Cuba: The Shaping of Revolutionary Consciousness* (1990), Tzvi Medin uses another metaphor—this one biological—to argue a similar point. The metaphor is one of grafting, whereby Marxism-Leninism is grafted onto Cuban nationalism:

> Cuban revolutionary leaders introduced Marxism-Leninism into the Cuban revolutionary message by grafting it onto the images, symbols, values, and concepts of Cuban nationalism. . . . Anti-imperialist nationalism became the vehicle of introduction, but it in turn began to take on a new meaning, like an orange tree onto which grapefruit is grafted: The graft will develop thanks to the orange tree, but in the end the tree will produce grapefruit.[24]

The use of a biological metaphor to describe a political phenomenon has the obvious drawback of reducing a complex and oftentimes subtle process into one that is deterministic and easily explained (away). However, the metaphor does contain a grain of truth. To the extent that the grafting metaphor is valid, then, it would be possible to simply cut off grafted branches so that the true Revolution, which is the rooted plant, could continue to grow and bear fruit. That was not the case in 1979, when the "grafted" Marxism-Leninism appeared to have overshadowed even Martían rhetoric, but it appears to be the case during the current Special Period. Indeed, after his initial Numantine statements to the effect that no matter what happened in Europe after the fall of the Berlin Wall, the Revolution would continue its Marxist-Leninist course, Castro has pretty much done away with that position. In July 1992, for example, references to Leninism were eliminated from the Constitution,[25] and Castro's speeches since then have instead concentrated on patriotism and anti-imperialism, two pillars of Martían discourse.

This move away from Marxism-Leninism is also prominent in the film. The only verbal mention of that discourse is indirect, when David claims to be a dialectical materialist. But as I have already pointed out, the context in which this claim is made makes David's statement a confession of faith, and not a gnostic claim. Moreover, Germán's statues of Marx as a suffering Christ, and of Christ as a victim of Marxism, are overtly subversive of Marxism-Leninism because they equate what is supposed to be a scientific gnosis with a religious faith (see the Conclusions chapter). Apart from these statues, however, none of the icons in Diego's apartment have to do with either Marx or Lenin. Diego's only possession of anything Marxist is a Marxist treatise on

sexuality by a Russian author, and even that has nothing to do with Marxism-Leninism as a means of explaining the need for an ideologically committed elite to direct and control all sectors of the economy and of the polity. In any case, what strikes me is the fact that even though the film deals in so many ways with Marxism-Leninism, this is nevertheless not as important as the question of pluralism.

Again, a key moment in the film gives us food for thought—in this case, the scene in which Diego toasts to "democratic communism" in response to David's opinion that "we all have the right to do what we want with our lives." Assuming that Diego is not being ironic, one may interpret this phrase as Diego's stripping away the "Leninism" from "Marxism-Leninism" so that grassroots pluralism may flourish. After all, it is Leninism, not Marxism, that stipulates the need for a prepared cadre of elite members of the Party to guide the masses. Unlike Leninism, which is imported, top-down, and theoretical, Diego's pluralism is home-grown, horizontal, and practical in that it responds to the reality of Cuba, not Russia. Diego's discourse, then, is more convincing than David's academic embrace of dialectical materialism because it is based on his own lived experiences as a Cuban revolutionary who has been marginalized by the very process he once embraced.

Another key scene in *Strawberry and Chocolate* may help explain what exactly Diego has in mind when he toasts to "democratic communism." It is the scene in which David places three icons of the Revolution among Diego's wall artifacts—a flag of the July 26 Movement, a portrait of Che Guevara, and a photograph of Fidel Castro as a guerrilla. David then asks rhetorically: "Aren't these also part of our history?" Diego's silence is enigmatic, his expression no less so. The previous discussion of grafting gives us a clue to a possible answer, in that these three icons correspond to what would be the trunk of the tree onto which Marxism-Leninism was grafted. This would also explain the emotion with which Diego reacts to David's attempt to remove them after a disagreement later in the film. It is as if David were telling Diego that by emigrating, he would give up the right to call himself Cuban, that he would no longer be part of that trunk of Cuban history that will outlive Marxism-Leninism and other imported models.

The intense emotions associated with these icons set the stage for the subsequent melodramatic union between David and Diego. This union, which culminates in the film's final embrace, in effect sublimates their mutual attraction by intellectualizing it, and thus opens the way for the chaneling of David's repressed sexuality toward a safer, heterosexual outlet in Nancy. In *The Melodramatic Imagination*, Peter Brooks has theorized about the political meaning of such unions by noting that "what is being blocked in melodrama is very seldom the drive toward erotic union . . . [but] virtue's claim to exist qua virtue. Thus with the triumph of virtue at the end there is not, as in comedy, the emergence of a new society formed around the united young couple . . . but rather a reforming of the old society of inno-cence."[26] In the case of *Strawberry and Chocolate*, the melodramatic union between David and Diego serves to recuperate a virtuous past defined as the early years of the Revolution, when the icons added by David did not conflict with the icons already in place on the walls of Diego's apartment. Politically, moreover, this synthesis of high and popular culture, of pre-Revolution and early-Revolution icons, effectively displaces David's academic Leninism and replaces it with Diego's virtuous politics of concensus (as when Diego toasts to democratic communism), of progressive ideals (i.e., the inclusion of homosexuals to the body politic), and of national sovereignty (as when Diego states that he doesn't want the Americans or anyone else telling Cubans what to do.) Consensus, progressive politics, and national sovereignty, then, seem to be what Diego stands for. But not the kind of concocted consensus that the government has fabricated in the Committees for the Defense of the Revolu-tion (CDR) and in "popular democratic" elections in which Communist Party elite always get elected. Rather, Diego stands for a consensus born of dia-logue and open discussion, of the kind that we see taking place between him-self and David.

There is yet another example of how the film delegitimizes Marxism-Leninism. It has to do with the changes in Miguel's position vis-à-vis David's position. Miguel's character is schematic, especially his adherence to the official Manichaeist interpretation of the Revolution and of Marxism-Leninism. In visual as much as in narrative terms, Miguel's position changes from one of dominance to one of insignificance. The first time we encounter him is in their dormitory room, as David recounts his encounter with Diego. The next time we see Miguel, he calls David from a second-story balcony. Firm in tone and with a gesture reminiscent of a *caudillo* addressing a crowd after a coup, Miguel tells David to come up to see him. In the bathroom scene, Miguel holds David from behind, while splashing him with water. The water, the half-naked bodies, and Miguel's position behind David eroticize the scene, while Miguel's pronouncements make the homoeroticism "safe."[27] Miguel's possessiveness of David also helps to account for his authoritarian-ism, while the washing underscores the Puritanism inherent in that attitude: Miguel literally washes David of such contaminants as hanging out with a confessed homosexual, drinking Johnny Walker (the drink of the enemy), being privy to a "strange" and potentially subversive exhibit of sculptures, reading censored novels, and even listening to Maria Callas, Ernesto Lecuona, and Ignacio Cervantes. Back in the dormitory room, David stands up for Diego, whereupon Miguel explodes into an invective against the impe-rialist enemy, thus conflating Diego's persona with Yankee imperialism. The next day, or a short time thereafter, Miguel decides to pay a visit to Diego, and has a verbal and physical fight with him. David arrives just in time to separate the two, and Miguel then accuses David of being Diego's lover.

David reacts violently, Diego holds him back, and Miguel begins to leave, launching more accusations and pointing his finger as he descends the stairs. The last time Miguel appears in the film is the day after the Lezamian lunch. David is beaming with the self-confidence and satisfaction of love, and after gleefully saluting some student companions, he casually walks by Miguel, who is squatting down on the stairs with a confused and defeated look on his face.

The mise-en-scenes—with their gradual displacement of Miguel from a position in the upper left corner of the frame to a position in the lower right corner of the frame—reflect these changes in the relationship between David and Miguel from that of equals (i.e., in their dormitory room when David recounts his first encounter with Diego), to one in which Miguel tries to wield power over David (i.e., when Miguel calls David from a second-story balcony at the university to give him instructions on how to frame Diego), and finally, to a relationship in which David reasserts his independence from Miguel, as when David intervenes to break up the fight Miguel and Diego are having over him, and Miguel leaves the scene (and the frame) as he walks down the stairs. This displacement may also be read allegorically, with Miguel representing Marxism-Leninism and David standing for the original revolutionary ideal of a sovereign Cuba, free from foreign meddling, yet open to new ideas. The reading would go as follows: In the beginning, Marxism-Leninism seemed very attractive. Soon enough, however, the Revolution found itself in the uncomfortable position of having to adjust its own convictions to those of a Manichaeist and belligerent ideology. In time, the Revolution began to reassert itself as separate from Marxism-Leninism, until Marxism-Leninism was eventually forced out of the picture.

Contrast this to the mise-en-scenes in which David and Diego interact. Whether at Coppelia, at Diego's apartment, or overlooking the Havana harbor, theirs is a dialogue between equals. Unlike Miguel's dogmatic and hierarchical rigidity, Diego's open-mindedness and pluralistic worldview promote a more flexible, tolerant, and self-critical revolutionary consciousness.

Hand in hand with this rejection of Marxism-Leninism as a defining feature of the Cuban Revolution is the concurrent revalorization of the Martían roots of the Revolution. Patriotism, anti-imperialism, and pan-Americanism are three key ideas that define current official discourse in Cuba. All of them are found in Martí's most famous essay, "Our America": on patriotism, for example, "Let the whole world be grafted onto our republics, but the trunk shall be that of our republics"; on anti-imperialism, "The disdain of our formidable neighbor, who does not know us, is the greatest danger of our America; it is urgent that he gets to know her, and gets to know her soon, so that when the day of reckoning comes, he will not disdain her. Out of respect, once he gets to know her, he would pull out his hands from her bosom"; and on pan-Americanism, "It is the hour of reckoning, and of the united march, and we shall march in close ranks, tight as the silver veins at the root of the Andes."[28] In *Strawberry and Chocolate* these three key elements of Cuban nationalism constitute the core of Diego's teachings to David, a gnosis that has been somehow lost because of the importance afforded to a Marxism-Leninism that is informed by the narrow and rigid ideological dictates of the Cold War. The Martían principles outlined here are presented in different forms. On patriotism, Martí's dictum of grafting the world onto the trunk of Cubanity (*cubanía* in Spanish, a term used to refer to a healthy pride in things Cuban) is evident in the prominence given to Cuban artistic tradition. Donne, Callas, Dos Pasos, and even Johnny Walker whiskey are creatively assimilated to a robust trunk of Cubanity represented by the likes of Lecuona, Cervantes, Lezama Lima, and Martí. On the second pillar of Martían discourse, anti-imperialism, Diego's assertion is clear enough: "I don't want the Americans nor anybody else to come here and tell us what we have to do." Finally, Diego's reading of Vargas Llosa and Goytisolo points to the third pillar of Martían discourse, with a show of pan-American (or in this case, pan-Hispanic) solidarity that transcends even differences over the Revolution.

Diego's open mind and David's engagement with Diego in those terms are conducive to precisely the kind of dialectic give and take that Alea defined in *The Viewer's Dialectic*, in which the truth is not in one or another position, but in the confrontation between them, and in what that confrontation suggests to the spectator. Applied to politics and sexuality, we can deduce from this that the meaning of *Strawberry and Chocolate* is neither with Diego nor with Miguel (i.e., homosexual or heterosexual, critical or dogmatic, exiled or not) but "in the confrontation between both and the main character [David], and what that suggests to the spectator within the general context of the film."[29]

Exile

Homosexuality and Marxism-Leninism are two central and emotionally charged topics in *Strawberry and Chocolate*. Exile, however, ignites even more passionate feelings among Cubans in the island and Cubans "of the community," as Cubans who have emigrated are called. In the film, this is reflected by the fact that the two most heated and passionate debates between David and Diego center on exile, both internal and external. The first of these two arguments takes place after David asks Diego why he is homosexual. The conversation quickly turns to the question of being or not being a revolutionary, whereupon Diego gives an impassioned defense of his credentials as a revolutionary and as an independent thinker. Because of that independence, Diego suggests, he has lost his illusions about the Revolution. His patriotism, however, remains intact. For someone who is strongly identified with his nation, the feeling of ostracism on political and sexual grounds is a heavy blow. But add to that the discrimination and rejection that homosexuality brings with it, and the two—ostracism plus discrimination—add up to internal exile.

The second impassioned argument between David and Diego takes place after Diego confesses "Me voy del país" ("I am leaving the country.") David reads in this pronouncement the words of a traitor, and Diego's response to that insinuation is one of the most memorable in the film. Diego's explanation of the consequences of speaking his mind—loss of career opportunities in the cultural sector and forced manual labor in agriculture or construction—effectively makes him a political dissident. Dissidence and treason, however, are shown to be quite distinct phenomena. As was the case with homosexuality, the film makes the issue of exile a much more complex phenomenon than the black or white, patriot or *gusano* dichotomy of official discourse. Exiles are not all counterrevolutionaries or traitors, as Cuban authorities paint them, but neither are all of them fleeing from terror and oppression, as the Cuban American National Foundation claims. Diego's fate inside Cuba is not much different from the fate of openly homosexual educators throughout Western democracies: stigmatization and loss of career opportunities. The difference is that in Cuba this was a matter of official policy, whereas in most other countries it is a matter of course. The more important issue is pluralism. In this respect it is revealing that Diego is going to Europe and not Miami, where political pluralism with regards to Cuba is as hard to come by as in Cuba proper, and where economic and family factors play a more important role in attracting Cubans than political factors. This choice of exile means that Diego, unlike the majority of exiles after 1965, was not an economic refugee who only needs to claim (no evidence needed) that he was "fleeing from Communist oppression" (under Eisenhower) or "escaping Communism" (under Johnson, Nixon, and Carter until 1980) in order to qualify as a political refugee in the United States. In a serious and balanced study of the Cuban migration to the United States from 1959 to 1995, Felix Roberto Masud-Piloto has the following to say about the logic behind this preferential treatment and the change that occurred in the reasons for exile after 1965:

> Many Cuban exiles, especially those who left between 1959 and 1962, were undoubtedly escaping political persecution, and they certainly deserved political asylum. On the other hand, the United States had its own political motives for accepting as many refugees from the revolution as possible. Unlike all pre-1959 Cuban governments, the revolutionary leadership refused to be dominated by the United States, and it posed a serious threat to U.S. economic and strategic interests, thus attracting the ire of successive U.S. administrations.

In response to the revolutionary government's "defiance," President Eisenhower initiated an unwritten open-door policy for Cuban refugees to weaken and discredit Castro and the revolution. The strategy was expected to cause a crippling "brain drain" and an embarrassing mass exodus. With a leftist revolution that was widely admired throughout Latin America, it was feared that Cuba would undermine the U.S. Cold War "sphere of influence." The policy worked in the short run by denying Cuba many of its best-trained minds. Ironically, the policy also worked to Cuba's long-run advantage by eliminating the most disaffected sectors of the old order and allowing the revolution a quicker and smoother consolidation of power. . . .

By the mid-1960s, the political motive of the Cuban migration declined. Thereafter, most Cubans who left the country did so for economic reasons or to reunify families. In the absence of regular migratory channels between the United States and Cuba, and to diffuse potentially serious internal discontent, the Cuban government decided to allow exiled Cubans to pick up relatives at the port of Camarioca in 1965, and at the port of Mariel in 1980. The two boatlifts and the airlift between 1965 and 1973 ultimately brought 400,000 Cubans to the United States.[30]

Diego, unlike many or even most of the Cuban refugees after 1965, but especially after 1980, was not fleeing for economic reasons but rather for political breathing space. His departure from Cuba is a double loss to the nation in the sense that it is part of a crippling brain drain, but also in the sense that it represents the elimination of an opposition that is sympathetic to many aspects of the Revolution. The brain drain caused by the departure of thousands of counterrevolutionary professionals in the early years of the Revolution was not lamented by many in Cuba, despite the accompanying loss in technical and entrepreneurial vigor. The loss of a truly patriotic, revolutionary, and anti-imperialistic professional twenty years into the Revolution, however, represents a dangerous squandering of Cuba's best and brightest hope for the future.

The politics of exile changed dramatically after the Mariel boatlift in 1980. This explains Alea's decision to situate the film in 1979. In his own words, "1979 represents the end of a historical period, because the Mariel boatlift occurred in 1980, and that caused many things to change. So we preferred not to burden our plot with additional complications."[31] The "additional complications" included several developments in the United States and several changes in Cuban domestic policy. On the U.S. side, the boatlift represented an ethical dilemma for the Immigration and Naturalization Program, which had to work out the double standard accorded to Haitians and Cubans arriving by the thousands into Florida. The temporary solution was the creation of a category called "Cuban-Haitian Entrant (status pending)." In the long term, Haitians arriving after 1981 were again deported to their country of origin to face almost certain imprisonment and probably death, whereas

Cubans were again automatically granted political asylum. The change to the status quo ante had much to do with the beginning of the Reagan-Bush conservative backlash and its escalation of the Cold War, especially in Central America. On the Cuban side, the consequences of the Mariel boatlift were even more pronounced, as befits a small country that suddenly, in a single year, lost over 125,000 people. Despite Castro's attempts to turn an embarrassing situation to his advantage by including several thousand "criminals" and "antisocials" among those leaving the island, the impression caused by thousands of ordinary Cubans sacrificing jobs, homes, and friends for an uncertain future in a strange land forced Castro to undertake a series of token measures to improve the conditions that led to that exodus. Some of these measures were the normalization of relations between Church and state,[32] the end of official discrimination against homosexuals,[33] and the partial regulation of the black market to allow the buying and selling of surplus produce on a small scale.[34] The film, therefore, would not have had the same poignancy had it been situated the 1980s as opposed to 1979, before all the changes that followed Mariel.

Notwithstanding the previous discussion, the fact remains: *Strawberry and Chocolate* was produced and directed in 1993, at a time of profound economic and ideological crisis in Cuba. In light of the changes in world politics brought about by the disintegration of the Soviet Union—independent Russia's disavowal of Marxism-Leninism and the subsequent end of subsidies to Cuba—the film takes on the very immediate task of formulating a Cuban nationalism that is no longer Marxist-Leninist but does not ignore the history of the previous thirty-some years of revolutionary experiment. In this sense, David and Diego represent the best of the two Cubas, the one inside and the one in exile, and their friendship symbolizes the aspired ideal of a Cuban nationalism that promotes unity of purpose while recognizing and accepting diversity in outlook. Their friendship is an example for all Cubans—those inside the island and those scattered around the world—to follow. It exhorts them to seek what is common to them and to develop a dialogue from there, with respect for each other's positions and, above all, with the willingness and the expectation to change in the process, much like David and Diego changed for the better as their friendship developed and deepened—in short, a call to reconciliation on an international scale.

Guantanamera

The idea for *Guantanamera* came in the mid-eighties from a newspaper article about a new plan to transport cadavers over long distances: "The idea was ridiculous, because in the end, with this relay you don't save any gasoline, and instead the whole operation gets complicated and creates more problems . . . and that was supposed to be a solution."[35] From this idea, Eliseo

Alberto Diego prepared a script and submitted it to ICAIC in 1986, but the project was shelved until after the success of *Strawberry and Chocolate*, when a Spanish producer secured the necessary funding. Alea, Juan Carlos Tabío, and Eliseo Alberto Diego then set to the task of updating the original script, and in less than a year they began filming.

The film begins with the upbeat tempo of Joseito Fernández's song from the 1950s, "Guantanamera," whose lyrics inform us that the plane on the screen is bringing Yoyita from Havana to her hometown to receive a cultural award. The song, here and elsewhere, functions as a chorus in a Greek tragedy, commenting and informing the spectator about the motivations and conflicts of the main characters. Georgina, Yoyita's niece and wife of Adolfo (the bureaucrat who comes up with the idea of the funeral relays), accompanies her to the ceremony, after which Yoyita visits her teenage sweetheart, Cándido, and dies of happiness in his arms.

Shocked but resigned, Georgina and Cándido accompany Adolfo in what he expects to be his ticket to political rehabilitation and what turns out to be, for the spectator, a road movie. As the two-car funeral cortege makes its way from province to province, having to change autos and fill out paperwork at each stop, a happy-go-lucky truck driver called Mariano crosses paths with them several times. Mariano, it turns out, had been Georgina's student at the university, and had even written a love letter to her on the last day of classes a few years back. But Georgina never went back to teach because her unorthodox economic views did not fit the official line. Instead, she returned to Guantánamo to become a subservient housewife. Predictably, Georgina (Gina) and Mariano end up together, while Adolfo ends up alone, poised on a pedestal and ready to be taken away by Ikú, a young girl who personifies Death. Interspersed throughout the film are some very keen observations about love and death and more than a few comic scenes in the style of customs and manners.

Guantanamera is full of self-references that allow Alea to rethink or revisit some of his past films. The most obvious self-reference is to *Death of a Bureaucrat*, with Alea poking fun at bureaucrats and at the solemnity of death. Other films, however, also come to mind. In the scene in Bayamo, for example, the tour guide explains how the city had survived and prospered through contraband in times past:

> Throughout the sixteenth, seventeenth, and eighteenth centuries, Bayamo was the most important smuggling center of the island, outwitting the restrictions and iron-fisted commercial monopoly of the Spanish Crown, which was putting the breaks on economic life. The illicit commerce with the English, the French, and the Dutch was practiced by all citizens, including the administrative, military, and ecclesiastic authorities. The dealings with the Protestants, who were stigmatized as being heretics, influenced not

only economic life, but also culture and politics. In this way, books which had been banned by the Inquisition entered, as well as the liberal and progressive ideas of the times. Not by chance was Bayamo the first city to rise up in arms against the colonial rule that was putting the brakes on the country's development.

The information is clearly a reference to the economic survival in contemporary Cuba, but it also takes us back to *A Cuban Fight against Demons*, in which the town contrabandist represented the best interests of the town, versus the authoritarianism and feudalism of the town priest.

Another example of self-referencing is the parable of death and immortality. As the funeral procession gets close to Havana, and with images of heavy rain followed by beautiful sunshine, the following legend of immortality is narrated off-voice:

> In the beginning, Oloffin called Oddua and asked him to create life. Oddua called Obbatala and told him: "The World is done. Done is the good and the evil, the beautiful and the ugly, the small and the big; now it is time to make Man and Woman." Obbatala made Man and Woman and gave them life; Obbatala made life, but he forgot to make death.
>
> Years went by, and the men and the women got older, but did not die. They were so old that they had to work together like little ants to move even a single tree branch, and over eighty arms were needed to cut a small pumpkin. The earth was filled with old men and women who were thousands of years old and who continued to govern according to their old laws; the young ones had to obey them and to carry them around, because that's how things had always been. The burden got heavier with each passing day.
>
> The young ones clamored so much that one day their pleas reached the ears of Oloffin, and Oloffin saw that the World was not as good as he had planned it. He saw that pain had taken over the World, and that everything crumbled under the weight of time, so that he himself felt old and tired to begin again what he had done so badly.
>
> Then Oloffin told Oddua to call Iku so that he could take charge of the matter. Iku saw that it was necessary to end the time when people did not die.
>
> Iku then proceeded to make it rain for thirty days and thirty nights nonstop, until everything was left underwater. Only children and the young could climb the highest trees and the tallest mountains. The whole Earth became a vast river with no shores.
>
> On day thirty one the rain stopped. The young then saw that the Earth was cleaner and more beautiful, and hurried to give thanks to Iku, because he had put an end to immortality.[36]

As in Sebastián's parable of Truth and Falseness in *The Last Supper*, this parable in *Guantanamera* transcends the narrative limits of the film to become a comment on contemporary Cuba and on Alea's own impending death. On the one hand, the parable points to a better future when the old guard finally gives way to a new generation with fresh ideas and newfound energy to tackle the very real problems facing contemporary Cuba. The message is clear: Cuba too will soon see the end of the current flood of problems, bury its dead, and go on with life without the burden of old ways that have become too heavy to carry. On the other hand, the parable alludes to Alea's own impending death from lung cancer:

> What one sees very clearly when faced with death is one's own life, but from a new perspective. You begin to take note of how marvelous it ought to be, which it is, in many ways, and how frustrating it is not to have lived it fully. Because so much is lost in trivialities, in stupid aggressions, in all those things that hurt us in vain, and things don't have to be that way. Life could be more beautiful, more fulfilling, if we filled it with those marvelous things it offers, like emotion . . . . But we turn it into a hell, with wars, with politics; with that enormous stupidity called politics, which makes us waste so much time.[37]

Clearly, Alea is thinking of his own death in *Guantanamera* but also, one may add, of his own politically motivated attacks against Néstor Almendros. Another notable example of self-referencing, this time with *Strawberry and Chocolate*, comes during the verbal fight between Adolfo and Gina after she gets fed up with his pedantry:

GINA: I'm tired of not thinking. If I make a mistake, well, I make a mistake, just like everybody else. Oh, and by the way, that radio program that José Luis has been offering me, I'm going to accept it.

ADOLFO: A radio program? And the kind that gives guidance to young people? Fuck! You were not able to guide your own daughter!

GINA: I'm fed up with your accusations that I'm the one responsible for Niurka's departure to Miami.

ADOLFO: Oh! And isn't it so? Who else let her hang out with all those long-haired intellectualloids?; who let her listen to all those puny little songs?; who let her read the perestroika magazines and all that other shit?! How the fuck was she not going to leave if you poisoned her brain?!

GINA: Oh, Adolfo! Niurka did not leave because of her friends, or because of any songs or because of what she read. She left because she had to do all of that in secret, and she was up to here (pointing to her neck) with it!

There are two reasons why this exchange is important. On the one hand, it reflects Alea's own experience with having a daughter living in Miami, sponsored by none other than Néstor Almendros. For Alea, then, exile was not simply a theoretical or political issue, but a very personal problem that affected family and friends. On the other hand, the dialogue between Gina and Adolfo drives home the point that many people who left Cuba did so to escape the imposed morality of an authoritarian patriarch(ism) and to enjoy freedom of expression. And yet, freedom of expression is not so much the problem as is the exercise of that freedom in the political and economic spheres. Alea has commented on this distinction:

> I don't think [cinema] has a very important impact on the changes in society. There are other weapons, instruments that are much more direct. Film works at a cultural level; its influence is large, but revolutions are not made from the theaters. Films reflect reality, they can stimulate thinking, point the way. But films are not harangues, nor will they make a people rise up and become aware of the injustice in which they live. It's a grain of sand.[38]

These remarks come from an interview in 1995, two years after *Strawberry and Chocolate* convinced Alea of the limited political impact of his films. They may make people think, but that may or may not translate into action. The unbridled optimism of *The Viewer's Dialectic*, in which Alea wrote of film's potential to effect changes in behavior, has, at the end of his life and in the middle of the worst crisis Cuba has seen since the Revolution began, transformed itself into a conditional optimism, a "grain of sand" in a vast sea of uncertainties. And yet *Guantanamera* is ultimately an optimistic film, with its parable of death and immortality reflected in the final scene of Gina and Diego riding together into the symbolically charged rain, as an upbeat version of the song "Guantanamera" comments on their love.

7
Conclusions

A diachronic view of Alea's films reveals two recurring themes: the role of the intellectual in a revolutionary society and religion and its place in Cuban history. These, in turn, are inseparable from the one event that informs all aspects of life in Cuba since 1959: the Cuban Revolution. The following concluding remarks are devoted to a discussion of these three central and recurring themes in Alea's filmography.

The Intellectual

In *The Lettered City*, Angel Rama's attempt to formulate a theory of Latin American intellectualism, the author traces the changing roles of Latin American intellectuals over six historical periods: conquest, colony, early republic, modernization, populist nationalism, and revolutions. Needless to say, these periods overlap and do not always follow in neat chronological order. Rama's thesis is that throughout these changes in political and economic circumstances, intellectuals have adapted to retain their privileged status relative to the majority of the population. As a group, Rama argues, intellectuals in Latin America have traditionally had special access to power, but have also depended on the state for a livelihood. This dependence began to crumble at the turn of the century, when advancements in public education created a domestic market of readers large enough to "enable some writers—formerly held in thrall by wealthy patrons or state sinecures—to shake off their economic dependence on the state and escape its tutelage."[1] Rubén Darío is the perfect example of this change. However, after the University Reform Movement, which began in Argentina in 1918 and spread rapidly throughout Latin America, the kind of independence from worldly affairs represented by Darío's *Azul* and, to a lesser extent, *Prosas profanas*, went out of fashion. Intellectual and artistic standing became increasingly tied to one's social commitment. Vallejo and Neruda in effect replace Darío as the new standards of excellence, not only because of the quality of their verse but also because of their progressive political views. In this new context, the Cuban Revolution presented Latin American intellectuals with the challenge to go beyond words and into action, to rethink their societal roles, and to take a strong stance either for or against the Revolution. The Bay of Pigs fiasco of 1961 and the Missile Crisis in October 1962 convinced most unconverted Latin American intellectuals, including unconvinced Cubans, of the moral obligation to support the struggling David against the Goliath of imperialism.

Ironically, the process of increasing intellectual independence that began at the turn of the century in the Southern Cone came to a halt and even reversed itself within Cuba. Intellectuals would slowly but systematically be brought under the tutelage of the state through preexisting organizations such as the University of Havana or through new ones such as the Cuban Film Institute, the Union of Writers and Artists, and Casa de las Américas, a sort of cultural clearinghouse that promotes pan-American dialogue through congresses, publications, and literary contests.

The one big difference between an intellectual's previous dependence on the state for livelihood and a Cuban intellectual who received his or her wages directly from the state was the idea that, instead of working for a privileged elite, intellectuals were now working for the masses, through largely independent state organizations. This situation was not new for Latin American intellectuals. José Vasconcelos, for example, was in a similar position when he acted as Mexico's Secretary of Education in the 1920s. Yet two things made the Cuban experience unprecedented: the extent to which all areas of intellectual activity were directed toward the overriding goal of promoting the Revolution and the enormous impression that the Revolution made on Latin American intellectuals.

The euphoria of the Revolution's early years, however, could not last forever. After 1970, Cuban intellectuals increasingly questioned the means by which the state controlled more and more aspects of life. The questioning turned into disillusionment in the 1980s, when thousands of intellectuals who had fought for the Revolution left the island, and carried into the 1990s, as increasing numbers of intellectuals who were born after 1959 decided to leave the island.

Through Alea's films one can trace these changes in the evolving role of the intellectual in revolutionary Cuba. *Stories of the Revolution* serves as a baseline. The first episode in this three-part film tells the story of an urban youth in 1957 who does not join the struggle against Batista, yet gets killed by Batista's police. The message is clear: Acquiescence amounts to collaboration with the enemy, and poetic justice calls for his death. *Memories* deals with a similar situation in that its main character, like the youth in *Stories of the Revolution*, does not join in the struggle. Now the struggle is *for* the Revolution as opposed to *against* Batista, but the basic idea remains: The intellectual faces the choice between social compromise and elitist isolation. Neither the youth in *Stories of the Revolution* nor Sergio in *Memories* chooses compromise. Sergio gets closer than the youth to revolutionary commitment, but in the end he also must die—if not literally, then figuratively through a *desgarramiento*. The story of Sergio is the story of an intellectual in transition from the prerevolutionary mentality that valued individualism above all else to a revolutionary mentality that emphasizes one's role within a much larger social project of social and economic justice.

The next three films by Alea—*A Cuban Fight against Demons*, *The Last Supper*, and *The Survivors*—were all made during the 1970s, a time when the Revolution turned authoritarian and intellectuals faced a new choice: to continue their support of the Revolution unabated or to denounce it for the growing evidence of *caudillismo*. It was a difficult decision, given the conservative backlash in Latin America: for example, the Chilean coup in 1973, the military dictatorship in Argentina, and Kissinger's ill-conceived policy toward Latin America in general. Not surprisingly, these three films explore the uneasy relationship between intellectuals and reactionary regimes. In *A Cuban Fight* the setting is the early colonial period, when priests were the intellectuals by default, and their subservience to Rome was matched by their servitude to the Crown. In *The Last Supper*, Alea explores a period of emerging bourgeois values during Spain's brief period of Enlightenment under Charles III, when scientists like Monsieur Ducle began to replace priests as the intellectuals par excellence. Here the role of the intellectual is more complicated because he becomes conscious of the conflicts between the Enlightenment ideals of freedom, equality, and fraternity on the one hand and the reality of slavery on the other. When Monsieur Ducle hides Sebastián from the *rancheadores*, for example, he could very well have asked who of the two was freer from the master. Finally, the intellectual in *The Survivors* is a historian at a time when social scientists were at the forefront of intellectual debates in Latin America. In all three cases, the intellectual serves the needs and purposes of a reactionary power: the Crown-Church alliance in *A Cuban Fight*, the emerging sugar aristocracy in *The Last Supper*, and the prerevolutionary industrial bourgeois in *The Survivors*.

The logical next step would be to explore the relationship between intellectuals and those in power in revolutionary Cuba, which is in fact what happens (up to a point) in Alea's next film, *Up to a Point* (1983). In this film Alea turns his analytical lens onto himself. The film's male protagonist is, like Alea, a Cuban filmmaker who decides to make a documentary as a way to explore an issue that has eluded the Revolution: sexism in the workplace and in the domestic sphere. Alea in this film recognizes himself as part of an intellectual tradition that includes priests, scientists, historians, and, now, artists. Yet unlike the intellectuals in his previous films, in *Up to a Point* Alea seems to be acutely self-aware of his own role as an intellectual and of the social commitment that comes with that role. And unlike the intellectuals in his previous films, with *Up to a Point* he gets the chance to please both his master, by addressing a subject of special concern to the revolutionary leadership (i.e., the integration of women into the work force), and himself, by exploring his own difficulties in accepting women as equal partners at work.

After the fall of the Berlin Wall, but especially since the beginning of the Special Period in 1991, Cuban intellectuals have increasingly questioned their assigned roles as promoters and guardians of the Revolution. Alea's last two films—*Strawberry and Chocolate* and *Guantanamera*—reflect this change in the role of the Cuban intellectual from apostle to apostate. As if to underscore the magnitude of this change, the intellectuals in these two films are no longer heterosexual white males, but rather a homosexual artist (Diego) in *Strawberry and Chocolate* and a woman professor (Gina) in *Guantanamera*. Like Sergio in *Memories*, both Diego and Gina criticize aspects of the Revolution that go against its spirit. The criticisms of Diego and Gina, however, carry more weight than those of Sergio. They have lived and fought for that spirit and don't like it being threatened (in *Strawberry and Chocolate*) by the intolerance of a machista establishment that sees homosexuality as a biological disease and artistic freedom as a bourgeois invention, or else undone (in *Guantanamera*) by the dogmatism and bureaucratism exemplified by Gina's husband.

Religion

In a memorable scene in *Strawberry and Chocolate*, Diego and his friend Germán fight over who can decide which sculptures will and will not be part of a planned exhibition. Germán holds a bust of Karl Marx, Diego holds a bust of Christ. At one point it seems as if Christ and Marx are the ones doing the fighting instead of Diego and Germán. Germán then becomes exasperated, takes a hammer, and hacks away at the bust of Marx, while Diego, devastated and pained to see his friend react so violently, salvages the Christ figure. The exhibition never takes place within the film, although I can imagine the possibility of one such exhibition materializing some day and including these statues as part of a larger exploration into the uneasy relationship between Christianity and Marxism in revolutionary Cuba. In this imagined exhibition, Alea's films would occupy a central space, as many of his films deal explicitly with Christianity and with Marxism.

The relationship between Christianity and Marxism in revolutionary Cuba has been a complex one. In the early months of the Revolution, before Castro declared the Revolution to be Marxist, relations between the different churches and the new government continued in a long Latin American tradition of friendly disagreement between freethinkers and believers, only this time freethinkers were in power and believers for the first time found themselves in an officially atheist state. After Castro's embrace of Marxism, relations between the different churches and the state deteriorated. Yet not all was confrontation. Some scholars even argue that what occurred in Cuba was an encounter of Marxism and Christianity from which Christians emerged with a stronger commitment to both the Revolution and their faith.[2] Whether one accepts this interpretation of the Marxist-Christian dialectic as a fruitful encounter or prefers the metaphor of confrontation, there is no denying the fact that both sides learned from each other and changed irrevocably in the process. This may even be the central message of Germán's sculptures, with the Christ figure pierced by the Marxist symbol par excellence—the sickle— and the Marx figure dripping blood from its forehead, as if he'd just taken off Christ's crown of thorns.

Alea's exploration of the parallels between Christianity and Marxism go beyond symbolism to questions of ideology and history. In *Memories of Underdevelopment*, for example, is a scene in which Sergio walks by a school where Hanna used to study. The school is named after Lenin, but in a flashback we find out that it used to be a Catholic school because in the place where a portrait of Lenin hangs, there used to be an altar to Our Lady of Fátima. In other words, Marxism has replaced Christianity as the moral and institutional base for education. The question that immediately comes to mind then is: How different will the Lenin School be from the old Catholic school? Will its secular teachers be just as orthodox as the priests who taught Sergio that might makes right?

In his next three films, Alea examines the role of Christianity in three different periods of Cuban history: the early colony, when the power of the Church matched that of the Crown; the beginnings of the sugar aristocracy, when priests began to be directly employed by the sugar mill owners; and under the commercial bourgeoisie, when priests' only function was to administer the sacraments. These three films in effect function together as a historical cycle that explores the larger issue of Cuban bourgeois identity; its origins in *A Cuban Fight*, its development in *The Last Supper*, and its decadence in *The Survivors*. Christianity is central to these films because it is pivotal in defining that developing identity. In *A Cuban Fight against Demons*, for example, the two protobourgeois Cubans (the freethinker and contrabandist Juan Contreras and the pious and royalist town mayor) are defined to a large extent by their relationship to the town priest, the mayor because he falls under the priest's spell and Juan Contreras because he is the priest's nemesis. Beyond these two individuals, however, the priest wields a power beyond anything imaginable in later times. Toward the end of the film, the priest succeeds in moving the town inland, and later returns to the coast to burn what is left of it. Christianity in *A Cuban Fight* is not a liberating religion but rather a tool for projecting the priests' own fears and zealousness onto the superstitious population. In *The Last Supper*, the priest loses his influence over the Count to the competing interests of an international sugar market based on a very un-Christian slave labor. Here the priest no longer serves his own interests, as in *A Cuban Fight*, but rather those of the Count. When the Count shifts his posture toward the slaves from that of steward to that of exploiter, the priest is right there next to him ready to bless the Count's new plans. The resulting hypocrisy continues under the commercial bourgeoisie, when priests like the one in *The Survivors*, or the one blessing Sergio's new furniture store in *Memories*, eased the conscience of the upper and upper-middle classes by attending to their empty rituals without the slightest concern for justice, spirituality, or brotherly love. To summarize, Christianity, or more specifically Catholicism, has been the single most important institution throughout Cuban history. As an institution it has served the Crown, the sugar barons, and the commercial bourgeoisie. The key to this survival has been its ability to adapt to the realities of each successive hegemony.

Could this also be the case in revolutionary Cuba? The Pope's visit to Cuba in January 1998 suggests so, yet Alea's films do not address Christianity as an institution when the action is set in revolutionary Cuba. Instead, one sees representations of Santería, which seems to have survived the Revolution's onslaught against organized churches in the early 1960s and even flourished to secure its place as the de facto religion of Cuba. In *Memories*, for example, a disoriented Sergio walks by a self-assured *iyabó*[3] before seeking refuge in a bookstore; in *The Last Supper*, Afro-Cuban religion and beliefs are given equal narrative weight to the Count's religion; in *Strawberry and Chocolate*, both Diego and Nancy keep home altars to Santa Bárbara-Changó; and in *Guantanamera*, Yoruban mythology (in the parable of death and immortality) has replaced the Bible as the source of moral teachings.

Unlike Catholicism or Marxism, Santería has never become old in the way that the men and women in the legend did. Rather, it has continued uninterrupted under Marxism because it is a truly popular religion with no conflict of interests with the spirit of the Revolution. Santería, Alea's films suggest, is the Cuban religion by birthright, one that grew out of the specific circumstances of Cuba and one that is free of the unproductive disputes over doctrine and orthodoxy that plague Catholicism and Marxism.

The Cuban Revolution

In the Introduction I postulated that the films of Alea are windows through which one can glimpse the Cuban Revolution from within. One of the principal reasons for focusing on *Memories of Underdevelopment*, *The Last Supper*, and *Strawberry and Chocolate* is the fact that each of these three films is symptomatic of an identifiable period in revolutionary Cuba. *Memories* corresponds to the period of triumph and reaffirmation of the Revolution, *The Last Supper* to the period of consolidation and institutionalization, and *Strawberry and Chocolate* to the period of crisis after the fall of the Berlin Wall. What each of these films says about each of these periods is as valuable to an understanding of the Revolution as what many studies of history, sociology, or economy may tell us.

In revolutionary Cuba, films are semi-official statements: "semi" because ICAIC is largely independent from meddling or interference by the central government, and "official" because it is an arm of the government nonetheless. Because of this, Alea's films can sometimes cut both ways. That is, they can be read as supportive of the central government and its policies, or as critical of that very same government, depending on how one interprets the film. In the following paragraphs I demonstrate how each of these two interpretations can be argued and upheld. First is a reading supporting the claim that Alea's films reflect the policies of the central government.

As products of a state-owned company explicitly created to "contribute to the development and enrichment of the new Humanism that inspires [the] Revolution,"[4] one would expect to find a correlation between the issues raised by government-produced films, such as Alea's, and the government's policies at the time each was produced. Indeed, one does. *Stories of the Revolution* (1960) tells three short stories of revolutionary struggle under Batista. There is a Western feel to these stories, in that there are the good guys (literally, since women play subordinate and insignificant roles) and the bad guys. And of course the good guys win, while the bad guys (whose ranks include those not fully committed to the struggle) lose or die. Two years later, *Cumbite* extolled the virtues of collective agriculture over independent farming just as the government began implementing the second and third phases of its agrarian reform program. The second phase effectively nationalized middle-sized farms, but the third phase of the program, which would have nationalized small farms, did not succeed because of strong grassroots opposition. *Death of a Bureaucrat* scoffs fun at—who else?—bureaucrats, at the same time that Fidel Castro was launching a campaign against bureaucracy.[5] In *Memories of Underdevelopment* (1968) the hero is a bourgeois who does not work and instead lives off the needs of others; in this case, the need for housing. These two facts make him suspect in a revolutionary society and help explain his alienation from the Revolution as well as his dispensability. This same logic—that having a private source of income is an obstacle to full integration to the Revolution and that it is at the root of alienation—was successfully used to justify the expropriation of the last thirty thousand small businesses remaining in Cuba in 1968. Two years later, *A Cuban Fight against Demons* (1973) portrayed a fanatical Catholic priest who used the pulpit for personal gain instead of for the promotion of the spiritual and material liberation of his flock. The film was released at a time when Fidel

Castro was working on a strategic alliance with Liberation Theologians such as Frei Betto in Brazil and Ernesto Cardenal in Nicaragua, an alliance that was to stand united against the already existing alliance between the Catholic Church and Latin American oligarchies. Fittingly, the priest in the film and his oligarch supporter die a justified death.

Alea's next film is possibly the best example of the coincidence in concerns between the central government and ICAIC. *The Last Supper* (1976), a film denouncing slavery, came out as Cuba began to send troops to help Angolan freedom fighters in their struggle against South Africa. When the Portuguese completely withdrew from Portuguese West Africa (Angola) in 1975, they left behind a country divided into two camps: the anti-Communists led by Jonas Savimbi (supported by the United States, Zambia, and South Africa) and the Marxist-oriented Popular Movement for the Liberation of Angola (MPLA), supported by Moscow money and Cuban soldiers. What had begun in 1965 as a small contingent of Cuban military advisers to the MPLA suddenly jumped in January 1976 to almost seven thousand Cuban troops and surpassed the thirty thousand level several times over the next ten years. In 1985 Fidel Castro stated that to date over 200,000 Cubans had served in Angola.[6] This level of involvement for a country of roughly ten million inhabitants is enormous and cannot have escaped Alea. Cuban artists, including Alea, embraced the subject of the African element in Cuban culture with the kind of vigor that characterizes works from the two other periods in Cuban history when Afro-Cubans took center stage in historical events and the political debates that informed them. The first of these events was the end of slavery in 1886, and it is within this debate that one should read *Francisco* (1839) by abolitionist Anselmo Suárez y Romero and *Cecilia Valdés* (1839–1879) by Cirilo Villaverde. The second of these events was the failed revolt of 1912, in which the Independent Party of Color resorted to armed rebellion after being banned. While the causal relationship between this second landmark in Afro-Cuban history and the literature produced at the time is not self-evident, the revolt is useful to help situate the works of two of Cuba's greatest writers, Lydia Cabrera and Fernando Ortiz. I submit that a third landmark in Afro-Cuban history is the deployment of tens of thousands of Cubans to Angola and Ethiopia in the 1970s and 1980s, a deployment that amounted to the first and so far only mass movement of people from the Americas to Africa, with the possible exception of the African-Americans who founded Liberia. The impulse behind this deployment was the tricontinental internationalism fostered by the recent and ongoing decolonizations in Asia, Africa, and Latin America. Not directly related to the African campaigns, but certainly important to the development of a historical consciousness needed to promote them, are Miguel Barnet's *Biografía de un cimarrón* (*Biography of a Runaway Slave*, 1967) and Fernández Retamar's essay "Calibán," (1971). In film, three works with an Afro-Cuban thematics (or *negrometrajes*) stand out: Sergio

Giral's *The Other Francisco* (1974), a feature-cum-deconstruction of Suárez y Romero's *Francisco*; Sara Gómez's incisive and moving *One Way or Another*, and Alea's *The Last Supper*.

Alea's next film, *The Survivors* (1978), is a virulent satire of an upper-middle-class family in postrevolutionary Cuba that decides to "wait it out." The film continues Alea's exploration, begun in the two previous films, of the Cuban bourgeoisie, also a favorite subject of scorn in official rhetoric. The origins of this class seem to go back to the end of the sixteenth century; on the walls of the mansion in *The Survivors* we see a portrait of the character named Evaristo from *A Cuban Fight* and another portrait of the Count from *The Last Supper*. The film also continues the previous two films' denunciation of placing individual interests over the needs of society, a "sin" committed by Evaristo in *A Cuban Fight*, the Count in *The Last Supper*, and the whole family in *The Survivors*. The message seems to be that unless present-day Cubans overcome this egotism, the Revolution will never progress, and may even end up, like Goya's *Saturn*, devouring its sons. *Up to a Point* (1983) may be seen as part of an on-and-off effort by the Cuban leadership to better understand and ultimately change the seemingly intractable problem of sexual prejudices and double standards. *Strawberry and Chocolate* (1993), for all its critiques against specific aspects of the system, actually follows the central government's lead in its calls for rectifications of past mistakes, one of the most notorious being the prosecutions of homosexuals. And finally, *Guantanamera* (1995) sings the praises of market-driven efficiency at a time when it was becoming increasingly common for the state to enter into partnerships with foreign capitalists.

The previous interpretation places Alea firmly within the category of "intellectual of the state." The other possible interpretation is more generous, and goes something like this: To call Alea (or ICAIC) a mouthpiece of the state would be a simplistic way of dismissing the fact that all of the films I just surveyed (with the exception of *Stories of the Revolution* and *Cumbite*) have enough in them to question the conclusion that they echo the policies of the central government simply because that's where the money comes from or because there exists a correspondence between some aspects of the films and some aspects of the official discourse. Looked at from a different angle, Alea's films reveal another reality: one of constructive criticism that nevertheless leaves enough interpretative room for contentious readings. For example, *Death of a Bureaucrat*, because it questions the wisdom of having the state control the ultimate destiny of one's body, could be construed as undermining the revolutionary wisdom of granting the state control over other more vital parts of citizens' lives. The case of *Memories of Underdevelopment* is more complex. Here we have a petit bourgeois who is sympathetic toward the Revolution. He does nothing to undermine or stop the revolutionary process, so his downfall is blamed on his inability to integrate as a revolutionary. The message is clear: If you are not with the Revolution, you are against it. This Manichaeism, which informs much of the revolutionary rhetoric, is undermined by people like Sergio, people who are neither *gusanos* nor revolutionaries. If the choice is between the state's ironclad Manichaeism and Sergio's more flexible if sometimes flawed worldview, an intelligent spectator would probably choose the latter. Alea's next film, *A Cuban Fight against Demons*, portrays a fanatical priest who, inspired by Divine Truth, succeeds in moving a coastal town inland. The ostensible reason is that on the coast, townspeople risk becoming infected with impure elements such as pirates or Protestants. A likelier reason is that on the coast it's becoming increasingly hard for the priest to impose his view of the world on the citizens. Here it is hard to resist drawing a parallelism with present-day priests, those party militants who instead of reciting the good news of Jesus Christ recite instead the good news of the New Man. The film ends with the priest gone crazy, preceded by an anachronistic montage featuring shots of Fidel Castro. Critics have expressed confusion over this anachronism, yet a likely explanation could be that Castro, like the priest, believes it his divine duty to purge Cubans from all impure influences and will even isolate Cuba from the rest of the world if that is what it takes. In 1973, this is certainly how things stood: a Cuba isolated from the capitalist world, for obvious reasons, but also isolated from most of the Third World for its support of the Soviet invasion of Czechoslovakia in 1968. As the state became more and more of an impediment to human development (official rhetoric notwithstanding), Alea's films became more and more critical. *The Last Supper*, filmed in 1975, may be read as an allegory of the quixotic 1970 sugar harvest. The Count in the 1790s, like Castro in 1970, focused all the resources at his disposal on increasing what would turn out to be a brutal sugar harvest. The price that each paid was not only monetary but also ideological: In both cases, Count and Castro, there was a marked shift from a humanist rhetoric to an authoritarian practice whose main purpose was to secure their respective positions of power and privilege.

Viewed today, *The Survivors* seems a caricature of the entrenched government in Cuba after the fall of the Berlin Wall. Like the patriarch in the film, Castro has decided for himself and for all the members of his household to wait out the Revolution—the one in Eastern Europe and the former Soviet Union, that is. Yet the Special Period is still in effect after more than a decade of increasing hopelessness. Will there be a rebellion, as in the film? Or is there still hope for a peaceful transition of power?

The 1980s were not a very productive decade for Alea as a director. His only two features during these years—*Up to a Point* and *Letters from the Park*—seem to have lost the edge of his previous films. At a personal level, however, the 1980s were Alea's happiest years, a time when his relationship with actress Mirta Ibarra blossomed and deepened. With the Special Period and the crisis in collective confidence that accompanied its implementation, Alea returned to directing overtly political films. *Strawberry and Chocolate*, the smash hit of 1993, criticizes state "mistakes" more than any previous film produced by ICAIC, with the exception of *Alice in Wondertown*. In fact, according to Alea, *Alice in Wondertown* paved the way for *Strawberry and Chocolate*.[7] Paulo Antonio Paranaguá has written the following about the events leading to the censorship of *Alice in Wondertown*:

> In May 1991 [immediately following the announcement of the Special Period], the authorities in Havana restructured the organization of film production: ICAIC was to merge with the television studio and with the Armed Forces studio under the direction of Enrique Román, the former director of the paper *Granma* [the official newspaper of the Cuban Communist Party]. ICAIC, the first cultural organization created by the Cuban Revolution, would thus lose the autonomy it had vigorously defended for all that time. Consequently, the filmmakers mobilized to contest such a decision while ICAIC's president, Julio García Espinosa, tendered his resignation. . . . The mobilization of filmmakers, ICAIC workers and artists in general was such that the reorganization [which had been] publicly announced and decided at the highest level was suspended—an event almost unheard of under Castro. Alfredo Guevara, fired ten years before under pressure from "hard liners" (dogmatists) and neo-Stalinists, was recalled to head ICAIC again. . . . One month later, tension mounted further: the film *Alicia en el pueblo de Maravillas* was withdrawn four days after its release in ten cinemas in Havana, on 13 June. *Granma* condemned the "exaggerated pessimism" of this political satire and resolutely rejected its "defeatism, hopelessness and bitterness." . . . In December 1991, the Festival of Havana was again held in spite of growing difficulties: passing from the defensive to rehabilitation in the space of a few months, Alfredo Guevara and Daniel Díaz Torres solemnly (ceremoniously) presented [there] *Alice in Wondertown*. However, the joint pressure of practically paralyzed production and of a rarefied political climate [did] not encourage production.[8]

With production practically paralyzed because of these events and the economic crisis, ICAIC began to look for partnerships for *Strawberry and Chocolate* as well as for Alea's last film, *Guantanamera*. For both, ICAIC was still the equivalent of the executive producer, yet the fact that most of the production money came from abroad meant that he and other directors at ICAIC were now de facto independent directors in an international market. This, along with the fact that Alea knew he would soon die, may explain the radical change between his last two films and the rest of his oeuvre. Gone was the need to allegorize, as in *The Last Supper*, *The Survivors*, and *A Cuban Fight against Demons*. Gone as well was the self-centered and alienated intellectual of *Memories of Underdevelopment* and *Up to a Point*.

Instead, the setting in *Strawberry and Chocolate* (notwithstanding the subtitle in the opening sequence that reads "Havana 1979") is contemporary,[9] and its main character an intellectual who is certain of his views and of the need for change in the status quo. The same may be said of Gina, the ex-professor of economics in *Guantanamera*. Like Diego, she has been pushed aside as much by her unorthodox economic, social, and political views as by a sexuality that crosses the strict boundaries set by those in power.

The two interpretations of Alea's oeuvre that I have just outlined may seem contradictory. Yet in many ways they actually complement and inform each other. It is not a question of *either* one *or* the other, but rather a realization that *both* present different sides of the same coin. As Alea wrote in *The Viewer's Dialectic*, the truth does not lie in one or the other position, "nor in the sum of both, but rather in the confrontation between both . . . and what that suggests to the spectator within the general context of the film."[10] Theoretically speaking, then, one may speak of Alea's "dialogism" or "double-voicing." In *Problems of Dostoevsky's Poetics*, Bakhtin defines double-voicing as "discourse with an orientation toward someone else's discourse."[11] The orientation may be one in which the author agrees with the other's discourse, in which case we're dealing with unidirectional double-voicing. (By citing Bakhtin, for example, I am entering a unidirectional dialogue with him because I agree with what he's saying.) When, on the other hand, the orientation toward the other's discourse is one of collision or disagreement, we're dealing with varidirectional double-voicing. Many of Alea's characters—Sergio in *Memories of Underdevelopment*, Monsieur Ducle in *The Last Supper*, Julio in *The Survivors*, and Diego in *Strawberry and Chocolate*, among others—are good examples of varidirectional double-voicing. All these characters are, in one way or another, disagreeing with the hegemonic discourse within the film and outside of it. It should come as no surprise, then, that with the exception of *Stories of the Revolution* and *Cumbite* (the two films Alea considered his least representative), all of Alea's films are parodic and/or ironic, precisely the kind of style associated with varidirectional double-voicing.

This does not mean that Alea was a dissenter. Without a doubt, Alea was committed to the Revolution, and his success as a director is inseparable from the success of the Revolution. On the other hand, Alea's political awareness dates to the 1940s and 1950s, so that his baseline for assessing the progress in Cuba was probably the short-lived presidency of Ramón Grau San Martín in 1933–1934. Compared to this brief period of political openness and economic improvement for the masses, the 1960s must have seemed to Alea the continuation of an interrupted project for national sovereignty, progressive politics, and economic justice. After 1970, when Castro took a visible authoritarian turn, the alternative must have seemed to be a return to the status quo ante, much as had happened with the Batista coup that toppled the Grau government in 1934, so Alea's continuing public support of Castro is at least understandable, especially in the context of U.S. aggression toward Latin America during the Nixon administration. All of this is of course speculation on a subject that Alea has never discussed in any of his published interviews. But it helps to make sense of what seems, from the outside, a struggle by Alea to balance support for the Revolution with criticisms to a central government that had turned against the Revolution in many ways.

The lesson to be drawn from Alea's films may be that the Revolution has been a partial success and a partial failure. In *Memories of Underdevelopment*, for example, the successes include a collective sense of purpose evident in the preparations for the Cuban Missile Crisis; the politicization of the masses evident in the street demonstrations as well as in Elena's innocent question to Sergio, "Are you a revolutionary?"; and the implementation of justice based on evidence rather than on influence, as Sergio's acquittal makes clear. On the other hand, one drawback of the Revolution that stands out in *Memories* is the inefficient and excessive bureaucratization of life, evident in the sequence in which housing inspectors ask Sergio (and the spectator) a series of questions that seem unnecessarily intrusive. The same may be said of *The Last Supper*. Viewed as an allegory, this film is a critique of the Revolution's authoritarian turn in 1970, yet the criticism is balanced by the implicit recognition of the Revolution's successes in improving the lot of Afro-Cubans and in defending the rights of the oppressed in Africa. And finally, in *Strawberry and Chocolate*, the continuing and ubiquitous presence of the Committees for the Defense of the Revolution and the possibility of going to jail for the "crime" of meeting with foreign emissaries stand out as unjustified relics of an earlier epoch when such things made more sense. At the same time, the fact that a poor country lad like David can get a university education—even if it is an education geared toward indoctrination into Marxist ideology—speaks volumes of a process that places a high priority on education.

Overall, the trend in Alea's films has been toward more open criticism of the central government. This makes sense, given the central government's emphasis on the creation of what Tzvi Medin calls a "monolithic democracy" whose aim is "to emphasize the importance of the involvement of the masses—but masses who are uniform in their revolutionary outlook."[12] In such a democracy, the pluralism and freedom necessary for personal creativity and socioeconomic development are increasingly hard to find. Yet Alea never lost hope. A humanist throughout, he always defended the ideals of the Revolution, if not always its methods. Even in 1993, with the economy in crisis and hardly any indications of impending changes in Castro's hold on power, *Strawberry and Chocolate* points forward to the day when heterodox Cubans will promote the spirit of the Revolution with greater individual freedom, a healthy dose of tolerance, and a sense of solidarity that transcends important but not insurmountable differences. In his last published interview,

Alea summed up his position as both apostle and apostate of the Revolution and explained why he remained in Cuba despite the ever-growing difficulties:

> Well, some say that I'm a dissident because I critique the Cuban reality, and others that I'm a propagandist for the government because with that criticism I try to make others believe that in Cuba there is liberty when in fact it does not exist. . . . The truth is, I am neither one thing nor the other. . . .
>
> Of course, I criticize everything within the Revolution that I think is a distortion of those objectives and those paths of hope; that is, I criticize everything that has sidetracked us to the point of placing us in the position we are in today, in a crisis that is very dangerous and very distressing. In that sense I am a critic, but I am not a dissenter. With regards to what the others say that I am a propagandist, . . . in that case I can only say that one would have to go directly to the content of my films. Ah, of course they are complex films, critical films, but precisely because of that, they are also an answer to the image that certain people give of Cuba from the outside, which is also a distorted image, a superficial image where our situation is not analyzed. . . .
>
> I've said everything I've wanted to say. And having the possibility of being much better off outside of Cuba, I have decided against it. . . . I haven't done it because of a problem of . . . I don't know how to explain it. Because it's not a rational decision, that's true, I could have lived better in other places, and in Cuba I submit myself to a routine that is very uncomfortable . . . . But I think that in Cuba there existed values that don't exist in other places, and I deeply lament the way those values are being perverted, and so I try to fight for their preservation . . . it's a vital necessity, and a very personal one.[13]

To view and study Alea's films is to see revolutionary Cuba through the eyes of the island-nation's most important and consistently critical filmmaker. On the whole, the picture that emerges is one of a complex reality that does not fit into the neat binarisms of the Cold War or the Manicheanism that has plagued discussions about the Revolution. Rather, all of his films give testimony to a collective project full of contradictions, a process that has been, successively, progressive and reactionary, machista and feminist, dogmatic and tolerant, heroic and tragic. To paraphrase Alea,[14] it is a project whose truth does not lie in any of these poles, but rather in their confrontation, and especially in what that confrontation suggests within a context that includes the Cold War, Latin America's revolutionary struggles for emancipation, and Cuba's own specific circumstances.

Notes

All translations from sources in Spanish and French are my own, with the exception of citations from Alea's *The Viewer's Dialectic*, for which I used the English translation.

Introduction

1. Of the first case, films such as *El otro Francisco* (*The Other Francisco*, 1974) or *Retrato de Teresa* (*Portrait of Teresa*, 1979) come to mind: well-made films whose didacticism was intended to help in the creation of a revolutionary consciousness. Of the second case, *P.M.* (1960) and *Alicia en el pueblo de Maravillas* (*Alice in Wondertown*, 1990) are the most notorious examples of films that were censured because they were deemed counterrevolutionary by well-placed people in the central government.

2. See Ambrosio Fornet, *Tomás Gutiérrez Alea: Una retrospectiva crítica* (La Habana: Letras cubanas, 1987); Silvia Oroz, *Tomás Gutiérrez Alea: los filmes que no filmé* (La Habana: UNEAC, 1989); José Antonio Evora's *Tomás Gutiérrez Alea* (Madrid: Cátedra, 1996); and its predecessor, *Tomás Gutiérrez Alea: poesía y revolución*, ed. José Antonio Evora (Huesca: 22 Festival de Cine de Huesca, Instituto de Cooperación Iberoamericana, Departamento de Educación y Cultura del Gobierno de Aragón, 1994).

3. Peter Brooks, *The Melodramatic Imagination. Balzac, Henry James and the Mode of Excess* (New Haven: Yale UP, 1976), 14–15.

4. Tomás Guitérrez Alea, *The Viewer's Dialectic* (La Habana: José Martí Publishing House, 1988), 81.

5. Eduard Said, *Orientalism* (New York: Pantheon Books, 1978), 3.

6. Román de la Campa, *Latin Americanism* (Minneapolis: U of Minnesota P, 1999).

7. Aníbal González, "Literary Criticism in Spanish America," *The Cambridge History of Latin American Literature, Vol. II: The Twentieth Century*, ed.

Roberto González Echevarría and Enrique Pupo-Walker (Cambridge: Cambridge UP, 1996), 425–57.
8. Ibid., 451.

Chapter 1: Context

1. Roberto Fernández Retamar, "Rushes of Titón," trans. Jane Marcus Delgado, *Cuba Update* (Summer 1997): 8.
2. Ibid., 8.
3. See Françoise Escarpit, " 'Je n'ai pas toujours été cinéaste': Les 'années Titón' avant la révolution," in *Cinemas d'Amerique latine* 5 (1997): 81–82.
4. Arturo Agramonte, *Cronología del Cine Cubano* (La Habana: Ediciones ICAIC, 1966), 116.
5. Julianne Burton, "Film and Revolution in Cuba. The First Twenty-Five Years," in *New Latin American Cinema*, Vol. 2, ed. Michael T. Martin (Detroit: Wayne UP, 1997), 126.
6. Ibid., 127.
7. Tzvi Medin, *Cuba: The Shaping of Revolutionary Consciousness*, trans. Martha Grenzback (Boulder, CO: L. Rienner Publishers, 1990), 169.
8. Ambrosio Fornet, *Alea, una retrospectiva crítica* (La Habana: Letras Cubanas, 1987), 9.
9. These are the project's principles as summarized by Ambrosio Fornet, cited in Zuzana Pick, *The New Latin American Cinema: A Continental Project* (Austin: U of Texas P, 1993), 20–21.
10. See Julianne Burton, "Modernist Form in *Land in Anguish* and *Memories of Underdevelopment*," *Post Scripts* 3.2 (1984): 65–84.
11. Thomas E. Skidmore and Peter H. Smith, *Modern Latin America* (New York: Oxford UP, 1989), 174.
12. Ibid., 209.
13. Ibid., 210.
14. Zuzana Pick, *The New Latin American Cinema: A Continental Project* (Austin: U of Texas P, 1993), 15.
15. Ibid., 4.
16. Fernando Birri, "For a National, Realist, Critical, and Popular Cinema," in *New Latin American Cinema*. Vol. 1, ed. Michael T. Martin (Detroit: Wayne State UP, 1997), 86–94.

Chapter 2: The Early Years

1. Silvia Oroz, *Los filmes que no filmé* (La Habana: UNEAC, 1989), 31.
2. Edmundo Desnoes, "Habla un director," *Revolución* [La Habana] January 8, 1963: n. pag.
3. "[*Cumbite*] was not a film that I sought out, but rather a film that fell on my lap. I made it without passion." Cited in Oroz, *Los filmes que no filmé*, 79.
4. R. Montero, "La muerte de un burócrata. Entrevista con Tomás Gutiérrez Alea," *Cine Cubano* 35 (1966): 14–19.
5. Oroz, *Los filmes que no filmé*, 93.

6. Ibid., 93–94.
7. Ibid., 40–41.
8. David Cook, *A History of Narrative Film* (New York: W.W. Norton & Company, 1996), 425.
9. Tomás Gutiérrez Alea, *Las 12 sillas* (La Habana: Ediciones ICAIC, 1963), 7.
10. Desnoes, "Habla un director," n. pag.
11. Ugo Ulive, "2 Historias de 12 sillas," *Cine Cubano* 6 (1962): 22.
12. Desnoes, "Habla un director," n. pag.
13. Oroz, *Los filmes que no filmé*, 79.
14. In José Antonio Evora, "Un cine de síntesis y revelación," in *Tomás Gutiérrez Alea: poesía y revolucion*, ed. José Antonio Evora (Huesca: 22 Festival de Cine de Huesca, Instituto de Cooperación Iberoamericana; Departamento de Educación y Cultura del Gobierno de Aragón, 1994), 156.
15. Michael Chanan, *The Cuban Image* (London: British Film Institute, 1985), 205.
16. Carlos N. Broullon, "Interview with Tomás Gutiérrez Alea" (press release), Berkeley, CA: Tricontinental Film Center, n.d: 3.
17. G. Colpart, *"Cumbite," Cine al Día* [Caracas] 12 (1971): 25–26.
18. B. R. Rich, "Death of a Bureaucrat: Madcap Comedy Cuban Style," *Jump Cut* 22 (1980): 30.

Chapter 3: *Memories of Underdevelopment*

1. José Antonio Évora, "El rábano por la raíz," *Juventud Rebelde* [La Habana], September 10, 1988, n. pag.
2. Julianne Burton, *"Memories of Underdevelopment* in the Land of Overdevelopment," *Cineaste* 8.1 (1977): 17.
3. Nelson Rodríguez, interview with Jorge Ruffinelli, n.d.
4. Burton, *"Memories of Underdevelopment* in the Land of Overdevelopment," 20.
5. Évora, "El rábano por la raíz," n. pag.
6. All of these examples are taken from Ambrosio Fornet, *Alea, una retrospectiva crítica* (La Habana: Letras Cubanas, 1987), 103–43.
7. Cited in Tomás Gutiérrez Alea, *The Viewer's Dialectic* (La Habana: José Martí Publishing House, 1988), 70.
8. See Don Allen, *"Memories of Underdevelopment," Sight and Sound* [London] (Fall 1969): 212–13; and Andrew Sarris, cited in Alea, *The Viewer's Dialectic*, 70.
9. Fornet, *Alea, una retrospectiva crítica*, 98.
10. Burton, *"Memories of Underdevelopment* in the Land of Overdevelopment," 16–17.
11. William Class Alexander, "Class, Film Language and Popular Cinema," *Jump Cut* 30 (1985): 47.
12. Sergei Eisenstein, "Un acercamiento dialéctico a la forma cinematográfica," *Cine Cubano* 54–55 (n.d.): 98.
13. Daniel Díaz Torres, "Encuesta sobre el cine cubano," *La Gaceta de Cuba* (August–September 1966): n. pag.

14. Cited in Burton, "*Memories of Underdevelopment* in the Land of Overdevelopment," 20.

15. Throughout the following description I will borrow from the continuity script as it appears in *Memories of Underdevelopment* (New Brunswick, NJ: Rutgers UP, 1990): 31–110. I will not use quotation marks, even though some of the descriptions that follow are verbatim or almost verbatim reproductions from this source. The reason is simple: If I use quotation marks, I will end up blocking the flow of the reading because I often change or rearrange the words and phrases in the original. In those cases where ideas come from sources other than the continuity script, I will note so with a footnote.

16. In the description of the first two sequences I borrow heavily and freely from Virginia Lin Keller, "Where Subject Meets Society: Modernist Narration and Bourgeois Alienation," in *Multiple Points of View: Dialectics of Film Narration*, Ph.D. diss., Northwestern U, 1989, 93–117. See explanation in previous note.

17. Burton, "*Memories of Underdevelopment* in the Land of Overdevelopment," 18.

18. Ibid., 20.

19. Évora, "El rábano por la raíz," n. pag.

20. I owe this information to Prof. Jorge Ruffinelli.

21. Nelson Rodríguez, interview with Jorge Ruffinelli, n.d.

22. E. Fernández, "Witnesses Always Everywhere: The Rhetorical Strategies of *Memories of Underdevelopment*," *Wide Angle* 4.2 (1980): 52–55.

23. Andy Engel, "Entrevistas con directores de largometraje, directores de fotografía, escritores, músicos," *Cine Cubano* 23–25 (1964): 68.

24. Julianne Burton, "Tomás Gutiérrez Alea: Más allá del reflejo de la realidad," in *Cine y cambio social en América Latina*, ed. Julianne Burton (México: Editorial Diana, 1991), 176–77.

25. Interestingly enough, a new translation of Aristotle's *Poetics* defines catharsis as the discovery of a deeper level of reality. Aristotle and Brecht, it seems, may not be as far apart theoretically as Brecht thought. See Cynthia Ramsey, "Third Cinema in Latin America: Critical Theory in Recent Works," *Latin American Research Review* 23.1 (Winter, 1988): 266–75.

26. Évora, "El rábano por la raíz," n. pag.

27. Sergei Eisenstein, in *Notes of a Film Director* (New York: Dover Publications, 1970), 54.

28. Ibid., 55.

29. Northorp Frye, *Anatomy of Criticism: Four Essays* (Princeton, NJ: Princeton UP, 1957), 41.

30. Ibid., 34.

31. Michael Chanan, *The Cuban Image: Cinema and Cultural Politics in Cuba* (London: British Film Institute, 1985), 218.

32. That is, it goes back to the first half of the nineteenth century, and to the novel *Cecilia Valdés*, by Cirilo Villaverde.

33. Steven Best, "Baudrillard, Jean," in *Encyclopedia of Contemporary Literary Theory: Approaches, Scholars, Terms*, ed. Irena R. Makaryk (Toronto: U Toronto P, 1993), 248.

Chapter 4: The Search for Cuba's "Intra-Historia"

1. Silvia Oroz, *Los filmes que no filmé* (La Habana: UNEAC, 1989), 142.
2. Isaac León Frías, ed. *Los años de la conmoción 1967–1973: entrevistas con realizadores sudamericanos* (México: Dirección General de Difusión Cultural/UNAM, 1979), 19.
3. Gerardo Chijona, "*La última cena*. Entrevista a T.G.A.," *Cine Cubano* 108 (1984): 87–88.
4. Tomás Gutiérrez Alea, "No siempre fui cineasta," *Cine Cubano* 114 (1985): 45.
5. José Antonio Évora, *Tomás Gutiérrez Alea* (Madrid: Cátedra, 1996), 135–38.
6. Miguel de Unamuno, *En torno al casticismo* (Madrid: Espasa-Calpe, 1972), 28.
7. Oroz, *Los filmes que no filmé*, 134.
8. Tomás Gutiérrez Alea, "Sobre un exorcismo necesario," in *Alea, una retrospectiva crítica*, ed. Ambrosio Fornet (La Habana: Letras Cubanas, 1987), 170.
9. Ibid., 172.
10. Sergio Roca, "Cuban Economic Policy in the 1970s: The Trodden Paths," in *Cuban Communism, Third Edition*, ed. Irving Louis Horowitz (New Brunswick, NJ: Transaction Books, 1977), 265–301.
11. José Antonio Évora, "Un cine de síntesis y revelación," in *Tomás Gutiérrez Alea: poesía y revolución*, ed. José Antonio Evora (Huesca: 22 Festival de Cine de Huesca, Instituto de Cooperación Iberoamericana; Departamento de Educación y Cultura del Gobierno de Aragón, 1994), 162.
12. Marcel Martin, "*Memoires du sous-developpement*," *Écran* [France] 31 (1974): 61.
13. Manuel Moreno Fraginals, *El ingenio: el complejo económico social cubano del azúcar, Tomo I (1760–1860)* (La Habana: Comisión Nacional Cubana de la UNESCO, 1964), 49.
14. Ibid., x.
15. Significantly, *The Last Super* is dedicated to Sara Gómez, Alea's protégée who died of asthma during the editing phase of her first feature, *One Way or Another* (1974).
16. Louis A. Pérez, *Cuba: Between Reform and Revolution* (New York: Oxford UP, 1995), 61.
17. Ibid., 60.
18. Ibid., 63, 86.
19. K. Jaehne, "*The Last Supper*," *Film Quarterly* 33.1 (1979): 48.
20. Fraginals, *El ingenio*, 49. The original reads: "Ustedes mismos tienen la culpa porque no todos cumplen con su obligación; ustedes son muchos; mayoral uno no más; hoy falta uno, mañana falta otro, otro día hace una picardía, otro día la hace otro: todos los días tiene mayoral que aguantar: esto todos los días, todos los días mas que no quiere, preciso, se pone bravo."
21. The original in Spanish goes as follows: "¡Ves, Sebastián, a dónde te ha llevado la soberbia! [Tornándose hacia los otros esclavos] Negro no aprende, tiene cabeza dura. Mayoral mande lo que mande, negro debe cerrar la boca y obedecer.

Negro no contesta al mayoral. Don Manuel es el mayoral y no se protesta cuando él manda a trabajar. Al negro le pasa esto porque son bruto. Entonces don Manuel tiene razón al ponerse bruto también. Negro coge monte, el mayoral lo coge y lo tiene que castigar bien duro, para que el negro no lo vuelva a hacer más."

22. Fraginals, *El ingenio*, 179.
23. The original reads as follows: "Olofi jizo lo mundo, lo jizo completo: jizo día, jizo noche; jizo cosa buena, jizo la cosa mala; también jizo lo cosa linda y lo cosa fea también jizo. Olofi jizo bien to lo cosa que jay en lo mundo: jizo Verdad y jizo también Mentira. La verdad le salió bonita. Lo Mentira no le salió bueno: era fea y flaca-flaca, como si tuviera enfermedá. A Olofi le dá lástima y le dá uno machete afilao pa defenderse. Pasó lo tiempo y la gente quería andar siempre con la Verdad, pero nadie, nadie, quería andar con lo Mentira . . . . Un día Verdad y Mentira se encontrá en lo camino y como son enemigo se peleá. Lo Verdad es más fuerte que lo Mentira; pero lo Mentira tenía lo machete afilao que Olofi le da. Cuando lo Verdad se descuidá, lo Mentira ¡saz! y corta lo cabeza de lo Verdad. Lo Verdad ya no tiene ojo y se pone a buscar su cabeza tocando con la mano . . . . [Sebastián tantea la mesa con los ojos cerrados] Buscando y buscando de pronto si tropezá con la cabeza de lo Mentira y . . . ¡ran! arranca cabeza de lo Mentira y se la pone donde iba la suya mismita [Sebastián agarra la cabeza del puerco que está sobre la mesa con un gesto violento, y se la pone delante de su rostro.] Y desde entonce anda por lo mundo, engañando a todo lo gente el cuerpo de lo Verdad con la cabeza de lo Mentira."
24. Mikhail Bakhtin, *Problems of Dostoevsky's Poetics*, ed. and trans. Caryl Emerson (Minneapolis: U of Minnesota P, 1984), 107.
25. Bertolt Brecht, *Mr. Puntila and His Man Matti*, trans. John Willet (London: Eyre Methuen, 1977), 92.
26. Dennis West, "Esclavitud y cine en Cuba: El caso de *La última cena*," *The Western Journal of Black Studies* 3.2 (1979): 132.
27. Fraginals, *El ingenio*, 34.
28. Carmelo Mesa-Lago, *Cuba in the 1970s: Pragmatism and Institutionalization* (Albuquerque: U of New Mexico P, 1978), 26.
29. Pérez, *Cuba*, 337–39.
30. Ibid., 339.
31. Ibid., 340.
32. Ernesto Guevara, "El hombre nuevo," in *Los dispositivos en la flor*, ed. Edmundo Desnoes (Hanover, NH: Ediciones del Norte, 1981), 525–32.
33. Ambrosio Fornet, *Alea, una retrospectiva crítica* (La Habana: Letras Cubanas, 1987), 316.

Chapter 5: *Up to a Certain Point*

1. Ugo Ulive et. al., "El Tercer Cine: el actor en la revolución," *Cine al Día* 15 (1972): 9.
2. The play in the film is a real play by Juan Carlos Tabío, the scriptwriter of *Up to a Certain Point* and director of its adaptation into film. The title of the play (and the film) is *Se Permuta*.

3. Gary Crowdus, "*Up to a Point*: An Interview with Tomás Gutiérrez Alea and Mirta Ibarra," *Cineaste* 14.2 (1985): 26.

4. Bernardo Marqués Ravelo, "Hasta (incierto) punto," *El Caimán Barbudo* [La Habana] 195 (March 1984): n. pag.

5. Silvia Oroz, *Los filmes que no filmé* (La Habana: UNEAC, 1989), 191.

6. Michael Chanan, "Tomás Gutiérrez Alea," *Encuentro de la cultura cubana* 1 (Summer 1996): 76.

7. E. Colina, "Entrevista a T.G.A. sobre *Hasta cierto punto*," *Cine Cubano* 109 (1984): 76; P. Aufderheide, "On Castro's convertible," *Film Comment* 21 (May–June 1985): 50.

8. Marvin D'Lugo, "Transparent Women. Gender and Nation in Cuban Cinema," in *New Latin American Cinema*, Vol. 2, ed. Michael T. Martin (Detroit: Wayne UP, 1997), 155–66.

9. Zuzana Pick, "Towards a Renewal of Cuban Revolutionary Cinema: A Discussion of Cuban Cinema Today," *Cine-Tracts* [Montreal] 3–4 (Summer 1979): 25.

10. Catherine Davies, "Modernity, Masculinity and Imperfect Cinema in Cuba," *Screen* 38.4 (Winter 1997): 354–55.

11. Ibid., 354–55.

12. Ibid., 356.

Chapter 6: Melodrama and the Crisis of the Revolution

1. Ambrosio Fornet, *Alea, una retrospectiva crítica* (La Habana: Letras Cubanas, 1987), 323–24.

2. Mirta Ibarra, "Titón: With My Heart," *Cuba Update* (Summer 1997): 7.

3. Gary Crowdus, "*Up to a Point*: An Interview with Tomás Gutiérrez Alea and Mirta Ibarra," *Cineaste* 14.2 (1985): 27.

4. Richard Goldstein, "Cuba Sí, Macho No!" *Village Voice* 29 (July 4, 1984): 43.

5. Néstor Almendros, "An Illusion of Fairness. Almendros Replies to Alea." *Village Voice* 29 (August 14, 1984): 40.

6. Tomás Gutiérrez Alea, "Cuba sí, Almendros no!" *Village Voice* 29 (October 2, 1984): 46.

7. José Antonio Évora, *Tomás Gutiérrez Alea* (Madrid: Cátedra, 1996), 53–54.

8. Cited in Enrico Mario Santí, "*Fresa y Chocolate*: The Rhetoric of Cuban Reconciliation" *MLN* [Baltimore, MD] 113.2 (1998): 424.

9. Sol Almeda, "Retrato de Cuba (*Guantanamera*)," *El País* [Madrid] (March 19, 1995): 49.

10. Rebeca Chávez, "Tomás Gutiérrez Alea: entrevista filmada," *La Gaceta de Cuba* (September–October 1993): 10.

11. The Special Period, a rationing program designed for wartime emergencies, began in 1991 after Russia announced an end to all subsidies to the island.

12. Susana Conde, "Readerly and Writerly Letters from the Park," *Journal of Film and Video* 44.3–4 (1992–1993):105.

13. Viviana Gamoneda León, "Las cartas de Gutiérrez Alea," *Revolución y Cultura* [La Habana] (December 1988): 22.

14. Roland Barthes defines a readerly text as one that has easily consumed conventions and stereotypes that require only acceptance or rejection. A writerly text, on the other hand, is a complex, avant-garde text that the reader has to engage and complete. See *S/Z, An Essay*, trans. Richard Miller (New York: Hill and Wang, 1974), 4. Julia Lasage translated Barthe's literary theory into film theory in "*S/Z* and Rules of the Game," in *Movie and Methods*, ed. Bill Nichols (Berkeley: U of California P, 1985); 476–500. For a "writerly" reading of the film, see Conde, "Readerly and Writerly Letters from the Park," 105–19, in which the author deconstructs the film's patriarchism.

15. José Antonio Évora, "Un cine de síntesis y revelación," in *Tomás Gutiérrez Alea: poesía y revolución*, ed. José Antonio Evora (Huesca: 22 Festival de Cine de Huesca, Instituto de Cooperación Iberoamericana; Departamento de Educación y Cultura del Gobierno de Aragón, 1994), 65–66.

16. The Coral Prize is the equivalent of the Oscars. It is given at the Latin American Film Festival held each December in Havana.

17. Cited in Tzvi Medin, *Cuba: The Shaping of Revolutionary Consciousness*, trans. Martha Grenzback (Boulder, CO: L. Rienner Publishers, 1990), 82.

18. Ibid., 23ff.

19. Carlos Alberto Montaner, "The Cuban Revolution and Its Acolytes," in *Cuban Communism: 1959–1995*, ed. Irving Louis Horowitz (New Brunswick, NJ: Transaction Publishers, 1995), 777.

20. For a discussion of Goytisolo's spirituality, see Javier Escudero, "Juan Goytisolo: De apóstata a iluminado" *Revista Hispánica Moderna* [New York] 51.1 (1998): 87–101.

21. Senel Paz, *El lobo, el bosque y el hombre nuevo* (Navarra: Txalaparta, 1995): 33–35.

22. Ibid., 36–37.

23. For two such interpretations, see, John Hess, "Melodrama, Sex, and the Cuban Revolution," *Jump Cut* 41 (May 1997): 119–125; and Paul Julian Smith et al., "The Language of Strawberry," *Sight and Sound* 4.12 (1994): 30–34.

24. Medin, *Cuba*, 53.

25. Oscar Quiros, "Critical Mass of Cuban Cinema: Art as the Vanguard of Society," *Screen* 37.3 (1996): 292.

26. Peter Brooks, *The Melodramatic Imagination*: Balzac, Henry James and the Mode of Excess (New Haven: Yale UP, 1976), 32.

27. Chris Berry, cited in Hess, "Melodrama, Sex, and the Cuban Revolution," 123.

28. José Martí, "Nuestra América," in *Literatura Hispanoamericana: Una antología*, ed. David William Foster (New York: Garland Publishing, 1994), 453–61.

29. Tomás Gutiérrez Alea, *The Viewer's Dialectic* (La Habana: José Martí Publishing House, 1988), 81.

30. Felix Roberto Masud-Piloto, *From Welcomed Exiles to Illegal Immigrants: Cuban Migration to the U.S., 1959–1995* (Lanham, MD: Rowman and Littlefield, 1996), 147–48.

31. Tomás Gutiérrez Alea, interview with Dennis West, *Cineaste* 21.1–2 (1995): 17.

32. John M. Kird, *Between God and the Party* (Tampa: U of South Florida P), 155–69.

33. Marvin Leiner, *Sexual Politics in Cuba* (San Francisco: Westview P, 1994), 21–51.

34. Jonathan Rosenberg, "Cuba's Free-Market Experiment: *Los Mercados Libres Campesinos*, 1980–1986," *Latin American Research Review* 27.3 (1992): 51–89.

35. Agencia France Press, "Gutiérrez Alea ironiza sobre la burocracia cubana en su filme Guantanamera," *Diario Las Américas* [Miami] (August 31, 1995): 8-A.

36. The original in Spanish is as follows: "Al principio del Mundo, Olofin llamó a Odduá y le pidió que hiciera la vida. Odduá llamó a Obbatalá y le dijo: 'Ya está hecho el Mundo. Está hecho lo bueno y lo malo, lo bonito y lo feo, lo chiquito y lo grande; ahora hay que hacer el Hombre y la Mujer.' Obbatalá hizo el Hombre y la Mujer, pero se le olvidó hacer la muerte. Pasaban los años, y los hombers y las mujeres cada vez se ponían más viejos, pero no se morían. Eran tan viejos que tenían que reunirse como hormigas para cargar entrre todos una ramita de árbol, y se necesitaban más de ochenta brazos para cortar una calabaza. La tierra se llenó de viejos que tenían miles de años y que seguían mandando de acuerdo con sus viejas leyes; los jóvenes tenían que obedecerlos y cargar con ellos, porque siempre habían sido así las cosas. Pero cada día, la carga se hacía más pesada. Tanto clamaron los más jóvenes que un día sus clamores llegaron a oídos de Olofin, y Olofin vio que el Mundo no era tan bueno como él lo había planeado. Y vio que el dolor se había adueñado de la tierra, y que todo se iba cayendo bajo el peso de tanto tiempo, y sintió que él también estaba viejo y cansado para volver a empezar lo que tan mal le había salido. Entonces Olofin le dijo a Odduá que llamara a Ikú para que se encrgara del asunto. Y vio Ikú que había que acabar con el tiempo en que la gente no moría. Hizo Ikú entonces que lloviera y lloviera sobre la tierra durante treinta días y treinta noches sin parar, y todo fue quedando bajo el agua. Sólo los niños y los más jóvenes pudieron treparse en los árboles gigantes y subir a las montañas más altas. Y la tierra entera se convirtió en un gran río sin orillas. Hasta que en la mañana del día treinta y uno paró de llover. Los jóvenes vieron entonces que la tierra estaba más limpia y más bella, y corrieron a darle gracias a Ikú, porque había acabado con la immortalidad."

37. José Antonio Évora, *Tomás Gutiérrez Alea* (Madrid: Cátedra, 1996), 168–69.

38. Sol Almeda, "Tomás Gutiérrez Alea," *El País* [Madrid] (March 19, 1995): 54.

Chapter 7: Conclusions

1. John Charles Chasteen, "Introduction," in Angel Rama, *The Lettered City*, trans. John Charles Chasteen (Durham, NC: Duke UP, 1996), xi.

2. Alice L. Hagerman and Paul Deats, "Cuba," in *Three Worlds of Christian-Marxist Encounters*, ed. Nicholas Piediscalzi and Robert G. Thobaben (Philadelphia: Fortress P, 1985), 176.

3. *Iyabó* is the term used for someone who is being initiated into Santería. As part of the initiation requirements, *iyabós* must dress in white for a full year.
4. Law for the creation of ICAIC, cited in María Eulalia Douglas, *La tienda negra* (Havana: Cinemateca de Cuba, 1996), 341.
5. See, for example, the speech in which Castro called for a "battle against bureaucracy," printed in *Verde Olivo* [La Habana] (March 5, 1967): n.pag.
6. Jay Mallin, Sr., "The Cuban Military in Angola," in *Cuban Communism, Eighth Edition*, ed. Irving Louis Horowitz (New Brunswick, NJ: Transaction Publishers, 1995), 551–68.
7. In an interview with Jorge Ruffinelli, Alea stated, "Hace algún tiempo, salió una película que se titula *Alicia en el pueblo de Maravillas*, una comedia satírica que hacía determinadas críticas que fueron mal entendidas, mal asimiladas y peor tratadas. A los cuatro días de su estreno la retiraron de la cartelera, lo cual originó una gran protesta por parte de quienes pensaron que ésa no era una manera de poner a discusión una expresión artística. Esa película después se ha vuelto a dar, pero nunca fue lo mismo, no tuvo ya una carrera normal, y se ha exhibido aisladamente, en festivales. Mucha gente se ha quedado sin verla, y se temía que con *Fresa y chocolate* pasara lo mismo. Pienso que mucha gente quiso verla durante el festival por temor a que después la quitaran. Nunca creí que la fueran a quitar, porque la torpeza cometida con *Alicia* no se puede repetir, sería suicida. Entonces, bueno, ése es un factor, creo, que exacerba un poco el interés de la gente. De todas maneras, la acogida que ha tenido y el entusiasmo que ha despertado entre la gente que la ha visto, sí es un fenómeno notable" (Jorge Ruffinelli, "Con Tomás Gutiérrez Alea: Sabores combinados para los años noventa" *Brecha* [Montevideo] [March 17, 1995]: 20–21).
8. Quoted in Paulo Antonio Paranaguá, "Cuban Cinema's Political Challenges," in *New Latin American Cinema*, Vol. 2, ed. Michael T. Martin (Detroit: Wayne UP, 1997), 167–90.
9. For a detailed analysis of the film's contemporaneity, see Jorge Yglesias, "La espera del futuro: el tiempo en *Fresa y chocolate*," *La Gaceta de Cuba* 4 (1994): 39–41.
10. Tomás Guitérrez Alea, *The Viewer's Dialectic* (La Habana: José Martí Publishing House, 1988), 81.
11. Mikhail Bakhtin, *Problems of Dostoevsky's Poetics*, trans. Caryl Emerson (Minneapolis: U Minnesota P, 1984), 199.
12. Tzvi Medin, *Cuba: The Shaping of Revolutionary Consciousness*, trans. Martha Grenzback (Boulder, CO: L. Rienner Publishers, 1990), 169.
13. Michael Chanan, "Tomás Gutiérrez Alea," *Encuentro de la cultura cubana* 1 (Summer 1996): 73–74.
14. Alea, *The Viewer's Dialectic*, 81.

Select Bibliography

The following bibliography is organized into three sections. The first section includes articles, books, and chapters of books dedicated to Alea in general; the second section lists interviews; and the third section includes works on individual films.

General

Anderson, Alexandra. Dir. *Tales from Havana.* Prod. Bandung Limited. Videocassette. Channel Four [England], 1993.

Almendros, Néstor. *Cinemanía. Ensayos sobre cine.* Barcelona: Seix Barral, 1992. 146–47.

Bernal, Augusto y Tapia, Carlos. "Del neorrealismo al subdesarrollo." *Arcadia va al cine* [Bogotá] (October–November 1986): n.pag.

Bilbatua, Miguel. "La complejidad del compromiso. Notas sobre el cine de T.G.A." *Viridiana* [Madrid] 7 (1994): 125–30.

Brouwer, Leo. "La música para el cine: dos experiencias." *Cine Cubano* [La Habana] 45–46 (1967): 23–24.

Burton, Julianne. "Film and Revolution in Cuba. The First Twenty-Five Years." In *New Latin American Cinema.* Vol. 2. Ed. Michael T. Martin. Detroit: Wayne UP, 1997. 123–42.

Casiraghi, Ugo. "Il regista no uno. Cinema Cubano." *Quaderni della FICC* [Roma] 1967: n.pag.

Chanan, Michael. *The Cuban Image.* London: British Film Institute, 1985.

———. "Remembering Titón." *Jump Cut* 41 (May 1997): 126–29.

————. "Special Report: The Changing Geography of Third Cinema."
Screen 38.4 (Winter 1997): 372–88.

Díaz Torres, Daniel. "Sobre vivencias y superviviencias: cinco respuestas."
Cine Cubano 89–90 (1979): 238–87.

Engel, Andy. "Solidarity and Violence. Three Cuban Directors. Tomás
Gutiérrez Alea, Humberto Solás, Santiago Álvarez." *Sight and Sound*
(Fall 1969): 196–200.

Escarpit, Françoise. " 'No siempre he sido cineasta.' Los 'años Titón' antes
de la revolución." In *Cinemas d'Amerique latine* 5 (1997): 79–82.

Évora, José Antonio. "El rábano por la raíz." *Juventud Rebelde* (September
10, 1988): n.pag.

————. "El mundo en la cabeza." *Noticias de Arte* [New York] (June 1992):
12–13.

————. "Poesía y dramaturgia en el cine de T.G.A.," *Cine Cubano* 137
(1993): 30–33.

————. "Evidencias del cine cubano." *Proposiciones* 1.2 (1994): 41–49.

————. "El premio del enemigo." *El Nuevo Herald* [Miami] (March 24,
1995): n.pag.

————. *Tomás Gutiérrez Alea: poesía y revolución.* Huesca [Spain]: 22
Festival de Cine de Huesca, Instituto de Cooperación Iberoamericana,
Departamento de Educación y Cultura del Gobierno de Aragón, 1994.

————. *Tomás Gutiérrez Alea.* Madrid: Cátedra, 1996.

Fernández Retamar, Roberto. "Rushes de Titón." In *Cinemas d'Amerique
latine* 5 (1997): 83.

Fornet, Ambrosio. *Alea, una retrospectiva crítica.* La Habana: Letras
Cubanas, 1987.

García Espinosa, Julio. "Nuestro cine documental: *Esta tierra nuestra* y *La
vivienda.*" *Cine Cubano* 23–25 (1964): 4–5.

González, Reynaldo. "Titón: artista-ciudadano." In *Cinemas d'Amerique
latine* 5 (1997): 98–100.

Gutiérrez Alea, Tomás. "El cine y la cultura." *Cine Cubano* 2 (1960): 3–10.

————. "El Free Cinema y la objetividad." *Cine Cubano* 4 (1961): 35–39.

————. "Cómo se mira una película." *La Gaceta de Cuba* (December 1,
1962): 9–10.

———. "Donde se habla de lo moderno en el arte y se dicen cosas que no fueron dichas en el momento oportuno." *Cine Cubano* 9 (1963): 48–49.

———. "Qué es lo moderno en el arte? (Referencia: el cine)." *Cine Cubano* 9 (1963): 33ff.

———. "Notas sobre una discusión de un documento sobre una discusión (de otros documentos)." *La Gaceta de Cuba* 29 (November 5, 1963): 5–6.

———. "Donde menos se piensa salta el cazador . . . de brujas." *La Gaceta de Cuba* 33 (1964): 6–8.

———. "Mi posición ante el cine." *Cine Cubano* 23–25 (1964): 68–71.

———. "Notas sueltas sobre un viaje." *Cine Cubano* 38 (1966): 35–43.

———. *Dialéctica del espectador*. La Habana: UNEAC, 1982.

———. "Dramaturgia (cinematográfica) y realidad." *Cine Cubano* 105 (1983): 71–77.

———. "No siempre fui cineasta." *Cine Cubano* 114 (1985): 43–52.

———. *The Viewer's Dialectic*. La Habana: José Martí Publishing House, 1988.

———. "Formación." In José Antonio Évora, ed., *Tomás Gutiérrez Alea*. Huesca: 22 Festival de Cine de Huesca, Instituto de Cooperación Iberoamericana; Departamento de Educación y Cultura del Gobierno de Aragón, 1994.

———. "Another Cinema, Another World, Another Society." *Journal of Third World Studies*. 9.1 (1994): 90–113.

Ibarra, Mirta. "Titón, with My Heart." *Cuba Update* (Summer 1997): 7.

Lundkvist, Artur. "El primer Tomás Gutiérrez Alea." In *Cinemas d'Amerique latine* 5 (1997): 86–88.

Marsolais, Gilles. "Un humour decapant: coup d'oeil sur quelques films de Tomás Gutiérrez Alea." *24 Images* 77 (Summer 1995): 37–39.

Martinez-Echazabal, Lourdes. "The Politics of Afro-Cuban Religion in Contemporary Cuban Cinema." *Afro-Hispanic Review* 13.1 (Spring 1994): 16–22.

Martínez Carril, Manuel. "Gutiérrez Alea observa a Cuba desde adentro." *Cinemateca Revista* 49 (1995): 15–20.

Meyerson, Michael. *Memories of Underdevelopment. The Revolutionary Films of Cuba*. New York: Grossman Publishers, 1973.

Oroz, Silvia. *Los filmes que no filmé.* La Habana: UNEAC, 1989.

Otero, Lisandro. "Titón, contra esto y aquello." *El Búho* [*El Excelsior*, México, D.F.] (April 28, 1966): 13.

Padura Fuentes, Leonardo. "Memorias de unos pasos perdidos. Making of de un filme que nunca se filmó." In *Cinemas d'Amerique latine.* Toulouse: Presses de l'Universite de Toulouse-le Mirail, 1997. 103–14.

Paranaguá, Paulo Antonio. *Le Cinéma Cubain.* Paris: Centre Georges Pompidou, 1990. 7–46.

———. "Cuban Cinema's Political Challenges." In *New Latin American Cinema* Vol. 2. Ed. Michael T. Martin. Detroit: Wayne UP, 1997: 167–90.

———. "Tensión y reconciliación." *El Amaute* [Buenos Aires] (September 1996): Sección Cine, 46–51.

Quiros, Oscar. "Critical Mass of Cuban Cinema: Art as the Vanguard of Society." *Screen* 37.3 (1996): 279–93.

Ramsey, Cynthia. "Third Cinema in Latin America: Critical Theory in Recent Works." *Latin American Research Review* 23.1 (Winter 1988): 266–75.

Rivero, Ángel. "Titón: un cine de ideas." *Revolución y Cultura* [La Habana] (March 1985): 26–33.

Rodríguez, Nelson. Interview with Jorge Ruffinelli. n.d.

Ruffinelli, Jorge. "Doce miradas (y media mirada más) al cine de Tomás Gutiérrez Alea." *Casa de las Américas* 36.203 (April–June 1996): 3–14.

Schumann, P. "Un cinéma qui ne change pas ne change rien." *Ecran* [France] (January 1977): 29–36.

Sigfrid. "Situación y perspectivas del cine en América Latina. Gustavo Dahl, Tomás Gutiérrez Alea, Fernando Solanas." *Hablemos de Cine* [Lima] 61–62 (1971): 27–36.

Vega, Pastor. "El cine de octubre y el Nuevo Cine Latinoamericano." *Cine Cubano* 93 (1979): 38–43.

Interviews

Ansara, Martha. "Tomás Gutiérrez Alea. Film Director." *Cinema Papers* [Melbourne] (May–June 1981): 209ff.

Ariel, M. "L'intellectuel et la révolution." *Cinema* [France] 192 (November 1974): 66–71.

Burton, Julianne. "Tomás Gutiérrez Alea: Beyond the Reflection of Reality." In *Cinema and Social Change in Latin America. Conversations with Filmmakers.* Ed. Julianne Burton. Austin: U of Texas P, 1986. 115–32.

———. "Tomás Gutiérrez Alea: Más allá del reflejo de la realidad." In *Cine y cambio social en América Latina.* Ed. Julianne Burton. México: Editorial Diana, 1991. 163–80.

Casiraghi, Ugo. "Cine Cubano encuesta. Respuestas de Julio García Espinosa, Miguel Torres, Tomás Gutiérrez Alea." *Cine Cubano* 54–55 (1969): 22–27.

Chanan, Michael. "Tomás Gutiérrez Alea." *Encuentro de la cultura cubana* 1 (Summer 1996): 71–76.

Chijona, Gerardo. "Gutiérrez Alea: An Interview." *Framework* [England] 10 (1979): 28–30.

Colpart, G. "Corteo funebre e d'amore per *Guantanamera.*" *Liberazione* [Italia] (September 1, 1995): 19.

Dahl, G. "T.G. Alea & Fernando Solanas. Situation et perspectives du cinéma d'Amérique Latine." *Positif* [Paris] 139 (1972): 1–18.

Ehrman, H. "El cine cubano enfrenta el desafío industrial: Entrevistas con Jorge Fraga y T.G.A." *Cine al Día* [Caracas] 19 (1975): 4–8.

Engel, Andy. "Entrevistas con directores de largometraje, directores de fotografía, escritores, músicos." *Cine Cubano* 23–25 (1964): 65–128.

Escobar Casas, Reynaldo. "Cara a cara con Tomás Gutiérrez Alea." *Cuba Internacional* [La Habana] (May 1987): 68–71.

Genaro, Jack. Interview with Tomás Gutiérrez Alea. Videorecording. Stanford U, 1993.

———. Interview with Ambrosio Fornet. Videorecording. Stanford U, 1993.

González Uribe, Guillermo. "Nuestro cine está regido por cineastas, no por burócratas." *El espectador* [Bogotá] (December 22, 1985): n.pag.

Gutiérrez Alea, Tomás. "Respuesta a Cine Cubano." *Cine Cubano* 54–55 (1969): 22–27.

"Interview with Tomás Gutiérrez Alea." *The Unesco Courier* (July 1, 1995): 53.

León Frías, Isaac. "Mesa redonda con Gustavo Dahl, Tomás Gutiérrez Alea y Fernando Solanas." In *Los años de la conmoción 1967–1973: entrevistas con realizadores sudamericanos.* Ed. Isaac León Frías. México: Dirección General de Difusión Cultural/UNAM, 1979. 17–39.

Pick, Zuzana. "Towards a Renewal of Cuban Revolutionary Cinema: A Discussion of Cuban Cinema Today." *Cine-Tracts* [Montreal] 3–4 (1979): n.pag.

Ruprecht, Alvina. "Interview with Tomás Gutiérrez Alea." *Ottawa Revue* (January 25–31 1979): n.pag.

Stone, Judy. "Cuba's Alea Talks about Fidel and Culture." *San Francisco Chronicle* (October 16, 1979): n.pag.

Tordera, Pilar. "Tomás Gutiérrez Alea." *El País* [Madrid] (October 6, 1987): Sección Cultura, 40.

Virgen, Lucy. "O reflexo, o eco e o verdadeiro sentido do cinema." *Cadernos de cinema e critica* [Rio de Janeiro] 6 (1994): 45–48.

Individual Films

Stories of the Revolution

Chanan, Michael. *The Cuban Image*. London, British Film Institute, 1985. 111–16.

Guevara, Alfredo. "Palabras de nuestro director (Première de 'Historias de la Revolución')." *Cine Cubano* 4 (1961): 58–59.

León, Eduardo Heras. "*Historias de la revolución* y 'El joven rebelde.' " *Pensamiento Crítico* 42 (July 1970): 128–34. [Reprinted in *Cine y Revolución en Cuba*. Barcelona: Editorial Fontamara, 1975.]

Mirphy, W. "Notas sobre la realización de 'Santa Clara.' " *Cine Cubano* 2 (1960): 17–21.

Oroz, Silvia. *Los filmes que no filmé*. La Habana: UNEAC, 1989. 39–52.

Richardson, Tony. "El cine cubano (*Historias de la Revolución*)." *Cine Cubano* 12 (1963): 6–7.

The Twelve Chairs

Chanan, Michael. *The Cuban Image*. London, British Film Institute, 1985. 124–27.

Desnoes, Edmundo. "Habla un director." *Revolución* [La Habana] (January 8, 1963): n.pag.

Díaz, Elena. "Las doce sillas." *Cine al Día* [Caracas] 12 (1971): 24–25.

Gutiérrez Alea, Tomás, and Ugo Ulive. *Las 12 sillas*. La Habana: Ediciones ICAIC, 1963.

Oroz, Silvia. *Los filmes que no filmé.* La Habana: UNEAC, 1989. 55–73.

Ulive, Ugo. "2 Historias de 12 sillas." *Cine Cubano* 6 (1962): 20–22.

———. *"Las doce sillas.* 'El heredero.' " *Cine al Día* [Caracas] 16 (1973): 40–41.

Cubmite

Chanan, Michael. *The Cuban Image.* London, British Film Institute, 1985. 122–24.

Colina, José de la. *"Cumbite."* *Cine Cubano* 14–15 (1963): 41–49.

Colpart, G. *"Cumbite."* *Cine al Día* [Caracas] 12 (1971): 25–26.

Oroz, Silvia. *Los filmes que no filmé.* La Habana: UNEAC, 1989. 77–88.

Death of a Bureaucrat

Baker, Bob. "Long Laugh the Revolution." *SoHo News Weekly* 6.34 (May 24–30, 1979): n.pag.

Broullon, Carlos N. "Interview with Tomás Gutiérrez Alea." Press Release by Tricontinental Film Center, Berkeley, CA, n.d.

Canby, Vincent. "Death of a Bureaucrat." *New York Times* (May 18 1979): C12.

Chanan, Michael. *The Cuban Image.* London: British Film Institute, 1985. 203–5.

Colpart, G. "La crítica italiana juzga los festivales internacionales y las películas cubanas (*La muerte de un burócrata*)." *Cine Cubano* 38 (1966): 18–23.

Gill, B. "The Current Cinema: Love and Death." *New Yorker* 55 (May 28, 1979): 122–23.

Kezich, Tullio. "Largometrajes (*La muerte de un burócrata*)." *Cine Cubano* 31–33 (1966): 4–27.

Montero, R. *"La muerte de un burócrata.* Entrevista con Tomás Gutiérrez Alea." *Cine Cubano* 35 (1966): 14–19.

Oroz, Silvia. *Los filmes que no filmé.* La Havana: UNEAC, 1989. 91–108.

Rich, B. R. *"Death of a Bureaucrat*: Madcap Comedy Cuban Style." *Jump Cut* 22 (1980): 29–30.

Seitz, Michael. "A Cuban Comedy Comes of Age." *The Chronicle of Higher Education* (May 29, 1979): Review Section, 26.

Tarratt, M. "*Death of a Bureaucrat.*" *Films & Filming* 9.4 (1973): 47.

Firk, Michele. "Cinéma et bureaucratie à Cuba. Entretien avec Tomás Gutiérrez Alea." *Positif* 85 (June 1967): 23–26.

Memories of Underdevelopment

Alexander, William Class. "Film Language and Popular Cinema." *Jump Cut* (March 1985): 45–48.

Allen, Don. "*Memories of Underdevelopment.*" *Sight and Sound* [London] (Fall 1969): 212–13.

Alonso, A. G. "Tras las huellas que conducen a la trascendencia." *Cine Cubano* 123 (1988): 2–10.

Ayala Blanco, Jorge. "*Memorias del subdesarrollo.*" *Siempre* [México] (November 26, 1969): 103.

Bassan, R. "*Mémoires de sous-developpement.*" *Téleciné* [France] 194 (1974): 24–25.

Bullita, Juan M. "*Memorias del subdesarrollo.*" *Hablemos de Cine* [Lima] 54 (1970): 20–21.

Burton, Julianne. "Modernist Form in *Land in Anguish* and *Memories of Underdevelopment.*" *Post Scripts* 3.2 (1984): 65–84.

———. "*Memories of Underdevelopment* in the Land of Overdevelopment." *Cineaste* 8.1 (1977): 16–21.

———. "Individual Fulfillment and Collective Achievement: An Interview with Tomás Gutiérrez Alea." *Cineaste* 8.1 (1977): 11–21.

Campa, Román de la. "*Memorias del subdesarrollo*: Novela/texto/discurso." *Hispamérica: Revista de Literatura* 15.44 (1986): 3–18.

Canby, Vincent. "Stink Bombs, Yes—Cuban Festival, No!" *New York Times* (April 2, 1972): 245–46.

———. "*Memories*, Cuban Film on Alienation." *New York Times* (May 18, 1973): n.pag.

Cooks, Jay. "Revolutionary Ennui: *Memories of Underdevelopment.*" *Time* (July 23, 1973): 80.

Chanan, Michael. *The Cuban Image*. London: British Film Institute, 1985. 236–47.

Colpart, G. "*Mémoires de sous-developpement.*" *Image et Son* [Paris] 290 (1974): 115–16.

Desnoes, Edmundo. *Memorias del subdesarrollo*. La Habana: UNEAC, 1965.

————. "Se llamaba Sergio." *Cine Cubano* 45–46 (1967): 26–28.

Díaz, Elena. "Memorias del subdesarrollo." *Cine Cubano* 52–53 (1969): 79–84.

Díaz Torres, Daniel. "Encuesta sobre el cine cubano." *La Gaceta de Cuba* (August–September 1966): n.pag.

————. "En busca del desarrollo fílmico." *La Gaceta de Cuba* (September–October 1968): n.pag.

————. "Cine Cubano en EE.UU." *Cine Cubano* 89–90 (1976): 65–71.

Fernández, E. "Witnesses Always Everywhere: The Rhetorical Strategies of Memories of Underdevelopment." *Wide Angle* 4.2 (1980): 52–55.

Fernandez, Henry, et. al. "3/on 2: Desnoes (and) Gutiérrez Alea." *Diacritics* [New York] 4.4 (1974): 51–64.

Gulliat, Penelope. "Thought's Empire (*Memories of Underdevelopment*)." *The New Yorker* (May 26, 1973): 122–23.

Gutiérrez Alea, Tomás. "*Memorias del subdesarrollo*: Notas de trabajo." *Cine Cubano* 45–46 (1968): 19–25.

————. "Vanguardia política y vanguardia artística." *Cine Cubano* 54–55 (1969): n.pag.

————. "Carta a Andrew Harris, re:censura de *Memorias* en EE.UU." *Cine Cubano* 89–90 (1976): 70–71.

Keller, Virginia Lin. "Where Subject Meets Society: Modernist Narration and Bourgeois Alienation." In *Multiple Points of View: Dialectics of Film Narration*. Ph.D. diss. Northwestern U, 1989. 93–117.

Kovacs, Katherine S. "Revolutionary Consciousness and Imperfect Cinematic Forms." *Humanities in Society* 4.1 (1981): 101–12.

Lesage, J. "*Memories of Underdevelopment*, Images of Underdevelopment." *Jump Cut* 1 (1974): 9–11.

Lieberman, Sharon. "Women: The *Memories of Underdevelopment*." *Women & Film* 2.7 (1975): 78–79.

López, Ana. "Parody, Underdevelopment, and the New Latin American Cinema." *Quarterly Review of Film and Video* 12.1–2 (1990): 63–71.

————. "Memories of a Home: Mapping the Revolution (and the Making of Exiles?)." *Revista Canadiense de Estudios Hispánicos* 20.1 (1995): 5–17.

Martin, Marcel. "*Memoires du sous-developpement.*" *Écran* 31 [France] (1974): 60–62.

Martínez Carril, Manuel. "*Memorias del subdesarrollo.*" *Cine al Día* [Caracas] 16 (1971): 27–29.

Memories of Underdevelopment. New Brunswick, NJ: Rutgers UP, 1990.

Meyerson, Michael. *Memories of Underdevelopment. The Revolutionary Films of Cuba.* New York: Grossman Publishers, 1973.

Murphy, Brian. "*Memories of Underdevelopment.*" *Films and Filming* [London] (September 1969): 64.

Murphy, William. "Two Thirld World Films." *Take One* 3.3 (Apr. 1972): 14–16.

Nussbaun, A. F. "*Memories of Underdevelopment.*" *Movietone News* [Australia] 39 (February 1975): 43.

Oroz, Silvia. *Los filmes que no filmé.* La Habana: UNEAC, 1989. 111–28.

———. "*Mémoires du sous-developpement.*" *Revue de la Cinémathèque* [Canada] 10 (1991): 4–6.

Roud, Richard. "Cuban 'Memories' You Won't Soon Forget." *New York Times* (May 20, 1978): 180.

Sánchez, Osvaldo. "Para no tocar de oído." *Cine Cubano* 107 (1983): 93–94.

Sarris, Andrew. "A Tale of Two Circles (Film in Focus)." *The Village Voice* [New York] (February 14, 1974): n.pag.

Spila, Piero. "*Memorias del subdesarrollo.*" *Cinema e Film* [Italia] 2.5–6 (1968): 51–52.

Ulive, Ugo, et. al. "El Tercer Cine: el actor en la revolución." *Cine al Día* [Caracas] 15 (1972): 5–9.

A Cuban Fight against Demons

Barnard, Timothy. "Death Is Not True: Form and History in Cuban Film." In *New Latin American Cinema.* Vol. 2. Ed. Michael T. Martin. Detroit: Wayne UP, 1997. 143–54.

Chanan, Michael. *The Cuban Image.* London: British Film Institute, 1985. 251–73.

Gutiérrez Alea, Tomás. "Presentación de *Una pelea cubana contra los demonios.*" *Cine Cubano* 78–80 (1971): 49.

Oroz, Silvia. *Los filmes que no filmé*. La Habana: UNEAC, 1989. 131–50.

Ortiz, Fernando. *Una pelea cubana contra los demonios*. La Habana: Editorial de Ciencias Sociales, 1975.

Paz, Senel. "*Una pelea cubana contra los demonios*. Entrevista a Tomás Gutiérrez Alea." *Cine al Día* [Caracas] 15 (1972): 10.

The Last Supper

Bosseno, Christian. "La última cena." *Revue du Cinema* 382 (April 1983): 39.

Castro, Carmen Lourdes. "La fotografía en *La última cena*." *Cine Cubano* 119 (1987): 50–57.

Chanan, Michael. *The Cuban Image*. London: British Film Institute, 1985. 271–73.

Chijona, Gerardo. "*La última cena*, el cine y la historia." *Cine Cubano* 93 (1979): n.pag.

———. "*La última cena*. Entrevista a T.G.A." *Cine Cubano* 108 (1984): 88–90.

Fraginals, Manuel Moreno. *El ingenio: el complejo económico social cubano del azúcar, Tomo I (1760–1860)*. La Habana: Comisión Nacional Cubana de la UNESCO, 1964.

Gilliat, Penelope. "Last Supper in Havana." *The New Yorker* (May 15, 1978): 121–23.

Hamilton, Ian. "Films: truly true." *New Statesman* 97 (9 May 1979): 336.

Jaehne, K. "*The Last Supper*." *Film Quarterly* 33.1 (1979): 48–53.

Kain, S. "*La última cena*." *Variety* 290.13 (May 3, 1978): 26.

Montero, R. "La última cena de una ética en crisis." *Cine Cubano* 98 (1981): 114–25.

Oroz, Silvia. *Los filmes que no filmé*. La Habana: UNEAC, 1989. 153–65.

Prochnow, C. "*Das letzte Abendmahl*." *Film und Fernsehen* 7.5 (1979): 15–16.

Pym, J. "*La última cena (The Last Supper)*." *Monthly Film Bulletin* [England] 46.543 (1979): 79–80.

Sanchez Crespo, Osvaldo. "The Perspective of the Present: Cuban History, Cuban Filmmaking: *The Last Supper*." In *Reviewing Histories. Selections from New Latin American Cinema*, ed. Coco Fusco. Buffalo, NY: Hallwals Contemporary Arts Center, 1987. 197–200.

"Selected Third World Classic Films." *Film Library Quarterly* 16.4 (1983): 53–68.

Tarqui, A. "*La última cena.*" *Cinema 83* 294 (June 93): 52–53.

Thirard, P. L. "*La última cena.*" *Positif* 267 (May 1983): 76.

Tesson, C. "*La última cena.*" *Cahiers du Cinema* 347 (May 83): 76.

Ulive, Ugo. "*La última cena.*" *Cine al Día* [Caracas] 22 (November 1977): 39–40.

"*La última cena.*" *Film und fernsehen* 7.2 (February 79): 27.

"*La última cena.*" *Cine Revue* 63 (March 24, 1983): 48.

West, Dennis. "Esclavitud y cine en Cuba: El caso de *La última cena.*" *The Western Journal of Black Studies* 3.2 (1979): 128–33.

The Survivors

Amig. "*Los sobrevivientes.*" *Variety* 295 (May 30, 1979): 24.

"Cuban Director Alea Scores with a Bourgeois Parody." *Variety* 295 (June 20, 1979): 40.

Díaz Torres, Daniel. "De *La última cena* a *Los sobrevivientes.*" *Cine Cubano* 97 (1980): 108–12.

Haustrate, G. "*Les survivants.*" *Cinema 79* 247–248 (July–August 1979): 25.

Oroz, Silvia. *Los filmes que no filmé*. La Habana: UNEAC, 1989. 169–84.

Paranaguá, Paulo Antonio. "*Los sobrevivientes.*" *Positif* 220–221 (July–August 1979): 66.

Predal, R. "*Les survivants.*" *Jeune Cinema* 120 (July–August 1979): 12–13.

Santos, Romualdo. "*Los sobrevivientes.*" *Bohemia* [La Habana] (January 12, 1979): 24–25.

Up to a Certain Point

Almendros, Néstor. "An Illusion of Fairness. Almendros replies to Alea." *Village Voice* 29 (August 14, 1984): 40.

Aufderheide, P. "On Castro's Convertible." *Film Comment* 21 (May–June 1985): 49–52.

Canby, Vincent. "Film: Alea's Certain Point from Cuba." *New York Times* (March 13, 1985): C19.

Chanan, Michael. "Tomás Gutiérrez Alea." *Encuentro de la cultura cubana* 1 (Summer 1996): 71–76.

Colina, E. "*Hasta cierto punto.*" *Cine Cubano* 108 (1984): 88–90.

———. "Entrevista a T.G.A. sobre *Hasta cierto punto.*" *Cine Cubano* 109 (1984): 73–77.

Crowdus, Gary. "*Up to a Point.*" *Cineaste* 14.2 (1985): 24–25.

———. "*Up to a Point*: An Interview with Tomás Gutiérrez Alea and Mirta Ibarra." *Cineaste* 14.2 (1985): 26–29.

D'Lugo, Marvin. "Transparent Women. Gender and Nation in Cuban Cinema." In *New Latin American Cinema*. Vol. 2. Detroit: Wayne UP, 1997. 155–66.

Davies, Catherine. "Modernity, Masculinity, and Imperfect Cinema in Cuba." *Screen* 38.4 (Winter 1997): 345–59.

Edna. "*Hasta cierto punto.*" *Variety* 314.10 (1984): 26.

Fernández, E. "Proper Conduct." *Village Voice* 30 (March 19, 1985): 58.

———. "Razzing the Bureaucracy: The Cuban Cinema of Tomás Gutiérrez Alea." *Village Voice* 30 (March 26, 1985): 45ff.

Gutiérrez Alea, Tomás. "Cuba sí, Almendros no!" *Village Voice* 29 (October 2, 1984): 46–47.

"*Jusqu' à un certain point.*" *Cinéma 72* 316 (April 85): 47.

Kopkind, A. "Films: *Memories of Underdevelopment, Up to a Point.*" *Nation* 240 (March 30, 1985): 377–78.

Llopiz, J. L. "El talón de Aquiles de nuestro cine." *Cine Cubano* 122 (1988): 6–12.

MacBean, J. R. "A Dialogue with T.G.A. on the Dialectics of the Spectator in *Hasta Cierto Punto.*" *Film Quarterly* (Spring 1985): 22–29.

Marqués Ravelo, Bernardo. "Hasta (incierto) punto." *El Caimán Barbudo* [La Habana] 195 (March 1984): n.pag.

Mason, J. "State Machismo: The Official Versions of the State of Male/Female Relations." *Cineaction* 5 (1986): 45–49.

Mendoza, Antonio. "Muestra de cine cubano." *Encuadre* [Caracas] 22 (1990): 64.

Oroz, Silvia. *Los filmes que no filmé.* La Habana: UNEAC, 1989: 187–201.

Paellink, Roselind. "Tomás Gutiérrez Alea." *Resumen* [Caracas] (January 29, 1984): 30–31.

Paz, Senel. "*Hasta cierto punto*: continuidad y ruptura." *Areíto* [New York] 10.37 (1984): n.pag.

———. "*Hasta cierto punto*: Entrevista a Tomás Gutiérrez Alea." *Areíto* [New York] 10.37 (1984): 44–47.

Pick, Zuzana. "Spectacles of Daily Life: *Up to a Point.*" *Canadian Journal of Film Studies* 2.1 (1992): 31–42.

Sesti, Mario. "Cinema cubano. Intervista a Tomás Gutiérrez Alea." *Cineforum* [Italy] 26.260 (December 1986): 32–34.

Tourne, A. "A Cuba, retour au réalisme critique: *Hasta cierto punto.*" *Jeune Cinéma* 159 (1984): 13–15.

Welsh, Henry. "*Jusqu' à un certain point.*" *Jeune Cinema* 166 (April 1985): 41–43.

Letters from the Park

Besa. "*Cartas del parque (Letters from the Park).*" *Variety* 332.11 (October 5, 1988): 19.

Chávez, Rebeca. "Filmar la intimidad." In *Cinemas d'Amerique latine* 5 (1997): 101–2.

Conde, Susana. "Readerly and Writerly Letters from the Park." *Journal of Film and Video* 44.3–4 (1992–1993): 105–19.

Gamoneda León, Vivian. "Las cartas de Gutiérrez Alea." *Revolución y Cultura* [La Habana] (December 1988): 22–25.

Larraz, Emmanuel. "Une collection hispanique: 'Amours difficiles.' " *CinemAction* [France] 57 (1990): 161–66.

Sánchez, Juan Carlos. "Cartas del parque." *Cine Cubano* 125 (1989): 87–88.

Sarusky, J. "Die Abenteuer eines Pianos." *Film und Fernsehen* 16.7 (July 1988): 66–67.

Strawberry and Chocolate

"IVXL Festival de Cine de Berlín." *ABC* [Madrid] (February 13, 1994): Suplemento Espectáculos, n.pag.

Almendros, Néstor. "An Illusion of Fairness. Almendros Replies to Alea." *Village Voice* 29 (August 14, 1984): 40.

Barquet, Jesús. "Paz, Gutiérrez Alea y Tabío: Felices discrepancias entre un cuento, un guión y un film: *Fresa y chocolate.*" *Fe de Erratas* 10 (May 1995): 83–86.

Behar, Ruth. "Queer Times in Cuba." In *Bridges to Cuba/Puentes a Cuba*, ed. Ruth Behar. Ann Arbor, MI: U of Michigan P, 1995. 394–415.

Bejel, Emilio. "*Strawberry and Chocolate*: Coming Out of the Cuban Closet?" *South Atlantic Quarterly* 96.1 (1997): 65–82.

Berry, Chris. "*Strawberry and Chocolate.*" *Filmnews* [Australia] 25.2 (April 1995): 13.

Birringer, Johannes. "Homosexuality and the Revolution: An Interview with Jorge Perugorria." *Cineaste* 20.1–2 (1995): 21–22.

———. "*Fresa y chocolate.*" *Sequences* 177 (March–April 1995): 41–42.

Chávez, Rebeca. "Tomás Gutiérrez Alea: entrevista filmada." *La Gaceta de Cuba* (September–October 1993): 8–11.

Chua, Lawrence. "I Scream, You Scream." *Artforum International* 33.4 (1994): 62.

Cuza Malé, Belkis. "Ni fresita ni chocolate." *El Nuevo Herald* [Miami] (April 4, 1995): n.pag.

"El discípulo, la amistad: Entrevista a Juan Carlos Tabío." In *Cinemas d'Amerique latine* 5 (1997): 90–96.

Évora, José Antonio. "Más fresas y chocolates." *El Nuevo Herald* [Miami] (May 14, 1994): 14A.

———. "Dios nos perdone; digo, Diego, en su nombre." In *Tomás Gutiérrez Alea: poesía y revolución.* Ed. José Antonio Evora. Huesca: 22 Festival de Cine de Huesca, Instituto de Cooperación Iberoamericana; Departamento de Educación y Cultura del Gobierno de Aragón, 1994. 203–12.

Feldvoss, Marli. "Auf verlorenem Postem." *EPD Film* 6.4 (April 1994): 10–11.

García, Ángeles. "Entrevista con Tomás Gutiérrez Alea." *El País* [Madrid] (March 7, 1994): Suplemento Cultura, 2.

Goldstein, Richard. "Cuba Sí, Macho No!" *Village Voice* 29 (July 4, 1984): 1ff.

González, Eduardo. "La rama dorada y el árbol deshojado: Reflexiones sobre *Fresa y chocolate* y sus antecedentes." *Foro Hispánico: Revista Hispánica de Los Países Bajos* 10 (1996): 65–78.

González, Reynaldo. "La cultura cubana con sabor a *Fresa y Chocolate.*" *Atlántica Internacional* [Las Palmas de Gran Canaria] 8 (1994): 100–9.

———. "Meditation for a Debate, or Cuban Culture with the Taste of Strawberry and Chocolate." *Cuba Update* (May 1994): 14–19.

Gutiérrez Alea, Tomás. "Cuba sí, Almendros no!" *Village Voice* 29 (October 2, 1984): 46–47.

———. "De *Fresa y chocolate.*" *Viridiana* [Madrid] 7 (1994): 119–24.

———. "*Fresa y chocolate* y una aclaración." *El Nuevo Herald* [Miami] (April 27, 1994): 14A.

———. *Fresa y chocolate.* Madrid: Fundación Viridiana, 1994.

Gutiérrez Aragón, M. "Insumisos en Numancia." *El País* [Madrid] (March 7, 1994): Suplemento Cultura, 3.

Hess, John. "Melodrama, Sex and the Cuban Revolution." *Jump Cut* 41 (May 1997): 119–25.

Jiménez Leal, Orlando. "Las adorables mentiras de Titón." *El Nuevo Herald* [Miami] (May 3, 1994): 12A.

Kunath, Sylke. "Lateinamerikas Cineasten melden sich zu Wort." *Film und Fernsehen* 22.2 (1994): 12–15.

Lavoie, André. "Viens chez moi, j'habite (peut-être) chez une copine . . ." *Ciné-Bulles* 14.2 (Summer 1995): 18–21.

Leclercq, Emmanuel. "Fraise et chocolat." *Positif* 404 (October 1994): 45–46.

Luque Escalona, Roberto. "Balada de Coppelia." *El Nuevo Herald* [Miami] (March 24, 1995): 12A.

Lux, Stefan. "*Erdbeer und Schokolade.*" *Film-dienst* 47.20 (September 27, 1994): 24–25.

Marin, Jairo. " 'Yo voto por la solidaridad humana.' Senel Paz en citas." *Kinetoscopio* [Medellín] 25 (1994): 10–13.

Martínez Carril, Manuel. "Todo empezó en Coppelia." *Cinemateca Revista* [Montevideo] 49 (1995): 55–56.

Matthews, Peter. "*Fresa y chocolate.*" *Modern Review* [United Kingdom] 1.18 (December–January 1994–1995): 17.

Monsiváis, Carlos. "*Fresa y chocolate.*" *Fe de erratas* 10 (1995): 82.

Montaner, Gina. "De fresas y chocolates." *El Nuevo Herald* [Miami] (March 7, 1994): n.pag.

Padieu, Helene. "*Fresa y chocolate.*" *Cinéma 72* 538 (September 17, 1994): 7.

Paz, Senel. "*Fresa y chocolate.*" [script.] *Viridiana* [Madrid] 7 (1994): 7–116.

Plasencia, Azucena. "*Fresa y chocolate.* Erotismo y cambio." *Bohemia* [La Habana] (February 4, 1994): 58–59.

Rother, Hans-Jorg. "Auf Wiedersehen, Kuba!" *Film und Fernsehen* 22.4–5 (1994): 74–75.

Ruffinelli, Jorge. "Con Tomás Gutiérrez Alea: sabores combinados para los años noventa." *Brecha* [Montevideo] (March 17, 1995): 20–21.

S. M. "*Fresa y chocolate.*" *Cahiers du Cinéma* 484 (1994): 68.

Santana, Gilda. "*Fresa y chocolate.* El largo camino de la literatura al cine." *Viridiana* [Madrid] 7 (1994): 131–40.

Santí, Enrico Mario. "*Fresa y Chocolate*: The Rhetoric of Cuban Reconciliation." *MLN* [Baltimore] 113.2 (1998): 407–25.

Serna Servin, Juan Antonio. "An Ideological Study of the Film *Strawberry and Chocolate.*" *Anuario de Cine y Literatura en Español: An International Journal on Film and Literature* [Villanova, PA] 3 (1997): 159–66.

Smith, Paul Julian, et al. "The Language of Strawberry." *Sight and Sound* 4.12 (1994): 30–34.

———. *Vision Machines. Cinema, Literature and Sexuality in Spain and Cuba, 1983–93.* London: Verso, 1996. 81–100.

Stratton, D. "*Fresa y chocolate.*" *Variety* 354.3 (1994): 48.

Thuna, Ulrich von. "*Fresa y chocolate.*" *EPD Film* 11.10 (October 1994): 43.

Toledo, Teresa. "Conversando con Senel Paz." *Viridiana* 7 (1994): 141–63.

Vicent, Maruricio. "*Fresa y chocolate*, el polémico helado cubano, llega a los cines españoles." *El País* [Madrid] (April 25, 1994): 36.

West, Dennis. "*Strawberry and Chocolate*, Ice Cream and Tolerance. Interviews with Tomás Gutiérrez Alea and Juan Carlos Tabío." *Cineaste* 21.1–2 (1995): 16.

Yglesias, Jorge. "La espera del futuro. El tiempo en *Fresa y chocolate.*" *La Gaceta de Cuba* 4 (1994): 39–41.

Guantanamera

Agencia France Press. "Gutiérrez Alea ironiza sobre la burocracia cubana en su filme *Guantanamera*." *Diario Las Américas* [Miami] (August 31, 1995): 8-A.

Almeda, Sol. "Retrato de Cuba (*Guantanamera*)." *El País* [Madrid] (March 19, 1995): 42–51.

————. "Tomás Gutiérrez Alea." *El País* [Madrid] (March 19, 1995): 52–56.

Boyero, Carlos. "Tierna y mordaz *Guantanamera*." *El Mundo* [Madrid] (September 3, 1995): Suplemento *Uve*, 5.

Bugeau, Florent. "*Guantanamera*." *Cinéma 72* 578 (July 1, 1996): 9.

Colpart, G. "Corteo funebre e d'amore per *Guantanamera*." *Liberazione* [Italy] (September 1, 1995): 19.

Fernández, Ángel. "La vida cotidiana." *El Mundo* [Madrid] (September 7, 1995): Suplemento *Metrópoli*, 4–5.

"*Guantanamera*." *Positif* 417 (September 1996): 52.

Index